THE KING'S ENGLISH

THE KING'S ENGLISH

[*Adventures
of an Independent
Bookseller*]

BETSY BURTON

Gibbs Smith, Publisher
Salt Lake City

First Edition
09 08 07 06 05   5 4 3 2 1

Published by
Gibbs Smith, Publisher
P.O. Box 667
Layton, Utah 84041

Orders: 1.800.748.5439
www.gibbs-smith.com

Designed by Maralee Lassiter / Lassiter Design
Printed and bound in Korea

Library of Congress Cataloging-in-Publication Data
Burton, Betsy.
The King's English : adventures of an independent bookseller / Betsy Burton.
— 1st ed. p. cm.
Includes bibliographical references and index.
ISBN 1-58685-687-1 (alk. paper)
1. King's English Bookstore—History. 2. Bookstores—Utah—Salt Lake City—History—
20th century. 3. Independent bookstores—Utah—Salt Lake City—Anecdotes. 4. Best
books—Utah. I. Title.

Z473.K54B87 2005
381'.45002'09792258—dc22

2004021518

[DEDICATION]

To ANN EDWARDS CANNON, who first suggested that The King's English Bookshop had other stories to tell besides the ones on its shelves; to Ann Berman and Barbara Hoagland, my partners past and present; to the dedicated booksellers who have made our store what it is today; and to independent bookstores all over the country, every one with tales to tell.

[CONTENTS]

[ACKNOWLEDGMENTS]

M Y THANKS TO ALL THE WONDERFUL BOOKSELLERS, past and present, at The King's English, especially to my partner, fellow reader, and dear friend Barbara Hoagland; my silent partner and close friend from childhood, Deon Hilger; my coeditor and best of friends, Kathy Ashton, who read this book so often and with such perception; the incomparable Anne Holman and Vicki Whitaker, whose management skills made it possible for me to spend so much time away from the store; and to independent booksellers everywhere.

My wonderful bookaholic husband Kit (who read my manuscript so many times he may give up reading altogether) and my lovely children Nicks and Amanda all have my undying gratitude and love.

And a particular thanks to fellow bookseller Gayle Shanks from Changing Hands Bookstore in Tempe, Arizona, who read this book more (far more) than once in its different incarnations and whose fabulous book list sparked the idea for the appendix; to Jeannette Haien for her life-sustaining friendship; and to both Jeannette and Jonathan Rabinowitz for all their support and help early on. Thanks to Margot Kimball, Stephanie Rosenfeld, Kate Woodworth, and Ann Cannon (again and again) for their input; to photographers Kent Miles, Michelle Macfarlane, Joe Marotta, and my lifelong friend Christina Papanikolas.

Thanks also go to my wonderful and persistent agent, Julie Popkin, who believed in me when it seemed no one else did; to Gibbs Smith for taking a chance on me; and to Jennifer Grillone, both for her patience with my stubbornness and for her subtle but artful editing; to

Ruth Greenstein for an insightful early edit; to my cohorts in the Salt Lake Vest Pocket Business Coalition and "Local First" for banding together in support of our community; to Chris Finan of ABFFE who knows more about censorship than anyone I've ever met; and to the staff of the American Booksellers Association: the indomitable Avin Mark Domnitz, who directs the ABA, the brilliant Oren Teicher, his second in command, Len Valhos, Dan Cullen, Mark Nichols, Kristen Gilligan, Jill Perlstein, and Meg Smith, all of whom have literally saved the lives of independent bookstores these past years—and all of whom seem to work 27 hours a day (then slip in another 7 hours of reading) and have each spent the majority of a lifetime working with, devoted to, books.

Thanks to authors Isabel Allende, Terry Tempest Williams, Jeannette Haien, Mark Spragg, and Mark Strand, and booksellers Cathy Langer of the Tattered Cover, Susan Wasson of Bookworks, and Meg Sherman, formerly of Chinook as well for their kind words about the book; and to the following independent booksellers for taking the time to compile and send their book stores' varied and interesting book lists:

Gayle Shanks, Changing Hands Book Store; Susan Avery, Ariel Booksellers; Cathy Langer and Margaret Maupin, Tattered Cover Bookstore; Dot Mccleary, John Doyle, and Thomas Talbott, Crawford and Doyle Booksellers; Andy Ross, Cody's Books; Lyn Roberts and Richard Howorth, Square Books; Clark Kepler, Kepler's Books; Jeannette Watson, Lenox Hill Bookstore; Gerry Donaghy, and Mimi Wheatwind, Powell's City of Books; Sheri Seggerman, Prairie Lights Books; Andrea Avantaggio, Maria's Bookshop; Linda Marotta, Shakespeare & Co.; Carla Cohen, Politics and Prose; Vivien Jennings, Rainy Day Books; Becky Anderson, Anderson's Bookshop; Linda Ramsdell, Galaxy Bookshop; Frank Kramer, Harvard Bookstore; Kelly Justice, Fountain Books; Gwen Marcum, Marcia Rider, Judy Stenovich, Kathy Kitsuse, Capitola Book Café; Chuck and Dee Robinson, Village Books; Neal Coonerty, Bookshop Santa Cruz; Rick Simonson, Elliott Bay Book Company; Kristine Kaufman, Snow Goose Bookstore; Leslie Ryan, Off the Beaten Path; Nancy Rutland, Bookworks; Linda Brummett, Brigham Young University Bookstore; Russ Lawrence, Chapter One Book Store; Daniel Goldin, Harry W. Schwartz Books; Mitchell Kaplan, Books & Books Inc.; Buster Keenan, Boulder Books.

Most of all, thanks to readers. Where would we be without you?

Chapter One

FROM *SUCH* RUDE BEGINNINGS

[*"Everybody's life has heroic dimensions. There is nothing like a common person or a dull life."*]

— Isabel Allende, *Deseret News*, February 7, 1991

[*"Harmless readers and copy editors are being defenestrated, even as we speak. We live in interesting times."*]

— A. L. Kennedy, *Everything You Need*

AMONG THE MORMONS

On any map of Salt Lake City, the Mormon temple is impossible to miss—not so much because Temple Square is the spiritual heart of a religious enclave as because the street system uses the temple itself as heart and hub: each address in the city-proper is plotted in terms of direction and distance from this one central point. Thus, The King's English Bookshop at 1500 East, 1500 South, is 15 blocks east and south of (you've got it) the Mormon temple.

In a town where every address is derived from its proximity to their spiritual mecca, Mormons are clearly not a force one can ignore. We Salt Lakers seem to define ourselves vis-à-vis the LDS (Latter-day Saint) church just as surely as we define our street numbers vis-à-vis the temple. The waxing and waning of our mutual hostility (Mormon and non-) make for a complicated social and professional life, but an endlessly interesting one, full of the crosscurrents—animosity, scorn, humor, respect, jealousy, distrust, grudging admiration—one might expect in what is essentially a petri dish for human comedy.

Comic or not, the fact is that every bookseller who tries to bridge the chasm between the two cultures in Salt Lake must (in addition to the dog and pony show carried out by any retailer) be a skilled high-wire artist, master of the artfully changed subject, and of spin—be, in fact, all things to all people. Such high-wire acts are what good independent booksellers do best. Contortionists one and all, we delight in climbing into other peoples' skins or clothes or shoes in order to walk a mile or two along another's path, view the passing scenery through another's eyes. We learn this skill from the books we read. We also learn it by studying the shoes or dress or expressions of the people who enter our stores. We chat them up, question them, and listen carefully to their replies, intent on deciphering what *they* want. We're natural-born matchmakers, and the truth is that most of us would do anything to sell a book. But not just *any* book, and not just to make a buck. Not even because we believe in certain books, although assuredly we do. The real pleasure in bookselling comes in pairing the right book with the right person. That's what drives us as we look, listen, assess, ask questions, and then quick-flip through the file of recently read and distantly remembered titles that are logged in every bookseller's beleaguered brain, until bingo! We come up with a match.

Say a conservatively dressed woman of a certain age comes in and wants a book for her elderly mother who has cancer and needs a laugh. Do we hand over *A Bit on the Side* by William Trevor because we consider him a genius, the stories haunting? We do not, although both of those statements reflect our beliefs. Instead we offer *I Capture the Castle* by Dodie Smith because it's light, funny, well written (that's one standard we try never to breach), guaranteed to give pleasure, but not to offend. We have a phrase for such books, coined by Kathy Ashton, the editor of *The Inkslinger*, a twenty-eight-page publication replete with interviews, book reviews, and author recommendations, which we publish biannually. "It's a book," Kathy will proclaim, waving a Barbara Pym or an Angela Thirkell, "perfect even for Great-aunt Heliotrope from Helper (a small rural Utah town), your maiden aunt who takes offense where none is intended and faints at the drop of a lilac-scented handkerchief."

If, conversely, a Mercedes SUV pulls into the parking lot and a young blond woman (not to stereotype) aglitter in (tasteful) gold climbs gracefully down and says she wants a stack of good beach reads for a month's sojourn in Hawaii—do we give her *A Bit on the Side*? No, again. In the first place, the last thing she wants is a hardcover, even if she can afford one, which she obviously can. She wants paperbacks she can sling into her string bag along with her Bain de Soleil, then toss when she's read (or rejected) them. For her, we might suggest a Janet Evanovich and a Sparkle Hayter, since she likes mysteries, likes to laugh, and doesn't shock nearly as easily as Aunt Heliotrope, or maybe a whodunit by Jamie Harrison or Ian Piers. Add a couple of amusing novels by Ann Tyler or Alice Hoffman, and perhaps a slightly wicked book like *Magdalena the Sinner* or *Lambs of God*, and her string bag's full. But wait, she tells us, her husband doesn't exactly like to read, but he might, if there's nothing else to do. And goodness knows he needs *something* to do besides . . . well, you know . . . She smiles an arch smile, and we smile back, adding to her pile a Carl Hiaasen and a James Hall, both funny mysteries, and, in a more serious criminal vein, a Dennis Lehane, along with one of James Lee Burke's. Next, some humorous (and terrific) fiction, two coming-of-age novels: *The Treatment* by Daniel Meneker and *High Fidelity* by Nicholas Hornsby. Finally we add *The Killer Angels* by Michael Shaara because she says her husband enjoys history, sort of, but never seems to finish nonfiction (besides, we've yet to meet anyone who didn't like *The Killer Angels*).

Would we ever give the above list to a Mormon? Or, for that matter, to a Baptist or a born-again Christian? Yes, of course, to a liberal Mormon or Baptist or born-again Christian possessed of a good sense of humor. Would we give Dodie Smith's *I Capture the Castle* to a nonbeliever? We do, all the time—it's the art of knowing when to and when not to that's the skill (and the joy) of bookselling, the art of *not* stereotyping (either Mormon or non-), but instead seeing people as individuals and trying to discern their wants and tastes. Putting the right book in the right hands at the right time can actually change lives. I like to think that the difference between booksellers and true believers—be they religious, political, or simply fixated—is that we try to give people what *they* want, not what we feel they ought to have.

So to whom do we sell William Trevor's books? Or Nadine Gordimer's or Shirley Hazzard's or Charles Baxter's or E. L. Doctorow's or Margaret Atwood's or Richard Powers'?

Oh, there are plenty of readers out there who love the world's truly great writers—passionate fiction lovers for whom novels of fine language and character, novels that deal with ideas as well as drama, are the staff of life. Long may they live.

Examining people's shoes, mentally stepping into them and strapping them on, seems to be an important skill—one that allows people to cross bridges, or to at least get to a midway point on some teetering plank of understanding. Salt Lakers used to possess this ability in good quantity, but right now it seems to be a dying art—one that ought to be fostered, preserved, taught. It is the skill of a good bookseller, and if more of us possessed it, quit foisting our own points of view on one other and began listening to other points of view with a degree of attention, maybe this city/culture/country/world would be less hostile, less riven, less dangerous. A bookseller can dream, right?

A SHORT HISTORY OF A SMALL PLACE

In the beginning, The King's English may have been born more in the spirit of avoidance than creation, but it was always predicated on an outsized passion for books. Ann Berman, my first partner and still good friend, loved books as much as I did, although the profession we both pursued with obsessive longing back then was writing. It was writing that had driven us away from our children several hours each day and into two of the four tiny offices in the cottage-like building in one of Salt Lake's many residential neighborhoods. And it was fear of being shut up in that room with the bad novel I was writing that prompted me to seize with such enthusiasm on Ann's idle comment that our location would be ideal for a bookstore, that the space was perfect.

"You're right—we could write in the back room and put bells on the door so we'd know when customers came in. Why don't we do it?"

"Bells?" Ann's face reflected her astonishment at my leap toward concrete (or rather auditory) reality. But perhaps because she was unwilling to write that day, she was willing to speculate, and when I said, "We could make it *different*, make it the kind of place we wish all bookstores would be," we began to list the things we *didn't* like about the ones we knew: aisles of shelves with no inviting nooks or crannies in which to linger, no way to flop and look, nothing to sip while flopping, snide looks and impatient coughs that discouraged browsing, shelves stacked with new "bestsellers" (we said the word with the contempt of the neophyte), and scant attention paid to the "good" books written recently or in years gone by. We weren't to learn for quite some time that terms like "midlist" and "backlist" apply to such titles.

"We could eliminate aisles, just have shelves against the walls like you would in your own house."

"And chairs, so you could sit down and really *look* at the books."

"And tables for coffee cups. And coffee to put in the cups."

"We can order books by the authors we love," Ann went on.

"*All* of the books by authors we love. Not just the ones everybody knows about. A really good store would have *all* of Graham Greene. And Anthony Trollope."

"Do you realize how many books Anthony Trollope wrote?"

"Yes."

There must have been glee in my voice because there was terror in Ann's. "We can't carry *everything*, you know."

Despite her obvious misgivings, Ann was hooked. I knew she was because she went on to speculate with an enthusiasm equal to my own as to how we would woo customers, how *nice* we would be to people when they came into the store, what we might say to them about various books, which ones we would recommend, the reviews we would write. We tossed around quirky titles like *Memoirs of a Midget*, *Cold Comfort Farm*, and *Cranford*, along with the standards, the classics, and lesser-known novels by well-known authors—Charlotte Bronte's *Villette*, Thomas Mann's *Joseph* quartet.

"We'll never give our customers dirty looks when they stay an hour to browse," I said. "Or be condescending if they like things we don't like."

"I draw the line at Danielle Steele, though."

"Don't be prejudiced."

"I'm not prejudiced, I'm a snob," said Ann. "That's different."

Ann and I were both recently divorced (I had one daughter, Mandy; Ann had four), and because each of us received alimony and child support payments marginally large enough to keep our children fed and clothed, neither had much to spare. We scraped up $6,000 apiece, however, and, realizing that our charge accounts at local department stores probably were not going to suffice by way of financials, we went to our bank where we managed to open a minuscule line of credit.

My ex-husband owned a lumber store, so shelves wouldn't be a problem; the room next door to the two offices we occupied happened to be available—plenty of walls on which to affix the bookcases—so space wouldn't be a problem. We already had two typewriters and one adding machine, and, in lieu of a cash register, we decided to use a money box. So much for the machinery of commerce—on to the books.

I had worked for several months in college for Sam Weller (owner of one of the West's best bookstores), and I knew of the existence of Bowker's *Books in Print (BIP)*. *BIP* consisted of six Yellow Pages-sized volumes listing every book that was in print at that time by title, author, and publisher. We obtained a copy of the author volumes from a wonderful book-crazed poet and employee of Sam's, John Schow, and began to read, filling out 3 x 5 file cards with author, title, price, and publisher information whenever we came across an author we knew and liked, or a title we recognized and liked or thought sounded interesting.

"I never guessed there were so many books in print in the world," Ann said one day, several weeks into this endeavor. "How will we ever finish?"

From this vantage point, nearly three decades later, I can't believe we did finish reading *BIP*. Ingrams, a major wholesaler, provides new stores with a suggested title list designed to serve as a basis for inventory, while the American Booksellers Association (ABA), the national association of which most bookstores in the country are members, offers bookseller schools for prospective bookstore owners—teaching some basic accounting and business techniques that we could have used, no question.

We hadn't heard of the ABA or Ingrams at that point, however, so we toiled our way through the rest of *BIP*, filling out title cards as we went. We actually enjoyed the process, scanning the columns of authors and titles, running across books we'd loved, books we'd meant to read but hadn't, books we'd heard about from friends, from classes, from other books. After we'd finally completed the Zs, we separated by publisher all the 3 x 5 cards we'd made, added up the totals, publisher by publisher, and began to weed. When we got to a point where we couldn't bear to throw out any more, we put all our cards in a shoe box and took them to John Schow, the mad poet who had already helped us. Together, we went through the titles, one by one. "You've got to have that," he'd say. Or, "Pitch that, it'll never sell." Or occasionally, "That one will sell like hotcakes. You'd better get two."

By the time we'd whittled the numbers down to $10,000, we had created an inventory that was highly idiosyncratic. Oh, we had holes, vast areas where our own ignorance was reflected on our shelves. But we had strengths, too. Our selection of fiction, of children's books, of mysteries, of letters and memoirs was distinctive and alluring. Or so we told ourselves. Back at the office, we typed up purchase orders, mailed them off, and hired a carpenter with the remaining $2,000 to build and install the shelves. The only things left were to await the arrival of the books we had ordered, name the store, and send out invitations.

By the Book, Book Nook, Booked, Pen and Ink, Pen to Paper, Bindings, Typed, Chapter and Verse, Volumes, Pages, Page One, The Writer's Den, Writers and Readers, Readers Inc., Readers Ink, etc. etc. etc.

"There's no zing to it . . ."

"That's so ordinary . . ."

"No lilt."

"Pedestrian."

"Dumb."

Or (after a few drinks), "That's the most ridiculous name I've ever *heard*."

We made lists, asked friends for lists, had a naming party and served vast quantities of cheap wine. All we got were headaches.

We tried a more philosophical approach. "How do we define what we're trying to do?" Ann asked.

"Carrying and selling good books, I guess."

"Maybe *that's* the answer. Name some good books. The ones that matter. That made a difference."

"*The Magic Mountain? Sound and the Fury?*"

"Too weighty, pretentious. You can't name a book store after a masterpiece."

Charlotte's Web? Too childlike. *Castle Rackrent?* Too Gothic. *Yoknapatawpha?* Too hard to pronounce—or spell for that matter.

"*Roget's Thesaurus?*" I venture.

"Too boring—but maybe *Roget* has some ideas . . ."

"Here's one under book lovers—how about *Bibliophile?*"

"Too Latin."

"*Bibliotheque?*"

"Too French."

"*Philobolist?*"

"Too obscure."

"*Bookworm?*"

"Too cute, try literature."

"*Scrivener?*"

"Too antiquated."

"*Belles Lettres?*"

"Too exclusive. Look up the word 'grammar.' Or try 'speech.'"

"Ahhh, I do love *Roget's*. Listen: 'The King's English.' Now that has a certain ring. Don't you think?

"Not bad, but is it *good?*"

"Well, it connotes proper diction. Proper use of language. And it's different."

Like our inventory, our name *was* different. And like our inventory, it was predicated on our love of reading. I've always thought it apt that after all our soirées and brainstorming sessions, we found the name we were looking for in a book. And we liked our name—although we were to pay a price for it in certain quarters.

Page ahead a few weeks. I'm by myself at the front desk when in walk two women wearing wire-rimmed granny glasses, tie-dyed skirts, cotton shirts (clearly no bras underneath), and sandals. Oh good, fellow feminists, I think. They'll love it here. I grin foolishly and get up, prepared to show off our women's section, the raft of feminist fiction we carry, from *Norma Jean the Termite Queen, Diary of a Mad Housewife,* and *The Golden Notebooks*, to forgotten classics like *Well of Loneliness, The Awakening, The Yellow Wallpaper* (this was 1977, remember, and forgotten masterpieces by women writers were just resurfacing). "And Virginia Woolf," I rehearse to myself. "Have you read *A Room of One's Own?*"

But before I can ask the question, they have one for me. "Why not the *Queen's* English?" the (natural) blond asks in a chilling tone while the one with (naturally) curly hair nods with such vigor that her brown curls bob.

"I beg your pardon?" I say, as much to stall until I can think my way to her intent as because of any problem I have hearing or understanding the blond's words. Although she fails to repeat her question I attempt an answer. "'The King's English' is a fairly common phrase," I tell her, "and it seems clear what the connection to—"

"So's 'The Queen's English.'"

"Your point?" My tone is still polite, but not very.

The brown curls bob and sway as the brunette woman shakes her head at me. "Why must it always be a man's world? Why can't our choices be based on equality rather than gender bias?"

I want to hector her right back. Me? Gender biased? I want to shriek. I mean here I am, a single mother, starting my own business with another single mother, and some damned woman is berating me about my faulty feminist values? What about solidarity? What about sisterhood? Damn it, I *am* a feminist! For a minute I almost say it all. But my nascent commercial instincts get the better of me. "Have you seen the new Judy Chicago?" I ask. "*The Dinner Party*, from that vaginal art show that's all the talk?" They nod uncertainly. "Are you going to love this," I tell them, and this time their nods are obedient.

And love it they did. They poured over the vaginal art with proprietary pride, thanked me profusely, and I learned a valuable lesson: There is a book out there for everyone. For a doctrinaire Mormon, the right book might be *Mormon Doctrine* by Bruce R. McConkie. For a '70s feminist it was *The Dinner Party*. For a sixth-grader who hates to read, it's *Harry Potter and the Sorcerer's Stone*, or if that doesn't work, maybe something by Gary Larsen. Finding the right book for the right person can be both an art and a vocation—an art and vocation all good independent booksellers share.

But page back to the beginning. Ann and I were still mulling names, and our carpenter hadn't yet finished building shelves to house our eagerly awaited inventory, when the books themselves began to arrive. Since we had already made a file card for every title ordered (computers weren't to darken our doors for years to come—in 1977 they were HAL-sized and wouldn't have *fit* in our offices), we marked the incoming quantity on the margin of each card. Then we filed these "inventory" cards in shoe boxes, piled the invoices on the desk in the back room to look at later, and began shelving—which had its interesting moments. When does a book leave fiction and become a classic? (It doesn't—since we have only *good* novels we don't need a separate section for classics. They're all classics, or classics in the making.) Should we shelve *The Petroglyphs and Pictographs of Utah* in Nature/Science because it's anthropology or in Western because it's about Utah? (Its location won over subject; don't ask me why.) We quarreled a bit, laughed a lot, and found a place for all the books. Finally, invitations went out.

The opening is attended by a host of curious friends, all of whom browse the shelves, asking about this book and that one. As we answer questions, make suggestions, ask what they like in order to decide what to recommend, we start talking faster and faster, pulling first this book and then that one off the shelves, brandishing titles in front of faces as we enthuse. When the last customer leaves (needing to imbibe something stronger than wine after a dose of our low-key bookselling style), we look at each other and say at the same time, "This is *fun*."

And it was. An average day's total that first year was forty dollars, but what a job. We sat at the front desk, nattering to customers about books, gleaning as many good titles from them as they did from us. For the first twenty-two years of our existence, there was a bench facing the front desk—the confessional bench, so-called because people who sat on it seemed compelled to pour out their hearts if not their souls to us (a fact that made us understand the importance of the self-help genre we'd initially scorned). One of those customers was Marilyn Warenski. She was a friend of Ann's and for several years she, like Ann and myself, had been working on a book. The difference was that she had actually finished hers and had found a national publisher. Its title was *Patriarchs and Politics: The Plight of Mormon Women* and it was an early harbinger of the rift that was to later widen so dramatically here in Happy Valley.

Marilyn had grown up Mormon, married a doctor, and embarked on the life of service that most Mormon women, not to mention doctors' wives, live—until it occurred to her that there ought to be more to her existence than canning peaches and driving car pools. A writer of grace and style, a feminist, and a skilled researcher, she wrote an insightful, lively book about our society that stands today as a definitive analysis of the position of women in the local culture.

Ann and I loved the book and begged Marilyn to become our first sacrificial victim in an attempt at an autograph party. She acquiesced, although she was as new to all of this as we were. None of us had any idea what to expect. What if only three or four people came? How many books should we order? We dithered (as we continue to dither before each signing and no doubt always will) and finally decided to go for broke, assume everyone we knew and everyone they knew would come.

We ordered a hundred copies—and sold them all. We had people lined up out the door and down the sidewalk carrying three and four books to have signed and give as gifts, people adding even more copies to the piles in their arms after imbibing several glasses of wine, people calling us to ask if we could get books signed for them because they couldn't be there. Everyone complimented us again and again on the party, the store, the books on our shelves. It was a success beyond our wildest dreams. Oh, did we love this business!

Not long after this, Karen Shepherd, then owner and editor of a feminist newspaper in Salt Lake City, organized a writer's workshop and invited Martha Lear as resident teacher. Martha's memoir, *Heart Sounds*, was the tale of her husband's death from heart disease, of his journey through the corridors of medicine as his heart weakened and failed—of the ways in which medicine failed him. Her husband was a doctor himself and knew the medical world from inside. Martha, a reporter for the *New York Times*, was a keen-eyed observer and an elegant prose practitioner. *Heart Sounds*, which received wonderful reviews, was a bestseller and was used in medical schools for years to induce, *introduce*, empathy and compassion to medical students, to interns and residents, to doctors. A profound and lovely book which said things that badly needed saying about death, about love, about medicine, it was a bestseller in our store, too. We hosted a party for Martha and it was another wild success. *Heart Sounds* is out of print now, more's the pity—we could sell copies by the gross if we only had them to sell (publishers, are you listening?). Martha remains a close friend of mine and of several other Salt Lakers whom she met on that intense, wonderful visit.

I'm not exactly sure why two women who thought they could run a store by writing books in the back room and coming out when the bells tinkled assumed their business could survive. The fact was that we were both business illiterates back then, and our new store was housed in a small building in an out-of-the-way neighborhood so short on traffic that friends snickered behind hands and whispered dire predications to one another. Ann and I were possessed of an outsized passion for books, true, but we were more interested in writing than in bookselling, and *no one* would have described us as masterful retailers. One of our first "customer relations" decisions was to serve coffee, despite the fact that it might well keep out the majority of the Mormons who comprise nearly fifty percent of the potential book-buying population of this religion-riven city. In the end, our Mormon customers grew to love the store despite the fact they didn't drink the coffee, and we ended up so in love with the art of bookselling, such trucklers to the act of matching books to people, that we let go of every other passion and prejudice (well, not quite all of them) in order to keep on selling books to readers. At The King's English we remain so obsessed still, that in these days of so-called—by their own hype departments—"superstores" whose investors demand no profit and who consequently "deep discount," some of them losing millions of dollars a year in the process, we carry on as if all's right with the world.

We must have known instinctively, all those years ago, that the love of books would see us through, that real readers love good books, and that if we stayed true to that one tenet, the bookstore would not only survive, but prosper. We're still banking on that premise, and, so far, it has stood us in good stead.

BOOK LIST
25 Favorite Books from the First Year of The King's English, 1977–78
(Most of Which Remain on Our Shelves Today)

1. *Song of Solomon*, Toni Morrison, 1977
2. *Daniel Martin*, John Fowles, 1977
3. *Ceremony*, Leslie Marmon Silko, 1977
4. *Harafish*, Naguib Mahfouz, 1977
5. *Dance Me Outside*, W. P. Kinsella, 1977
6. *Shosha*, Isaac Bashevis Singer, 1978
7. *Tirra Lirra by the River*, Jessica Anderson, 1978
8. *The World According to Garp*, John Irving, 1978
9. *The Sea, The Sea*, Iris Murdoch, 1978
10. *Legends of the Fall*, Jim Harrison, 1978
11. *An Imaginary Life*, David Malouf, 1978
12. *Excellent Women*, Barbara Pym, 1978 (reprint)
13. *The Cement Garden*, Ian McEwan, 1978
14. *The Coup*, John Updike, 1978
15. *In Patagonia*, Bruce Chatwin, 1977
16. *The Dragons of Eden*, Carl Sagan, 1977
17. *A Rumor of War*, Philip Caputo, 1977
18. *Samuel Johnson*, W. Jackson Bate, 1977
19. *A Distant Mirror*, Barbara Tuchman, 1978
20. *Wind in the Rock*, Ann Zwinger, 1978
21. *This House of Sky*, Ivan Doig, 1978
22. *The Snow Leopard*, Peter Matthiessen, 1978
23. *American Caesar*, William Manchester, 1978
24. *Letters of E. B. White,* 1978 (paperback)
25. *Rumpole of the Bailey*, John Mortimer, 1978

Chapter Two

A FINE FICTION

[
*"Shelf for shelf, The King's English is
the best bookstore I've ever been in."*

— E. L. DOCTOROW, 1979
]

E.L. Doctorow's remark may not be as flattering as it sounds, since in 1979 The King's English was undoubtedly the smallest bookstore he had ever been in. Had Mr. Doctorow been a historian, say, or a chef, he would never have made such a comment in the first place—but he was a novelist. And if there was any subject about which Ann and I were ardent it was fiction. It was our first and fiercest love, and we both knew that if our store were to make its way in the world, it would be on the strength of that passion for—and knowledge of—fiction. Oh, we had a smattering of history, of poetry, some biography, a shelf of regional books, a *great* selection of mysteries, some good children's books. But fiction was our obsession and it showed on our shelves.

THE WORLD ACCORDING TO HIMSELF

Not long after E. L. Doctorow made his flattering comment (he had been in town for a university appearance and had come by the store), Ann and I, bedazzled by our initial forays into the world of book signings, seized upon the next opportunity that presented itself. A splendid poet, Dave Smith, who was teaching at the University of Utah, told us about a close friend of his who had just completed his fourth novel. Not particularly well-known, although he had garnered a fair amount of review attention, said novelist had made arrangements to take a ski vacation with Dave as a way of breaking the publicity tour his publisher had arranged.

We were wowed by a review copy of this author's book, and we called Dave. Could his friend come and sign books for us while he was in town? No way he'll agree, Dave told us. But I'll give you his address and you can ask him yourselves. Dave did, we wrote a letter, and the answer was, "Sure, put some beer in the snow and I'll come in one night after we get off the slopes."

Invitations have gone out, but no matter how we enthuse, no one seems ecstatic at the prospect of meeting this little-known novelist. Nonetheless, given what has happened with Marilyn's book and with Martha's, we decide to order more than we think we'll need. Again, we get 100 copies. Then the national reviews appear. Rave reviews. The book, *The World According to Garp*, hits the bestseller list and, almost simultaneously, John Irving hits The King's English.

On the night of the signing it's snowing. Hard. The door bangs open, the bell tinkles, and in walks Dave Smith. Behind him is America's newest literary sensation. He's dressed in a parka and a striped turtleneck—true to his word, he's fresh off the slopes and looking around for the beer we've promised. What he sees is women. Scores of women. They are beaming at him as if the force of their smiles will pull him into one of their competing orbits. He sits on the bench that has been the scene of so many confessions, and they surround him, gather, hover, perch near him, touch his arms, stick as close to him as iron filings to a magnet. It's a phenomenon unlike any we've seen before. Some gush and blink their eyes in a caricature of flirtation; others, unable to say anything, merely blush and gape.

And Irving talks to the women. Aside from being handsome, he's *nice*. He asks them polite questions while he signs their books. All their books. The books are gone in minutes. So is the beer. And before long, John Irving is gone as well—but not forgotten.

The best part is yet to come. A friend, Lonnie Chipman, is at a party that same snowy evening, and because John Irving is so suddenly and ferociously famous, rumors are flying.

"It's such a tiny store," a woman with red lipstick says. "And this is Salt Lake, after all. No *way* someone like that would come here. Unless . . ."

"I heard Betsy . . ."

"Oh, you don't think . . ."

Lonnie tells me later that my name has been part of at least four separate conversations he's overheard; that it's been linked with John Irving's knowingly; that a man we both know, a neighbor of mine, claims he's seen someone he's sure now must have been John Irving stealing away from my house in the wee hours of the morning, that he's seen him more than once . . .

Lonnie, who knows that the first time I laid eyes on John Irving was that very night, says he almost interrupted the conversation. Then he reconsidered. "What the hell," he told me later. "Nothing like a good scandal to get people talking, and this one is better than anyone could invent. Free advertising."

TALES OF A THOUSAND NIGHTS

Although at the time I was stunned by John Irving's star power, I understand it better now than I did then. It's both similar to and different from the sort of magnetism actors have—different because one sees the inside rather than the outside, the thought process rather than the physical image of the author; similar because people feel they have been privy to both novelists' and actors' lives in some personal way, watched them laugh and cry and swear and make love. It's amazing how few people understand that fiction really is usually just fiction, not autobiography.

But the real source of authorial star power is that reading a brilliant novel can be exactly like falling in love, *is* falling in love. Falling into a book, reveling in its language, recognizing its truth, reading on and on in a state of absolute rapture, unable to pull yourself away from the story . . . Reading *The House of the Spirits* was such an experience for me. I wanted to meet the woman who wrote that book, see for myself if her presence was as magical as her words. My desire to sell her novel became positively messianic. This was something I hadn't felt before, this fervor to make people see, experience a book the way I had seen and experienced it. It was as if I were giving them a gift just *telling* them about *The House of the Spirits*.

In a kind of rapturous daze I wrote a fan letter to Isabel Allende and sent it via her publisher, Random House at the time—sent it because I wanted her to know how much her book had moved me. To my astonishment, she wrote back. Not knowing she responded to *every* letter she received, I took her reply as a sign she had been somehow touched by my words, and I wrote again. Again she replied, and, after a pause of a few weeks, I wrote once more. A sporadic correspondence was established, and at some point, perhaps one of my letters did touch her, or maybe she was just impressed by my persistence. But in any event, when I read, in 1988, that she was going to be at the American Booksellers Association convention and wrote to ask if it were true, she replied that it was, that she was, and that she would love to meet with me.

My new partner Barbara (a tale for another chapter) and I are at the convention in Anaheim. It is May 1988, and not my first book convention, but it is Barbara's. We are both overwhelmed with the books, the people, the noise spilling from room to room at the hall, the sheer staggering commotion of it all. Having been on the floor, looked at maybe a tenth of the thousands of books on display, talked to dozens of writers, hundreds of publicists, reps, editors, we are exhausted. We check our messages for perhaps the twenty-seventh time, to see if Ms. Allende has called. And she has. She's left a message saying that she would be glad to visit with us and please, would we call her in her room.

Allende's voice is soft, her English good but cadenced, laced with Latino inflection. "I have some time right now, if you do also, but I must come to you. Willie is napping, and the rooms here are so tiny.

"He's exhausted," she goes on, as if we are already in complicity with her in her efforts to protect this new husband of hers. And we are more than willing to be whatever she wishes us to be—until I realize what she has just said.

Come to us? *Now?* My brain is short-circuiting in alarm as I look wildly around the room, trying, among other things, not to meet Barbara's eye.

Barbara is tidy, organized, a neatnik, while I, very emphatically, am anything but.

"In five minutes?" I recognize the question in my voice as rude and say, "Five minutes is perfect."

"She's coming here in five minutes?" Barbara asks when I hang up the phone. Her tone is ominous.

I nod and look at the floor.

"Well you'd better hurry then, hadn't you?"

There are clothes everywhere, hanging off the chair, oozing from my suitcase, the drawers. I'd been looking for a sweater that morning, a notebook later on, and then there was the shoe I couldn't find. There are books, papers, strewn about, stacked helter-skelter on the nightstand, the dresser, and I start organizing, piling, then give up and pitch everything into the closet. Barbara has to help me shut the door. She is opening a bottle of no-name wine (no-name wine is better than no wine, she points out) which we have stashed in the fridge, when we hear a knock on the door.

Isabel Allende is beautiful. We have seen her picture on the dust jacket of *The House of the Spirits*, but pictures can lie, often make people appear more glamorous than they actually are. In her case, the opposite is true—the photograph on the jacket of her books is a dim reflection of reality. Her eyes are enormous, liquid, she wears bright lipstick and exotic clothes (remember, we're Salt Lakers, and almost anything seems exotic to us), and she is tiny, iridescent, moves like a hummingbird or a dragonfly. She seems eager to meet us, although we can't believe that this is actually the case.

Generous as she is lovely, she takes charge of us, asks us questions about ourselves until, gathering our wits, we offer wine. She sips politely and so do we, and she insists that we call her Isabel.

I have little memory of what else we said that day. Both Barbara and I were in a kind of starry-eyed stupor, at least when we managed to forget what lay behind that closet door. But I recall the sympathy and interest apparent in Isabel's wide eyes, the intensity with which she listened to us. And I remember her talking with surprising frankness about her own life, telling us how, after so many years of dutiful marriage, when she had finally obtained her freedom, she had planned, like Eva Luna, to use that freedom well. Then she had met Willie, she said, and here she was a wife once more. We laughed at the irony of it.

I know one of us must have asked her, at some point, if she would ever consider coming to the store, because I do remember that she promised to try. It was kind of her to say so, we both agreed, knowing it would never happen. Not many writers came to Salt Lake in those days. Why would they, unless they happened to be on a ski vacation? We asked her to sign the copies of *Eva Luna* and *The House of the Spirits* we had hauled from home.

Page ahead a year. Barbara and I are in the store when the phone rings. It is a publicist from Harper and Row. Ms. Allende would like to do a signing at The King's English, are we interested?

Yes, we tell them, we're more than interested, we're ecstatic. We call the papers, write reviews, call the TV stations, the radio. We send out invitations and I call Emy, a friend from Seattle who had recently adopted a Chilean child whom she had named Clara, after Clara Trueba in *The House of the Spirits*. "Would you like to come to the signing?" I ask her. "And would you like to bring Clara?"

It is the morning of the autograph party at last. When Isabel gets off the plane Barbara and I lead her toward the baggage area. As we stand by the carousel, our august author asks if we are meeting someone else.

"No, just waiting for your luggage."

"This is my luggage," she says, holding up a carpet bag not much larger than a purse.

"But haven't you been on this tour for two weeks?" I ask, knowing from her publicist that she has.

She hefts the bag. "One dress, washable, two pair of underpants, also washable, and a necklace, because when I'm signing books I like to dress up." She flashes one of her magnificent grins.

Isabel has an interview scheduled with KUER, the local public radio station, an hour later. I leave her at her hotel, pick up Emy and Clara, and before long, it's time to get Isabel again. When she climbs in the car I make introductions all around.

"She looks Chilean," Isabel says, nodding toward Clara.

"She is," Emy answers, and a solicitous look from the author launches my friend into the tale of Clara's adoption, to which Isabel listens intently, empathy apparent in her large eyes. We arrive all too soon at the station, where Isabel smiles her electric smile at Clara; two-year-old Clara gives her one right back. As Isabel disappears inside I take mother and child home to await the reading.

Five p.m. and the reading is scheduled for five-thirty. I've dropped Emy and Clara at the store, helped Barbara put out wine (this time better than the last) and cheese and left her there ushering people into the restaurant above the bookstore, seating them. At the hotel, I search the lobby, call Isabel's room, but no one can find her. Finally, I see her tiny form coming from the hotel gift shop. She is holding two large bags. I know she can't have brought whatever she's carrying with her—the sacks are far larger than that carpet bag she had on the plane. There's something red poking out of one bag, and as she draws closer I recognize it for what it is— the yarn-topped head of a Raggedy Ann doll. In the other nestles a Raggedy Andy. "For Clara," she says, giving the "a" the long rolling "ah" of her native tongue.

Allende's speech that day surprised us all. We were prepared for a glorious reading and for a certain amount of sexuality, given the nature of *Eva Luna*. But we were not prepared for her joyous, bawdy humor, nor for the way she courted the audience, wooed and conquered them as if they were lovers. She was serious, heartbreaking one minute, then arch, as she talked about the disappointing truth behind the Latin myth of male machismo. Her delivery deadpan, she told us that her mother edits all her manuscripts, described the agony of waiting for maternal reaction to the sex scenes.

I've not met an author with more crowd or media savvy. Allende said once that writing *The House of the Spirits* was like opening a vein and letting the blood flow. Her appearances are a bit like that in the sense that she seems to hold nothing back, hide nothing. What she gets in exchange for her openness, her humor, and her courage is mass adoration—roomfuls of people so mesmerized they forget to breathe, so enraptured they watch her every gesture, every expression with intensity, not wanting to miss a heartbeat. Star Power. The power of genius. It's intoxicating stuff. Hard to resist. Who wants to resist? Not I.

A friend once called me to task for toadying up to authors, engaging in a sort of self-effacing, adolescent hero-worship. So what, I said then, still say. It's true, I worship at the feet of the best of them. Why ever should I not? I've dedicated my entire adult life to telling customers about the books of writers I admire. So yes, authors—at least the truly great ones—are my gods. They can craft words into sentences that make music and at the same time shed light on the human condition, can make the heart and the mind sing the same heady song. They are geniuses deserving of worship, the Mark Strands, E. L. Doctorows, Margaret Atwoods; the Gabriel Garcia Marquezes, Shirley Hazzards, Nadine Gordimers; the Jeannette Haiens, the Ian McEwans, the Isabel Allendes. So what's not to worship? It's what I care about most in life outside the confines of my family and close personal friendships.

Perhaps if I knew them better I wouldn't be so dazzled, or at least so the argument goes. But I do know some of them better, well enough to know that although occasionally quirky (who among us is not?) and often arrogant, they are also kind, generous, loyal, and deeply honest people, used to looking life in the eye, assessing, then defining, often cold-bloodedly, exactly what they see. They are a stalwart, courageous bunch, hounded by worshippers ("droolers" is the rock term for such groupies, and the image the word evokes is repellent enough that I refuse to go so far as to put myself in that category), and if they carve out a private patch, throw up fences to keep out strangers, who's to blame them? What use to claim they are unjustly proud? Why not defend their right to *be* proud? Why not sell their books well and passionately—at least if they are good books? That is, after all, the point of this blessed business.

Isabel Allende has come back to The King's English five more times over the years. Her audiences have grown so large we have to rent an 800-chair auditorium to seat everyone. And each appearance is the same—a tiny dazzling figure up on the stage, standing on two phone books to reach the mike. A feminist flirt, she pokes fun at the male of the species, Latin lovers, movie stars (this one isn't so gorgeous *off*-screen, that one's teeth are yellow), while maintaining that bawdy, flirtatious air. She has all of us weeping along with her as she reads from *Paula*, has us in gales of laughter as she recites a recipe for a love philter from *Aphrodite*. With *Daughter of Fortune* and *Portrait in Sepia*, Oprah and the chains have claimed her as their own, but she's loyal to us, to independent bookstores. And we are loyal to her. We sold *My Invented Country* with as much passion as we did the transcendent *Paula*, and so did other independent booksellers I know. Indeed, when I attended a committee meeting of independent booksellers gathered to choose speakers for the Book Expo (our annual trade show), the one author everyone agreed on unanimously (did so by proclamation as soon as they saw her name) was Isabel Allende.

MY DINNER WITH ISABEL

A final tale regarding Isabel Allende. She came back to Salt Lake not long ago for the Salt Lake City Library's gala celebration of its new building. TKE had invited her for the occasion and, feverish with excitement when she accepted, I had the chutzpah/gall/hubris/sheer unadulterated stupidity to invite her to dinner—worse, to invite her when my husband, Kit (the house chef, and the man to whom I had by now been married for some years), was out of town.

It is 7:50 p.m. and we've been to the airport to collect Isabel and Willie. The table is set for ten, the side dishes are wrapped in foil and refrigerated, the salmon safe in the oven, the salad and hors d'oeuvres made. Everything seems to be running smoothly; we have drinks in the front room, and the conversation is lively. I leave to put on the couscous—and Isabel follows me into the kitchen, sits down at the counter. "I like kitchens," she tells me, and sips her wine.

She's going to watch *me* cook? I think and swallow hard. Pulling down a pot, I fill it with water and reach for the lid. It isn't there. My daughter, Mandy, had "straightened" the kitchen earlier, and the stack of stainless-steel lids usually nesting between the pots and pans has vanished. Isabel's quiet presence does nothing to calm my nerves as I rummage frantically through the cupboards, attempting to second guess Mandy's tidy mind. No lids present themselves—until Isabel points to a blue one atop a cast iron pot, saying in a sweet voice, "I think that one would work, don't you?"

She's right, it fits. I breathe a sigh of relief, thank her and put my hand on my head to pull down my glasses so that I can read the directions on the couscous box. No glasses. I look frantically to right and to left, all the while trying (and no doubt failing abysmally) to make witty conversation, It's then that Isabel says, "I think perhaps a little flame under the pot would help to boil the water." Her tone is careful—she's not trying to hurt my feelings, just to increase the chances of dining before midnight. I look at the stove. Sure enough, I've forgotten to turn on the burner.

I do so, laugh a weak laugh and pick up one of the couscous boxes, trying, with eyes that need 2.25 power reading glasses, to decipher the fine print, figure out the ratio of couscous to water. I make out the word "boil," but I already know that part, and after a minute she takes pity on me. "I'll do this, you take care of the asparagus," she says and over she bustles.

The large cookie sheet on which I had planned to cook the asparagus, is, of course, missing as well, so I improvise with two broiler pans. The basting brush isn't in the drawer where it commonly resides (I really should cook more often, so I know where Kit keeps things, I tell myself) so I begin spooning olive oil over the spears. Isabel's brow goes up, but kind enough not to show her doubt, she continues stirring couscous without comment while I sprinkle Kosher salt over the asparagus and surreptitiously wipe sweat from my neck. Reaching for the temperature knob (which has long since broken off the second oven, but which resides on top of the toaster), I discover to my horror that it's not there.

I can't bear this, I think, and, perhaps anticipating another of my mad rampages through cupboards and drawers, Isabel says with a wave of her hand, "Never mind, Willie will fix this."

She calls him in, and while he studies the oven as if it were a witness he's deciding how to cross-examine (he's a lawyer, a good one, I suspect), I tell my friend Emy sotto voce (she has flown in for the occasion, bringing along her daughter Clara, now fourteen) to check the salmon, and ask her if she'll carve it when it's done.

"Me?"

"You told me you do this all the time at home. I've got to finish the asparagus and—"

"Steve does it, not *me*."

Steve is Emy's husband. He's in Seattle and no help at all.

I can't bear this, I think again, and say, fighting for an even tone, "So what does he do with the bones? I mean how does he avoid serving them up with the fish"

"Well, he sort of—"

"Willie will do it," says Isabel firmly (perhaps because she's thinking that if Willie doesn't deal with the salmon, there won't *be* any dinner, or perhaps she's alarmed at the word "carved").

Willie looks up from the stove. "Do what?"

"*Fillet* the salmon," Isabel says, and he dutifully examines the fish, pronounces it too rare, and then returns to his oven adjustment efforts while I carry on setting things on the table and Chris, another friend (if truth be known much of what *is* finished the two of them, Chris and Emy, accomplished while I was at the airport), serves the appetizers. Checked again, the salmon proves done and I don mitts to haul it out, making an executive decision to start the asparagus in the same oven. Isabel, meanwhile (I've described the recipe which calls for baking the asparagus at 500 degrees for five minutes), looks dubiously at the temperature gauge which is still set at 350. Ignoring her concern I crank up the temperature and pop in the pan without waiting for the oven to preheat.

Five minutes later Chris enters the kitchen, commenting astutely, "That seems to be smoke billowing from your oven, non?"

She's right, it is smoke, and although I'm not worried, since olive oil always smokes at that temperature, still, bedlam seems to have reached a new level. In addition to me, Emy, Willie, and Isabel, now Chris, my partner Barbara, and Clara have all entered the fray, ferrying salads into the dining room as fast as Chris can ladle dressing onto the greens. When yet another friend wanders in to freshen her wine, eight of the ten people at the party are in the kitchen—in what is in fact a very small space. Thanks to two ovens, one cranked to 500 degrees, the other to God knows what, the temperature is rapidly rising; I only hope it isn't rising in my guests as well, since at any second the asparagus is going to burn. (Even if it's all right thus far, it won't be for long, since I can't open the oven without hitting Isabel's derriere. Do I tell her to move? Let it burn?)

Luckily, Isabel and Willie finish filleting the fish, and as they proudly bear the salmon platter into the dining room, I tong asparagus onto a serving dish, wipe my dripping brow (I'm longing to stick my head in the sink, but I resist), and follow them, wondering how Isabel, who has spent as much time in the kitchen as I, worked as hard, if not harder, manages to look so cool and so lovely.

The actual dinner goes swimmingly. Everyone's adrenaline is up from the experience of cooking, from the narrow escapes from disaster some among us have experienced, and from relief that the food is actually edible. Isabel still remembers that evening; while signing books at The Changing Hands Bookstore in Tempe, Arizona, a few months later she was asked by owner Gayle Shanks whether she knew me. Her reply? "Oh yes, I love Betsy. She's not really a very good cook though, is she?"

HALCYON DAYS ON THE PATIO, OR RUB-A-DUB-DUB, THREE MEN . . .

Over the years, and thanks in no small part to John Irving and Isabel Allende, we began to entice more writers to appear at the store. In the glory days of the late eighties and early nineties, before the advent of so-called superstores, Barbara and I added three spacious (by our standards) new rooms to the building, doubling our size to a whopping 2,000 square feet. We now had eight rooms and plenty of shelf space. We also built a brick patio large enough to seat 100 people (150 if we put chairs in the adjoining driveway as well) and planted a garden around it. We have held many readings on that patio over the years, some more memorable than others.

Sherman Alexie read and signed out there one summer afternoon. He was, in fact, a one-man show, chanting instead of reading, playing his guitar, badgering members of the audience—including my own mother. An aging anthropologist with as much respect for Native Americans as anyone I know, she asked him some question about a ceremony which didn't apply to his own locale and people; asked it hesitantly because she was elderly and trying to get what she meant straight in her own head while she was speaking.

"Do you think because I am Indian I know about *all* Indians?" he interrupted her, before she could finish the sentence that would presumably have tied what she had said thus far with precisely what he was demanding—a connection to/comparison with his own culture.

Mom fiddled with her hearing aid and, too polite to ask him to repeat himself, nodded her fluffy white head as if she had heard and agreed. The audience was deathly still, Mom oblivious, I speechless. And he rode roughshod over all of us, daring us, anyone white, to step to the plate. Sherman Alexie is a brash, defiant young man who loves to give offense and is quick to take it. He is an author with a chip on his shoulder, a raw, astonishing imagination, and an absolute genius for language and for storytelling. His was not the easiest reading in the patio's history, but it was certainly one of the more intense.

Another patio star, and one I deem to be among the West's best living practitioners of the art of fiction, is Ivan Doig. He's a quiet man with a beard that seems grown to insure privacy of expression, and he doesn't sing at his readings (although he came close the last time he was here), but his language sings for him. His modest exterior hides a depth of feeling, a hard, searching honesty, an ear for the cadenced beauty of Western speech, and an eye for the land and its people unlike anything else the West has produced. I've fallen in love with Doig's chronicles—one after the other—of the McCaskill family: of their move to Montana from Scotland in *Dancing at the Rascal Fair*; of McCaskills, father and son, on a Montana ranch in the '30s in *English Creek*; of the clan's involvement in the building of the Fort Peck Dam in *Bucking the Sun*. Perhaps even more remarkable are his works of nonfiction, the National Book Award-winning *This House of Sky*, and the lyrical *Heart Earth*. He read from *Heart Earth* the first time he came to the store, and I can still remember the startling changes he made in language, can hear that gentle voice with its insistent western rhythm unleashing active verbs from quintessentially western nouns as he conjured life out of air. When *Bucking the Sun* was published, he returned to TKE and the language in that piece of fiction once again startled. Montana's Fort Peck Dam was built in the 1930s, and he captured the street argot of that time and place so exactly that to listen to him read was to be catapulted into another world altogether. The audience on the patio was mesmerized by the lilt of it as well as the words themselves, ensnared by the narrative, as he squinted against the sun and spun his tales. The characters he described were clearly people he liked and respected, people who mattered to him, and it became plain to all of us who watched him just what a kind and loyal man Ivan Doig is—as good, I suspect, as any of his characters. Better, perhaps. Less flawed, at least as far as any of us could see. He came again to read from *Prairie Nocturne*, a sequel to his incandescent *Dancing at the Rascal Fair*. The warp of this stunning novel is music, the weft the history of a West in which the Ku Klux Klan, Black Cavalry units, white ranchers, World War I and grand opera all play a part. Doig's book is so infused with music in terms of theme and plot, that it (music) comprises a pervasive piece of the story. While discussing this fact after the reading, we almost convinced Doig to sing some of the songs his characters had composed. Almost, but not quite—grinning, he intoned them but never actually broke into song, more's the pity.

Mark Spragg didn't sing when he came to TKE either, but his prose, like Doig's, is so musical he doesn't need to. He read from his memoir, *Where Rivers Change Direction* and immediately attracted a huge following in Salt Lake, a following which multiplied when Spragg returned with the publication of *The Fruit of Stone*, a supremely lyrical novel of landscape with a quirky, memorable cast of characters and a plot involving reckonings, redemption, and the responsibilities of friendship. Spragg's audience grew to rock star–proportions (by Salt Lake standards) when he read from his next book. *An Unfinished Life* is one of those quintessential American novels that comes along about once every decade and reminds us why we love this land (and why, sometimes, we hate it). One voice in the book is that of a young girl, Griff; it's a Scout sort-of voice, frank, naïve, revelatory in ways that make the reader's heart ache. Another is that of Griff's mother, a woman who's seen more of life than she wants, and who is on the run from her past. Then there's the girl's grandfather, who doesn't like his daughter-in-law one bit; he lives on a Wyoming ranch with another old man, and the two have the sort of friendship that lies more in action than words, more in being than telling. These characters come together in a story so fast-paced and compelling that it is impossible to put down, yet one which tunnels so deep that it is equally impossible to forget. I read it in manuscript some time ago, and the characters still pop in and out of my consciousness like family. Spragg and his wonderful wife, Virginia, also wrote the screenplay for a movie by the same name directed by Lasse Hallestrom and starring, among others, Robert Redford, Morgan Freeman, and Jennifer Lopez. Mark Spragg, along with Ivan Doig, Sherman Alexie, yes, and a handful of other novelists—including Kent Haruf, author of National Book Award nominee *Plainsong* and the more recent but equally luminescent *Eventide*, and another writer we love and have hosted at TKE—have huge careers out here in the West and across the nation, each of them living proof that the American novel is alive and well.

BOATS THAT FAILED TO FLOAT

Signings aren't all songfests of course. There are always the famous authors who turn out to be pills, not to mention the not-so-famous authors and the mid-famous authors who expect more in the way of audience than we can provide. In the first category, a few awful examples come to mind, but perhaps the most noxious in the fiction category was a Midwestern novelist who shall remain nameless, and who is far too unreflective a man to see any personal resemblance in my description. His chronicles of small-town life and small-time sports teams, some of which have been both bestsellers and films, are deft and quirky, and for some reason we assumed he would prove to be as good-humored as the characters he limned with such affection. Instead, he shook hands as if certain that germs were passing, was punctilious in expressing his list of (high) expectations and his disapproval of our (sadly inadequate) efforts to meet those expectations, and was so utterly incapable of carrying on a conversation about anything other than himself that he brought his wife along as a sort of social translator/intervention facilitator. In the course of the dinner following his reading, whenever the chatter (I hesitate to call it conversation) veered away from himself, his face shut down as visibly as did Gielgud's in *Brideshead Revisited*.

There are, of course, other bloodcurdling examples of well-known authors-as-pills, although surprisingly few of them. Among the not-so-famous, the proportion of pills to polite people is far greater, perhaps because new authors are often too frightened to be entirely polite—are as afraid of failure as are the booksellers who host their readings.

The trick and the terror of such events lie in the size (and quality) of the audience. We wring our hands at the thought of an audience of one, and try as we might to publicize, promote, and otherwise pimp our author events, sometimes the worst occurs. When it does, we've learned the hard way that there are ways and means to avoid a debacle.

Rule I for publicists and booksellers alike: Never schedule a reading at a neighborhood bookstore the night before Halloween because: (a) all the mothers in the universe, or at least in the country, are home frantically putting together costumes made from bed sheets and shoe polish; (b) all the fathers in the world (country) are either performing like tasks, assisting their spouses in performing said tasks, or skulking in the TV room, hoping the rest of the family has forgotten their existence; while (c) don't ask me where the single people are, but believe me, they're not out and about attending readings. This same rule can be applied to almost any other holiday eve for exactly the same reasons: think Easter, Valentine's, Thanksgiving—you get the drift.

Example? Judith Freeman had, with *Chinchilla Farm*, received lovely reviews. When her next novel, *Set for Life*, was published, she went on tour, and we were delighted at the prospect of her appearance at TKE, far too green at that point to appreciate the awfulness of the news that she would appear at the store on October 30th. Having duly advertised, we sent out the usual invitations, called in the media, along with babysitters to help craft costumes for our own neglected children (that should have been our first hint), and sat back complacently to await the successful event we thought we had every reason to expect. We sat and sat, waited and waited, while no one—and I do mean *no* one—came. Half an hour into this nightmare of a non-event, I had proffered to our lovely, congenial, discomfited author every conceivable excuse and explanation, uttered banalities ad tedium on every subject from literature to the book business to life in general. Finally, although nothing would have relieved me by this point but a crowd of thousands surrounding Judith Freeman shouting hosannas, I excused myself to go to the bathroom. Instead, I fled to the office, called two women who lived in the area, writers both, and begged them to come. Promising to babysit their children, buy them books, dinner, playing on their own fears—should they ever publish—of finding themselves in like circumstance, I begged, bribed and otherwise encouraged them to fly to our rescue, and to call any friends who lived nearby and beg them to come along.

Leaving hearth and children behind, these kind literary friends of mine not only came but lingered, asking Ms. Freeman to sign several copies of her book and engaging in a writerly conversation that salved her dignity and salvaged the remnants of the store's reputation in the authors' network where word can spread so quickly.

Miraculously, considering her experience here, Judith Freeman returned to TKE some years later, and we managed to redeem ourselves in her eyes, working hard on publicity for the event, attracting a large crowd, and selling a satisfying number of copies of her novel, *Red Water* (although in fairness to the author, it was her splendid reading from the book that deserves credit for selling copies, the glowing reviews that helped attract the audience). Nevertheless, I learned yet another lesson from the earlier disaster, one that I haven't forgotten: have a flotilla, a battalion, a guerrilla band of reinforcements to call should the worst occur—employees who will come disguised as audience, friends willing to leap to the rescue, browsing customers who don't mind being strong-armed into sitting for a half-hour listening. I've even snagged diners waiting for a table upstairs at Fresco's Italian Restaurant a time or two, pouring them a glass of Pinot Grigio and promising to flag them when their table was ready.

Rule II: Never host an event for a book you aren't passionate about. This is a harder rule to follow than at first might seem the case, since books usually aren't published until long after the author tours are established. Often, all we can do is judge by the previous books of that same author—something which in general practice works splendidly. There are, however, exceptions.

Example? A book about a disabled child written by an established, talented novelist. I was certain the book would be perfect for an event in our store. The writer in question had received rave reviews for all his previous work, and more than one of his novels had won awards. Budding novelists would flock to the store to hear him. I had given birth to a disabled child a few years before and could easily tap into that world, since parents in our predicament love to read about others dealing with the same issues, and draw strength, wisdom, hope from doing so.

Wrong, wrong, wrong. Long after the time, date, and publicity were on track, I received a review copy of the book, read it, and was horrified. The protagonist had given up on the kid. Sent him away. With reason, sure. But where were the funny or oddly endearing or simply mundane stories that give disabled children character and substance? Where were the telling tales of behavior that elucidate the contrary mix of trying and touching, heart-warming and heart-wrenching, that is so much a piece of life with such children? Where were the scenes that illustrated their (our) common humanity?

Tap into the special-needs community for an audience? Not on your life. To make matters worse, the narrative was defensive and so hopelessly, haplessly dark in the telling that the local reviews were lukewarm at best. Exit writers-as-audience. Could I call in my battalions, flotillas, guerrillas? Not in good conscience.

Result? An audience of three: one an expert on the particular medical condition from which the child in the book suffered, and two chance browsers curious about the man on the patio. Consequence? The worst forty-five minutes I have ever spent outside the delivery room.

Rule III: Never host an event for a first novel (or a first anything) without some outside mechanism for bringing in an audience. Why? Give me one reason for anyone to attend a signing or reading for a first novel unless he or she (a) knows the writer, is related to the writer, or is unusually curious about new authors; (b) loves the subject; or (c) is bored or lonely. So (a) invite the writer's friends, relatives, business peers, fellow writers; (b) tap into organizations that might have any sort of tie to the subject of the book; and (c) schedule all first-time or lesser-known mid-list authors on a regular roster, so that the lonely, bored, or curious can mark their calendars accordingly.

This advice might sound harsh, and I mean no disrespect to either writers *or* customers—

in my late twenties, blasted by divorce and loneliness, I attended strings of such events on the evenings my daughter was with her father (there might be worse prospects to a twenty-something single than a weekend evening home alone, but not many). Mind-centered events that fill such evenings with social commerce and interest are, among other things, a community service *and* a service to writers trying to establish names—matters of no small import. In fact, author events are a large and vital piece of what booksellers do, and for the most part we love doing them. It's just that there are ways to make them work, ways to avoid causing them to fail.

THREE OLD(ISH) BROADS IN A BOAT

As eastern as Doig is western, Jeannette Haien's language has something in common with Doig's, a musicality, a cadenced flow, an attention paid both to the exact meaning of a word and to the singing sound of it. *The All of It* came out in 1988. I stumbled across a galley and read it in two or three hours. My God, I said aloud in bed, waking my husband. He rolled over and went back to sleep. I read it again.

A tiny book, a perfect book, a book with heart, with soul, it tells the tale of a man on his deathbed relating to a priest "the all of it"—and of the wife who must finish this tale after the man's death. It is a truth-telling book and is written in language so unbelievably musical, so completely Irish, that I still can't believe its author is American. Again, wanton that I am, I fell in love. I sold the book to everyone, talked about it at dinner parties, on the phone to my friends, to every customer who walked in the door asking for good fiction.

Then, wonder of wonders, its author came to Salt Lake. Mark Strand was new on the faculty at the University of Utah then. He loved our store, and when he scheduled Jeannette Haien to read at the U, he agreed to bring her by for a signing afterward.

She came in a voluminous cape. It was November and cold. The reading had been luminous; her big rich voice seemed to surround her words in a nimbus, and her diction was like her writing, exact but full of implication. Her Irish dialect had been so pure during the reading that her reversion to American English was a shock, one leavened by her broad, salty humor. The crowd was as enamored as I was. Everyone trooped over to the store en masse, wanting, needing, a signed copy of her book.

Later, I went to dinner with Mark and Jeannette. The conversation was general in that way conversations can be when people don't know each other well, but there was a purpose to it, an honesty, that made it seem far from the chitchat that usually marks such occasions. I asked if she'd come back when her next book was done. She said yes, and I knew she meant it.

She did mean it. In 1997, when *Matters of Chance* was finished, she called me. We had kept in touch through Mark Strand over the course of that decade, and when the manuscript was in its final stages, she sent it to me. It is a big family novel that is also a social history of a time and place. The time is the era that begins with the forties and World War II, spans the complacent fifties, rowdy sixties. The book's pace is stately—like *Dance to the Music of Time*, it treats the decades as movements in some magnificent symphony. She captures the essence of the era she portrays in its voices and in a web of plot that is at once as inevitable and surprising as life itself.

Jeannette's reading from *Matters of Chance* at TKE was, if possible, even more compelling than her reading from *The All of It* had been ten years earlier. I can still hear that rich, generous voice of hers, the tears in it as she *became*, one after another, the characters she'd come to love like family over the years she'd spent with them. She lives in her art, I realized. And it lives in her.

By the end of her second visit to TKE, Jeannette had become a friend. We kept in touch from that time forward via phone and letter, and three years later she returned to Salt Lake to teach at an annual writer's workshop called Writers at Work. That visit was, for me, one of those pivotal times we all experience at least once or twice in our lives.

Jeannette stayed with me and my family, which by then included my second husband, Kit, and our young son, Nick. Nick had been born brain-damaged and had an intractable seizure condition. While Jeannette was here, he came down with pneumonia; his seizures, exacerbated by spiking fevers, were frequent, terrifying, the house hushed. Kit and I spelled each other at his side, keeping watch day and night.

No prima donna she, Jeannette moved around as quietly as we did, offering to help, empathizing, bringing us drinks, keeping us company. She told us funny stories to cheer us up, brought Nick presents to cheer him up, was, in short, the perfect guest in the most trying situation imaginable. Most people in her place would have fled to a hotel, claiming they wished to make life easier for us, when their actual motive would have been to make life easier for themselves. I know this to be true because I've watched people flee my son's problems for years. Jeannette stayed. Not only stayed, but made life infinitely more bearable by so doing.

She had workshops to conduct in the daytime, so I ferried her back and forth to the conference when Kit was with Nick, attended a couple of readings with her. The flip side of Jeannette's honesty is that she does not suffer fools and, although never unkind, is dead honest in her assessment of her students' work. She is adamant about right usage, intolerant of unnecessary verbiage (she would no doubt deplore the use of "unnecessary" here, saying that "verbiage" *means* wordiness, that the adjective "unnecessary" *is* unnecessary), and she calls unessential adverbs "Tom Swiftys," insisting that except in unusual cases a verb that cannot stand alone should be replaced by one that can.

Jeannette Haien's passion for the miraculous potential for meaning that is language's blessing, the potential for misuse that is its curse, could be seen as arrogance, her high standards as intolerance. But Jeannette is a woman of extraordinary integrity who applies her exacting standards to herself more rigorously than to anyone else. She does not (has never I suspect) view her work as something to which she can apply herself when not otherwise engaged with those things most of us use to postpone the realization of our secret desires. Yet her dedication is not self-seeking. Honesty is at the core of Jeannette Haien. However musical her writing—and after four decades spent in the concert halls of the world performing Bach, Beethoven, Mozart on the piano, having as students the likes of Murray Perahia, how could music *not* pervade her writing—musicality is never achieved at the expense of meaning. Her every effort is directed toward using the word that exactly fits the meaning she seeks, cadence and pitch not-withstanding. Her every word is directed toward what matters.

I don't know what her students picked up from Jeannette's classes, but what she taught me was that I count, that what I agonize over on paper counts—especially if I take the trouble to agonize, to be exact, honest, and only then to commit the words to paper. I began to write regularly after that visit, to take myself seriously again, to carve out a little bit of time for my own pursuits. Reading her books has changed my idea of what art is. Knowing her has changed my idea of who I am.

Why did I put Jeannette Haien in a section entitled "Three Old(ish) Broads in a Boat"? Because I choose to define "old broad" as a woman who is (1) wise and experienced enough to recognize the truth about humankind when she sees it, (2) fearless enough to tell that truth straightforwardly, and (3) honest enough to regard language with the same frankness, giving artistry and meaning equal weight. And I use the phrase "in a boat" in connection with her because of Jerome K. Jerome's *Three Men in a Boat*, yes, but also because Jeannette is one of three such women who have come to The King's English over the years, each in the same boat not only in terms of age, but of talent, all having published their first fiction when well into the second half of their lives (Jeannette had published something in her youth, but claims it doesn't count)—in their sixth, seventh and eighth decades respectively.

The first of the three to visit the store was Harriet Doerr. Married to a mining engineer, she had lived a life similar to that of Susan Burling Ward in Wallace Stegner's *Angle of Repose*, moving around the West with her husband, dragging children from mining camp to mining camp. *Stones for Ibarra*, set in a small Mexican village, details the life of such an American woman, a wife and mother, beginning, after decades of selflessness, to regard life and death from fresh angles. Doerr was 74 when *Stones* was published and well into her 80s when *Consider This, Señora* came out. She visited the store for both books, frail, white-haired, kind, but possessed of a steely spine and an aristocratic manner that impressed those prepared to dote, kept them at a polite distance and on their best behavior.

When attending an ABA convention in California, we stopped to visit her in Pasadena. She received us with that same impeccable formality, pouring us tea and chatting with us. Her eyesight now failing, she mistook me for Eve Leonard, our publicist at the time, and directed most of her conversation Eve's way, speaking of books, of Wallace Stegner (under whom she studied) of the business of writing, the business of books. I sat quietly in the corner marveling at Doerr's acuity as a reader and writer, her startling intelligence, her wit. Her books, now three in number, combine the carefully observed detail and the fully examined life in wonderful ways. Like Jeannette, she was a wise and candid observer. She was well over 90 when she finally passed away.

Olive Ghiselin's collection of short stories, *Testimony of Mr. Bones*, is one of the best story collections I've read in the years TKE has been open. Married to poet and academician Brewster Ghiselin, she, like Doerr, moved through much of her life in her husband's wake. She taught English at the University of Utah, then left to raise two children and to help

Brewster entertain and host every famous author of their time, from Dylan Thomas to John Dos Passos. Knowing Olive, I am sure she held her own with all of them. I've never met anyone with literary acumen or a mordant wit equal to hers. A quiet feminist in her ironic way, she knows more about well-known, not to mention obscure, women writers of the twentieth century than anyone I've met inside or outside academia. At 96, she is still as droll, as curious, as discerning as ever, shooting me laudatory comments on Margaret Atwood's *The Blind Assassin*, some not-so-laudatory comments on a couple of other novels I sent her which, she told me, "went on (and on and on)." Or "didn't seem to go anywhere at all, for all the huffing and puffing." A natural heir to Jane Austen, Olive's own stories are beautifully wrought, delicately written, and yet tough-minded, carefully crafted, brimming with irony. Life is for her a feast of human comedy, yet like Jane Austen, she balances her critical eye with a compassionate sensibility, is possessed of consummate narrative skill and uncanny facility with language.

Jeannette Haien, Harriet Doerr, Olive Ghiselin. All three are, in a sense, navigators of the unknowable just as surely as is Margaret Atwood, attempting to chart the universe—and the course of humankind across its unfathomable surface.

THIS BOY'S LIFE

We've had other wonderful novelists at the store, of course, and this chapter could go on indefinitely (as the lists at the end of it may seem to do). But there are three authors I cannot omit, the first of whom is Tobias Wolff. Wolff is a wonder of a writer of fiction and nonfiction alike, a master of the short story and a man who took memoir to a new height in his tale of growing up in a peripatetic and sublimely dysfunctional family, *This Boy's Life*, and of coming of age in Hell, *In Pharaoh's Army*. Wolff's style is deceptively simple; he writes in clear prose, using subterfuge and wit to deliver invidious papercuts, the pain of which we feel only pages later. A master of the short story, he came to TKE when his sublime collection, *The Night in Question*, was new; he's a stunning writer and a marvel of a teacher as well, judging by the way he responded to the students' questions at TKE. Indeed, he holds the Wallace Stegner chair at Stanford University and heads the creative writing program there. Geoffrey Wolff, another spectacular writer and Tobias Wolff's brother, came along with him to Salt Lake City and the two of them ended the trip with a week of skiing.

Wolff came again to TKE and to the Salt Lake City Library when *Old School: A Novel* was hot off the press. The tale of a boy not of the establishment (indeed, a boy who hardly knows, in the beginning, how to define establishment) who attends an Eastern prep school where he learns what separates those for whom class is second nature from those who simply try to ape class, this is a witty and hugely intelligent (and affecting) book. Wolff manages to mine school-life for all it's worth, telling what is, on the face of it, a simple coming-of-age tale, while he develops theme after intriguing theme: writing, what works and why (or why not); truth, the effect not telling it can have on one's life or one's work; class, in terms of academia as well as society. Wolff's own writing is at once as simple and as complex as life itself; *Old School* is another book that, like *This Boy's Life*, will live on on the shelves of good bookstores, of libraries, of readers.

P OSEIDON

Speaking of living on, of becoming part of the canon of contemporary literature, E. L. Doctorow is a novelist whose work obviously will do so. I met him when he was teaching at the University of Utah in 1975. He had lived next door for several months, but emerging from the pain of divorce, I was oblivious to his presence—until, just before he was due to leave, my neighbor Milt Voigt invited me to a party. Milt was chair of the English Department, and there were so many members of his faculty milling around the living room that night that once inside, all I wanted to do was go home. This was before my bookselling days, and dismayed by the gap that dissociated my straightforward love of books from the more academic take on things literary, I was gazing around, wondering what in the world I could contribute to a discussion in which deconstruction, Eliade, and Derrida were prominent themes, when a bearded man with a crooked grin mentioned a novel and asked me if I'd read it. I hadn't, but not wanting to appear dumb I named another one, told him I thought it was good. He disagreed, and we began talking books in earnest, passing a pleasant half-hour. I finally asked what he was teaching, and when he said a creative writing course, it came out that he had recently published a novel, was working on another. He described the one already published, and when I left, I was proud that I had managed to stay the respectable period of time that cocktail parties require. I had a copy of his latest novel under my arm and planned to read a chapter before bed. I stayed up all night.

It was *The Book of Daniel*, and I felt like I'd been poleaxed when I finished it. In fact, outside of adolescence, when I fell in love with books as frequently as I developed crushes on boys, I hadn't been struck so all-of-a-heap by anything I'd read except *Gravity's Rainbow* and *Beyond the Bedroom Wall* (why are we so deadly serious when we're young?). I felt, after I'd finished *The Book of Daniel*, that there had been some fundamental shift in the way I viewed the world, politically, historically, and in terms of art. I leafed back through it just to make sure I hadn't made it up and was more certain than ever that the man was a genius. I met him again the next day, on the sidewalk. He was packing up to leave town, and this time I was so tongue-tied that I probably wouldn't have spoken, but he saw me. He smiled and asked if I'd read that first chapter like I'd promised.

Ever a fool for a good book, I was stunned, staggered. And mute. This was one of the best contemporary novels I'd ever read. I don't remember how long I stood, red-faced and speechless, or what my exact words were when they finally emerged, but today's equivalent would probably be something brainy like, "Oh my God."

Then, suddenly, I couldn't *stop* talking. I told him I'd read the whole thing. I told him it was brilliant. I told him I'd never thought about the Rosenbergs as *people* before, not really, and I'd never even considered the fact that they had a son.

"It's a novel, not history," he said with his wry smile. "It's loosely based on the Rosenbergs yes, but it's fiction, not fact in any way."

I said that, novel or not, it had made me see life, see history, question history, observe its currents at work from some point above like no book ever had before. God only knows what else I said that day—I don't. But I do know that I went on and on and on.

He was pleased. Who wouldn't be? He promised he'd send me a copy of the novel he was currently working on when it was finished. Then he left, waving as he drove down the street where he'd lived all those months unbeknownst to me, and I went inside to reread *The Book of Daniel*.

Two months later, I was in Aspen, Colorado, taking a writer's workshop and beginning my bad novel. I'd sent Doctorow a fan letter, reiterating my admiration for his book, and back in the mail came a copy of *Ragtime*. Oh my God, I thought after I'd read it. He's not only a genius, he's a genius who doesn't repeat himself. I sent him a rave review that he read before all those rave reviews hit the papers. I said that in an entirely different way from *The Book of Daniel*, *Ragtime* was just as brilliant—a tour de force, in fact, that was going to have a powerful effect on literature in our country. How stupidly brash I was, I think now, how callow he must have thought me. I was right about that book, though, with its inventive mix of history and fiction; its fictive, fresh-angled interpretation of history's famous, their relationship to the world they lived in, to the characters he invented; its depiction of the patterns individuals can impose on the vast canvas of human history, the scars history can carve on the hearts of individuals.

He visited the store when he was in town a few years later to read at a college, and he liked TKE, small as it was back then. He's returned a time or two since, when he was lecturing in Salt Lake, but there was never a new book, or even a book newly out in paperback at the time, on which to pin an event. I read his novels with admiration, sometimes with awe. *Billy Bathgate* and *Loon Lake* with their fabled, notorious Depression-era casts of characters; *World's Fair*, an incandescent coming-of-age story set around the 1939 World's Fair; *The Waterworks*, the darkly horrifying and perversely fascinating tale of the evil that rich, powerful men wrought in post-Civil War New York (and a book which so far transcends *The Alienist*, which came out the same year, that I can hardly believe the latter was a bestseller) . . . But what am I thinking? *Doing?* If he thought me callow before—here I am, rendering his brilliant novels in five-word phrases. Ghastly, true, but unfortunately the very nature of the business of bookselling, this casting out of phrases, pheneromes, in hopes that some reader will catch a scent of narration in the air and take a bite.

Every two or three years when Ron Smith, the Random House rep, told me that Doctorow had a new book out, I wrote or called the author to beg yet again—but he goes to only a handful of cities on a given book tour these days, and Salt Lake has always been out of the question. At the end of 1999, I called him as usual, lamenting, as I do all too frequently these days, the state of the book industry, the way the chains are gobbling us up. Hearing the self-pity in my voice, I began giving him all the positive reasons for coming to The King's English. We could do a fund-raiser for the English department, hold the event at the university, bring in classes. Charles Berger, the chair of the department, actually taught *Daniel* in class every year and was an ardent admirer. I would get huge articles in both papers, call Doug Fabrizio at our public radio station, it would be glorious, fun—

"I'll come," he said.

What?

"Call publicity to get a date. I'll come."

Oh, my God.

City of God is, like all of Doctorow's work, brilliant, thought provoking. A book which eschews the rampant narcissism of most American fiction and relates the lives of its characters to the larger concerns of social, political, and in this case, theological, history, it is a complex novel, as fragmented and yet inescapably interlinked as our age, as our communication systems, as our every exchange, be it through E-mail or text messaging or fax. Its rhythms are as fractured, frantic as the jazz that is the trademark music of our nation, as the quantum theories that mark the beginning (or is it the end?) of physics as we know it. This quality of interruption, truncation, makes the book more difficult to read than other of Doctorow's novels, at least until one gets the knack of it, learns to make the requisite leaps. It doesn't take long to do, some twenty or thirty pages, although for some reason the *New York Times* reviewer couldn't manage. (Could it have been because said reviewer was a film critic rather than a book critic by trade?) *Time*, *Newsweek*, and most of the other newspapers and magazines in the country loved the book.

We worried about that wretched *New York Times* review, dithered and stewed about how many people might attend the reading, what space to use. Since the University of Utah was on spring break on the date the publicist had given us, we couldn't involve the campus as we had planned. There are two private high schools that kindly allow us to host events in their auditoriums—the capacity of one is twice the size of the other. The public would come, of course. Doctorow was, is, one of our country's finest living novelists. But with the university out of session, weather beckoning people to the southern part of the state, how many would attend? Finally we decided to go for broke.

It is 6:45 p.m. I pick Doctorow up at his hotel and on the way to the school manage to take two wrong turns. It's hard to get lost in Salt Lake, unless you're as lacking in directional instinct as I am. I finally pull into the parking lot at two minutes of seven, but there are no free spaces. A good sign, but I can't drop off E. L. Doctorow and leave him to wander the corridors of a huge high school alone. Then I see a spot, clearly marked BUSES ONLY.

It's night, I reason, surely no buses will appear this late in the evening. I park, walk him in and through the back halls, rehearsing my welcoming remarks in my head. Duly terrified at the prospect of introducing one the country's great authors, I have funked it, have asked Charles Berger, the chair of the English department and the man who teaches *The Book of Daniel* in his classes, to do it for me; my sole duty is to welcome the crowd, introduce Charles.

I am sitting backstage, eyeing the far-too-empty auditorium, praying it will fill, wondering what Doctorow is thinking, will think if more people don't show up in the next three minutes, when an announcement comes over the loudspeaker. "Will the person whose Toyota is blocking the bus parking area please move his or her car? There is a busload of children waiting. Will the person whose . . . "

The nightmare is, or at least so it seems to me, Shakespearean in dimension. I want to dive into the orchestra pit, drop through the trap door in the stage floor and hit concrete, oblivion. Until I look up to see Doctorow's mouth uptilting in that half smile of his. I walk out to the mike, confess to the audience that I am the guilty party, the owner of the offending Toyota. As Barbara grabs my keys, shaking her head, and the audience laughs, more people begin streaming in, taking seats—over five hundred of them. Thank God, I tell myself. They settle in, and I belt out my welcome, introduce Charles.

A few minutes later, Doctorow emerges, grinning. He strides to the podium and proceeds to give the most stirring speech in defense of independent bookstores in general and The King's English in particular that I've ever heard in my life. Independents are the ones who take the time to read our books, he says. The ones who think about what they read, know what's good and what isn't; who pass that knowledge on to readers; who find talented new authors to tell readers about, rediscover authors long-forgotten. Independent bookstores matter. The King's English matters. He carries on in this vein, eliciting a storm of applause from the audience. Then he delivers a reading that no one in the room will ever forget. There's a story fragmented throughout *City of God* which tells of an orphan, a Jewish tailor, and an SS major in a Lithuanian ghetto where Jews were forced to police themselves *for* the Nazis on the one hand, protect their inhabitants from the Nazis (as best they could) on the other. Doctorow read that tale in a seamless piece, and there was such a stillness in the audience by the time he was finished that it was plain everyone had been imprinted indelibly with his narrative. The only other time I ever heard such stillness in an audience was at a concert here recently when Rostropovich, after an overwhelming ovation, played as an encore a minor-key Sarabande from a Bach Suite. There was that same absolute hush afterward, as a stunned audience tried to swim back to the present, to the reality of clapping hands, of coats and gloves and scarves.

SURFACING

Two months after E. L. Doctorow's reading, I was in New York visiting relatives and had coffee with him. He was his usual genial self and said that in Canada he'd run into Margaret Atwood at some literary affair and that she'd asked him about his tour. When he told her he'd gone to Washington, D.C., Los Angeles, San Francisco, and Salt Lake City, she said, "Why in the world did you go to Salt Lake City, of all places?" To show solidarity with a friend who's having trouble with the chains, he told her. When he'd finished describing The King's English, she announced that she, too, wanted to go, to show solidarity.

I don't know whether she'll actually manage it, he told me. But that's what she said she'd do.

I marveled at the implication—that two of the best novelists on our continent are champions of Independents, willing to come to Salt Lake City, of all places, to "show solidarity." Then I went home and called my sales rep at Margaret Atwood's publishing house who, as all of a twitter as I was, called the publicist to tell her the tale. But the publicist's reply was "Sorry, Atwood's tour is booked. It's set in stone." So, alas, we gave up the idea.

A couple of months passed, and a prerelease copy of *The Blind Assassin* came in the mail. It was fabulous. I've always loved Atwood's books, was first captured by the scene in *The Edible Woman* where the narrator/protagonist is sitting on the floor in a bedroom listening to a conversation in which she has no part and feels so invisible she slides quietly under the bed (no one notices). Then there was *Cat's Eye*, the most vivid evocation of the cruelty of teenage girls I've ever read. Like Doctorow's fiction, each of Atwood's fifteen novels is different, this one delving into history, as does the brooding, mysterious *Alias Grace*; that one making darkly speculative forays into the future like the inventive, chilling *The Handmaid's Tale*; toying with the present, the reader's head, as does *The Robber Bridegroom* . . .

Like Doctorow, Atwood is stylistically unpredictable, allying form with content in such a way that as one changes, so does the other. She's brave, creative, and brilliant, just as

Doctorow is. Even for her, however, *The Blind Assassin* is a tour de force. A story within a story within a story that contains the seeds of yet another tale, it is a blindingly complicated and completely enthralling book about which I wrote a short blurb for Book Sense. (A blurb is the sort of mini-review I've been indulging in in these pages, consisting of a couple of not-very-long sentences that convey story and merit—or lack of merit. Book Sense is an alliance of independent booksellers more completely defined in a later chapter.)

I sent the blurb off, and then the review by Thomas Mallon, hardly the world's most scintillating novelist, appeared in *The New York Times*. Mallon said, among other things, that *The Blind Assassin* was flat. Flat? I fumed. This book I couldn't put down, that wowed me with its language, its stories, its history, its sheer unadulterated virtuosity? Flat? I wanted to scream my indignation, but instead I wrote it. I do occasional reviews on our local public radio station and I did one—not of Atwood's book, but of Mallon's review of it—working off my spleen at the all-too-similar review of Doctorow's book at the same time, wondering on the airwaves why *The New York Times* found major books by two of the world's best novelists "too difficult" and whether this said more about the publication than it did about the books.

Page forward another month. Karen Hopkins, the Doubleday rep, is in the store, and I ask her if she'd consent to pose to Atwood, via her publicist, a question for the holiday edition of our store newsletter, *The Inkslinger*. The question: What is the thing you'd least like to receive as a gift this holiday season, and when (inevitably) you receive it, what will you trade it in for?

"I'll deliver the question to Atwood myself," Karen told me. "She's slated to visit Denver's Tattered Cover Bookstore and I'm going. So send me your Book Sense review and your radio review of that dumb Mallon pan, too."

Atwood came to Denver, was both witty and compelling, according to Margaret Maupin, the fiction buyer at The Tattered Cover. Atwood told Karen that she was sorry she hadn't been able to make The King's English after all. "But I will come," she said. "In the future. I know about the store now; I'll be there." She signed a book for me, signed bookplates for the store and answered the question we asked. Here is her reply:

"As to the unwanted Xmas object—a set of electric hair curlers would top the list. What would I trade them for? Almost anything else. How about a book certificate for The King's English? That would be an added incentive for going there."

Margaret Atwood finally did appear at TKE when her next book, a darkly brilliant futurist tale entitled *Oryx and Crake*, was new in paperback. She read in the same auditorium in which Doctorow appeared. Like Doctorow she delivered a wonderful paean to independent bookstores, and like Doctorow she read with transfixing power, mixing in a delicious wit that sent seven hundred people into paroxysms of laughter—something no one who had read that chilling book expected. She was a trooper, too, not only signing over six hundred books for the people in the audience, but (when I discovered to my horror that a bookseller had taken the rest of our stock back to the store) also offering to drive over to TKE on her way to the airport to sign the rest of the books. Her plane was due in less than an hour, but even though her driver and I both protested that she might miss her plane, she insisted. We swung by the store, loaded up several boxes of *Oryx and Crake*, and she autographed madly all the way to the airport, talking books as her pen flew. At the terminal she leapt from the limo, bent down and promised to return, saying she had had a wonderful time and thanking me.

Thanking *me*? I wondered. What made her come to this out-of-the-way city, anyway? And what made her promise solidarity with such fervor? What made Rohinton Mistry agree, as he did (see Chapter 7), that he'd visit and read at TKE? My guess would be that the idea of our store pleases them—the idea of a store somewhere west of the Hudson where booksellers read, sell, and care passionately about good books. And that, at a guess, is what engages E. L. Doctorow's sympathy and support, and Isabel Allende's as well—not The King's English per se, but all the TKEs, the independent bookstores across the country, that are engaged in this happy business of finding new books to admire, fanning the embers of admiration that keep alive an abiding passion for the glorious old ones. These authors—so famous they don't need to go anywhere, do anything, to publicize their books except to write them well and truly—are paying tribute to all of us when they visit any of us, recognizing the fact that we are, collectively, a vital part of the book industry, one that must not be lost.

That is not just a guess, but a deeply held belief—that we are all in this together, and that independent booksellers do what chains and dot-coms, with their obsessive attention to the bottom line, can never do as well. And I believe that writers, along with those readers who are passionate about books, recognize this fact—or soon will, if enough voices are raised, speak with appropriate fervor on the subject.

※

Book Lists
25 Favorite Novels from the First 25 Years of TKE in a Bewildering Variety of Categories

25 Novels That Stood the Test of Time and Stand Out Still
1. *Song of Solomon*, Toni Morrison, 1977
2. *The Sea, The Sea*, Iris Murdoch, 1978
3. *Shosha*, Isaac Bashevis Singer, 1978
4. *The Burger's Daughter*, Nadine Gordimer, 1979
5. *The Second Coming*, Walker Percy, 1980
6. *The Transit of Venus*, Shirley Hazzard, 1980
7. *Midnight's Children*, Salman Rushdie, 1980
8. *Smiley's People*, John Le Carre, 1980
9. *A Chain of Voices*, Andre Brink, 1982
10. *Unbearable Lightness of Being*, Milan Kundera, 1984
11. *The House of the Spirits*, Isabel Allende, 1985 (U.S. edition)
12. *World's Fair*, E. L. Doctorow, 1985
13. *The All of It*, Jeannette Haien, 1986
14. *Moon Tiger*, Penelope Lively, 1987
15. *Crossing to Safety*, Wallace Stegner, 1987
16. *Dancing at the Rascal Fair*, Ivan Doig, 1987
17. *Love in the Time of Cholera*, Gabriel García Márquez, 1988
18. *Possession*, A. S. Byatt, 1990
19. *The English Patient*, Michael Ondaatje, 1992
20. *Consider This, Señora*, Harriet Doerr, 1993
21. *The Cunning Man*, Robertson Davies, 1994
22. *Corelli's Mandolin*, Louis De Bernieres, 1994
23. *The Moor's Last Sigh*, Salman Rushdie, 1995
24. *A Fine Balance*, Rohinton Mistry, 1996
25. *The Blind Assassin*, Margaret Atwood, 2000

15 Newer Novels That Will Stand the Test of Time

1. *Bel Canto*, Ann Patchett, 2001
2. *The Gardens of Kyoto*, Kate Walberg, 2001
3. *Atonement*, Ian McEwan, 2002
4. *Family Matters*, Rohinton Mistry, 2002
5. *The Lost Garden*, Helen Humphreys, 2002
6. *The Story of Lucy Gault*, William Trevor, 2002
7. *The Great Fire*, Shirley Hazzard, 2003
8. *Any Human Heart*, William Boyd, 2003
9. *Old School: a Novel*, Tobias Wolff, 2003
10. *The Curious Incident of the Dog in the Night-Time*, Mark Haddon, 2003
11. *The Master*, Colm Tóibín, 2004
12. *An Unfinished Life*, Mark Spragg, 2004
13. *Heir to the Glimmering World*, Cynthia Ozick, 2004
14. *Banishing Verona*, Margo Livesey, 2004
15. *The Plot Against America*, Philip Roth, 2004

25 Irresistibly Madcap, One-of-a-Kind Reads
(Beware: some have dark underbellies)

1. *The World to According to Garp*, John Irving, 1978
2. *Confederacy of Dunces*, John Kennedy Toole, 1980
3. *Water Music*, T. C. Boyle, 1981
4. *Dinner at the Homesick Restaurant*, Anne Tyler, 1982
5. *Handling Sin*, Michael Malone, 1983
6. *Not Wanted on the Voyage*, Timothy Findley, 1984
7. *The Alley Cat*, Yves Beauchemin, 1986
8. *The Hearts and Lives of Men*, Fay Weldon, 1988
9. *Good Omens*, Terry Pratchett and Neil Gaiman, 1990
10. *Foolscap*, Michael Malone, 1991

11. *The Wilde West*, Walter Satterthwaite, 1991
12. *Lempiere's Dictionary*, Lawrence Norfolk, 1991
13. *A Dubious Legacy*, Mary Wesley, 1992
14. *Green Grass Running Water*, Thomas King, 1993
15. *Crazy in Alabama*, Mark Childress, 1993
16. *Gospel*, William Barnhardt, 1993
17. *White Man's Grave*, Richard Dooling, 1994
18. *Wicked: The Life and Times of the Wicked Witch of the West*, Gregory Maguire, 1995
19. *Reservation Blues*, Sherman Alexie, 1995
20. *St. Burl's Obituary*, Daniel Akst, 1996
21. *Human Croquet*, Kate Atkinson, 1997
22. *My Heart Laid Bare*, Joyce Carol Oates, 1998 (hard to believe, but this owes more to Dickens than Dostoevsky)
23. *Horse Heaven*, Jane Smiley, 2000
24. *The Amazing Adventures of Kavalier & Clay*, Michael Chabon, 2000
25. *The Miracle Life of Edgar Mint*, Brady Udall, 2001

25 Unforgivably Strange, Relentlessly Cynical, Unforgettably Good Novels
1. *The Cement Garden*, Ian McEwan, 1978
2. *The Second Coming*, Walker Percy, 1980
3. *The White Hotel*, D. M. Thomas, 1981
4. *Pilgermann*, Russell Hoban, 1983
5. *The Bone People*, Keri Hulme, 1985
6. *Perfume*, Patrick Suskind, 1986
7. *Handmaid's Tale*, Margaret Atwood, 1986
8. *The Twenty-Seventh City*, Jonathan Franzen, 1988
9. *The Book of Evidence*, John Banville, 1989
10. *Life with a Star*, Jiri Weil, 1989
11. *Because It Is Bitter and Because It Is My Heart*, Joyce Carol Oates, 1990
12. *Headhunter*, Timothy Findley, 1993
13. *The Waterworks*, E. L. Doctorow, 1994

14. *In the Lake of the Woods*, Tim O'Brien, 1994
15. *Felicia's Journey*, William Trevor, 1995 (U.S.)
16. *Galatea 2.2*, Richard Powers, 1995
17. *Heat Wave*, Penelope Lively, 1996
18. *A Debt to Pleasure*, John Lanchester, 1996
19. *The Sparrow*, Mary Doria Russell, 1996
20. *Lives of the Monster Dogs*, Kirsten Bakis, 1997
21. *The Night Inspector*, Fredrick Busch, 1999
22. *Pilgrim*, Timothy Findley, 1999
23. *Being Dead*, Jim Crace, 1999
24. *Anil's Ghost*, Michael Ondaatje, 2000
25. *Oryx and Crake*, Margaret Arwood, 2003

25 One-of-a-Kind, Huge and Hugely Wonderful Books That Embrace a Particular Time or Place

1. *Year of the French*, Thomas Flanagan, 1979
2. *Name of the Rose*, Umberto Eco, 1983
3. *Winter's Tale*, Mark Helprin, 1983 (nothing wrong with fantasy)
4. " *. . . Oldest Living Confederate Widow Tells All*," Allan Gurganus, 1984
5. *Bonfire of the Vanities*, Tom Wolf, 1987 (although I would have preferred to *like* some-one in the book)
6. *Oscar and Lucinda*, Peter Carey, 1988 (ditto)
7. *The Quincunx*, Charles Palliser, 1989
8. *A Suitable Boy*, Vikram Seth, 1993
9. *Nobody's Fool*, Richard Russo, 1993
10. *Stones from the River*, Ursula Hegi, 1994
11. *The Unconsoled*, Kazuo Ishiguro, 1995
12. *Discovery of Heaven*, Harry Mulisch, 1995
13. *Alias Grace*, Margaret Atwood, 1996
14. *Matters of Chance*, Jeannette Haien, 1997
15. *Poisonwood Bible*, Barbara Kingsolver, 1998

16. *An Instance of the Fingerpost*, Iain Pears, 1998
17. *Colony of Unrequited Dreams*, Wayne Johnston, 1999
18. *Music and Silence*, Rose Tremain, 1999
19. *Everything You Need*, A. L. Kennedy, 2000
20. *Jayber Crow*, Wendell Berry, 2000
21. *Corrections*, Jonathan Franzen, 2001
22. *Fortress of Solitude*, Jonathan Lethem, 2003
23. *The Time of our Singing*, Richard Powers, 2003
24. *The Falls*, Joyce Carol Oates, 2004
25. *The Divine Husband*, Francisco Goldman, 2004

6 Collections (Mostly Reissues) That Embrace a Particular Time or Place

1. *Memory of Fire Trilogy*, Eduardo Galeano, 1980s
2. *The Deptford Trilogy*, Robertson Davies, 1983
3. *Regeneration Trilogy*, Pat Barker, 1990s
4. *The Man Without Qualities*, Robert Musil, 1995 (new translation)
5. *A Dance to the Music of Time*, Anthony Powell (1995 reprint)
6. *The Joseph Quartet*, Thomas Mann (2005 reissue)

25 Small But Stunning Novels

1. *When the Tree Sings*, Stratis Haviaras, 1979
2. *Dogs of March*, Ernest Hebert, 1979
3. *Ghost Writer*, Philip Roth, 1979
4. *On the Black Hill*, Bruce Chatwin, 1982
5. *Light*, Eva Figes, 1983
6. *Stones for Ibarra*, Harriet Doerr, 1984 (short stories woven into a novelistic whole by a central thread)
7. *English Creek*, Ivan Doig, 1984
8. *The Lover*, Marguerite Duras, 1985
9. *The All of It*, Jeannette Haien, 1986
10. *Hour of the Star*, Clarice Lispector, 1992 (1977 in Portuguese)

11. *The Following Story*, Cees Nooteboom, 1994
12. *Remains of the Day*, Kazuo Ishiguro, 1989
13. *Wartime Lies*, Louis Begley, 1991
14. *Einstein's Dreams*, Alan Lightman, 1993
15. *Reef*, Romesh Gunesekera, 1994
16. *Morality Play*, Barry Unsworth, 1995
17. *Elena of the Stars*, C. P. Rosenthal, 1995
18. *I Never Came to You in White*, Judith Farr, 1996
19. *Summer at Gaglow*, Esther Freud, 1997
20. *Mariette in Ecstasy*, Ron Hansen, 1991
21. *The Far Euphrates*, Aryeh Lev Stollman, 1997
22. *The Whereabouts of Eneas McNulty*, Sebastian Barry, 1998
23. *Lying Awake*, Mark Salzman, 2000
24. *Loving Graham Greene*, Gloria Emerson, 2000
25. *Eva Moves the Furniture*, Margot Livesey, 2001

50 That Are Equally Luminescent and Only Slightly Longer
(Anyway, I couldn't leave them off)
1. *Ceremony*, Leslie Marmon Silko, 1977
2. *Dubin's Lives*, Bernard Malamud, 1979
3. *A Bend in the River*, V. S. Naipaul, 1979
4. *Housekeeping*, by Marilynne Robinson, 1980
5. *Ah, But Your Land is Beautiful*, Alan Paton, 1981
6. *Book of Ebenezer Le Page*, G. B. Edwards, 1981
7. *The Good Son* by Craig Nova, 1982
8. *Obasan*, Joy Kogawa, 1982
9. *During the Reign of the Queen of Persia*, Joan Chase, 1983
10. *Disturbances in the Field*, Lynn Sharon Schwartz, 1983
11. *Summons to Memphis*, Peter Taylor, 1986
12. *Beloved*, Toni Morrison, 1987
13. *The Joy Luck Club*, Amy Tan, 1989

14. *The Things They Carried*, Tim O'Brien, 1990
15. *The Shipping News*, E. Annie Proulx, 1993
16. *Remembering Babylon*, David Malouf, 1993
17. *Wolf Whistle*, Louis Nordham, 1993
18. *The Buccaneers*, Edith Wharton, 1993 (no, she didn't come back from the dead; she was writing this novel when she died, and in 1993 Margaret Mainwaring finished it for her—we thank her for doing so)
19. *The Stone Diaries*, Carol Shields, 1994
20. *The Bird Artist*, Howard Norman, 1994
21. *The Soloist*, Mark Salzman, 1994
22. *Private Altars*, Katherine Mosby, 1995
23. *To the Wedding*, John Berger, 1995
24. *Fugitive Pieces*, Anne Michaels, 1996
25. *Last Orders*, Graham Swift, 1996
26. *Santa Evita*, Thomas Eloy Martinez, 1996
27. *Birdsong*, Sebastian Faulks, 1996
28. *Dreams of My Russian Summer*, Andrei Makine, 1997
29. *The God of Small Things*, Arundhati Roy, 1997
30. *Blindness*, Jose Saramago, 1997
31. *Martin Dressler*, Steven Millhauser, 1996
32. *Bucking the Sun*, Ivan Doig, 1996
33. *Cold Mountain*, Charles Frazier, 1997
34. *The Magician's Wife*, Brian Moore, 1998
35. *The Way I Found Her*, Rose Tremain, 1998
36. *Mark of an Angel*, Nancy Huston, 1999
37. *Cinnamon Gardens*, Shyam Selvadurai, 1999
38. *A Gesture Life*, Chang-Rae Lee, 1999
39. *The River Midnight*, Lilian Nattel, 1999
40. *Waiting*, Ha Jin, 1999
41. *Plainsong*, Kent Haruff, 1999
42. *Feast of Love*, Charles Baxter, 2000

43. *Prince of the Clouds*, Giannie Riotta, 2000 (1997 in Italy)
44. *Place Last Seen*, Charlotte Freeman, 2000
45. *Gertrude and Claudius*, John Updike, 2000
46. *Sweet Hearts*, Melanie Rae Thon, 2001
47. *Last Report on the Miracles at Little No Horse*, Louise Erdrich, 2001
48. *In Sunlight in a Beautiful Garden*, Kathleen Cambor, 2001
49. *The Seven Sisters*, Margaret Drabble, 2002
50. *Prairie Nocturne*, Ivan Doig, 2003

25 Slight in Size, Sometimes Wicked, But Funny
1. *Excellent Women*, Barbara Pym, 1978
2. *Simon's Night*, Jon Hassler, 1979
3. *Like Water for Chocolate*, Laura Esquivel, 1980
4. *Household Saints*, Francine Prose, 1981
5. *Loop's Progress*, Chuck Rosenthal, 1986
6. *Walking Across Egypt*, Clyde Edgerton, 1987
7. *The Commitments*, Roddy Doyle, 1987
8. *Postcards from the Edge*, Carrie Fisher, 1987
9. *A Far Cry from Kensington*, Muriel Spark, 1988
10. *Nice Work*, David Lodge, 1989
11. *Someone Is Killing the Great Chefs of Europe*, Nan Lyons, Ivan Lyons, 1990
12. *Goodbye without Leaving*, Laurie Colwin, 1990
13. *The Tenured Professor*, John Kenneth Galbraith, 1990
14. *Buster Midnight's Café*, Sandra Dallas, 1990
15. *The Queen and I*, Sue Townsend, 1992
16. *The Treatment*, Daniel Menaker, 1998
17. *Red Eye*, Clyde Edgerton, 1995
18. *High Fidelity*, Nicholas Hornby, 1995
19. *Le Divorce*, Diane Johnson, 1997
20. *The Traveling Horn-Player*, Barbara Trapido, 1998
21. *Chocolat*, Joanne Harris, 1999

22. *Headlong*, Michael Frayn, 1999
23. *Ella Minnow Pea*, Mark Dunn, 2001
24. *The Clothes They Stood Up In*, Allan Bennett, 2001
25. *The Finishing School*, Muriel Spark, 2004

5 Funny Novels for Women
(And Men with a Sense of Humor about Feminist Issues)

1. *Heartburn*, Nora Ephron, 1983
2. *Splitting*, Fay Weldon, 1995
3. *Lambs of God*, Marele Day, 1998 (wicked—may make men uncomfortable)
4. *Magdalena the Sinner*, Lilian Faschinger, 1997 (ditto)
5. *Turning on the Girls*, Cheryl Benard, 2001

5 Funny Novels for Men
(And Women with a Sense of Humor)

1. *Black Mischief*, Evelyn Waugh, 1977 (reissue)
2. *Pale Fire*, Vladimir Nabokov, 1978 (reissue)
3. *Portnoy's Complaint*, Philip Roth, 1983 (reissue) (*guaranteed* to make women uncomfortable)
4. *Witches of Eastwick*, John Updike, 1984 (ditto)
5. *Pastoralia*, George Sanders, 2001

25 Short-Story Collections and Novellas
(Smaller *Can* Be Better)

1. *Moons of Jupiter*, Alice Munro, 1983
2. *Legends of the Fall,* Jim Harrison, 1979
3. *Collected Stories of Eudora Welty*, Eudora Welty, 1980
4. *Collected Stories of Elizabeth Bowen*, Elizabeth Bowen, 1981
5. *Cathedral*, Raymond Carver, 1983
6. *Levitation*, Cynthia Ozick, 1982
7. *The House on Mango Street*, Sandra Cisneros, 1984
8. *Last Worthless Evening*, Andre Dubus, 1986

9. *Rock Springs*, Richard Ford, 1987

10. *Emperor of the Air*, Ethan Canin, 1988

11. *Testimony of Mr. Bones*, Olive Ghiselin, 1989

12. *Collected Stories*, William Trevor, 1992

13. *Lone Ranger and Tonto Fist Fight in Heaven*, Sherman Alexie, 1993

14. *Matisse Stories*, A. S. Byatt, 1993

15. *Collected Stories*, Grace Paley, 1994

16. *Stories of Vladimir Nabokov*, 1995

17. *All The Days and Nights: The Collected Stories*, William Maxwell, 1995

18. *The Night in Question*, Tobias Wolff, 1996

19. *Collected Stories*, Mavis Gallant, 1996

20. *Women in Their Beds*, Gina Berriault, 1996

21. *Believers*, Charles Baxter, 1997

22. *Birds of America*, Lorrie Moore, 1998

23. *Close Range*, E. Annie Proulx, 1999

24. *Collected Stories*, Richard Yates, 2001

25. *Sweet Land Stories*, E. L. Doctorow, 2004

25 Novels That Are Easy to Read and Hard to Put Down

1. *Tirra Lirra by the River*, Jessica Anderson, 1978

2. *Lonesome Dove*, Larry McMurtry, 1985

3. *Rich in Love*, Josephine Humphries, 1987

4. *The Bean Trees*, Barbara Kingsolver, 1988

5. *A Short History of a Small Place*, T. R. Pearson, 1985

6. *Chinchilla Farm*, Judith Freeman, 1989

7. *A Woman of Independent Means*, Elizabeth Haily, 1989 (reprint 1995)

8. *Daddy*, Loup Durand, 1988

9. *China Boy*, Gus Lee, 1991

10. *Brothers K*, James Duncan, 1992

11. *I Been in Sorrow's Kitchen and Licked Out All the Pots*, Susan Straight, 1992

12. *Ruin Creek*, David Payne, 1993

13. *A Big Storm Knocked It Over*, Laurie Colwin, 1993
14. *Charms for the Easy Life*, Kaye Gibbons, 1993
15. *Soldier of the Great War*, Mark Helprin, 1991
16. *Ladder of Years*, Anne Tyler, 1995
17. *Power of One*, Bryce Courtenay, 1989
18. *Range of Motion*, Elizabeth Berg, 1995
19. *Hanging Tree*, David Lambkin, 1996
20. *I Capture the Castle*, Dodie Smith, (reissue 1998)
21. *Armadillo*, William Boyd, 1998
22. *Confessions of an Ugly Stepsister*, Gregory Maguire, 1999
23. *Peace Like a River*, Leif Enger, 2001
24. *Secret Life of Bees*, Sue Monk Kidd, 2002
25. *Broken for You*, Stephanie Kallos, 2004

— Chapter Three —

FRIENDLY PERSUASION

[
*"Am I related? . . . By work you are.
It's the next step down from blood."*

— MARK SPRAGG, *The Fruit of Stone*
]

I n business, as in life, a couple of obvious truisms prevail: one is to expect the unexpected and the other is that, in the end, it's the people who count. Whatever visions one may possess, plans one may conceive, goals one may set, it's the people who make any business work— or not work. I've already admitted another truth concerning the book business in particular—that independent booksellers are an odd lot and the book business an odd business, since for most engaged in the industry, the book is the thing, their first loyalty, their passion. Also, like most independent business owners, we're exactly what our name implies—independent. We hate outside control, will do almost anything to avoid it.

Case in point concerning my own borderline behavior in this respect: During the years I've been in business, I've done one thing above all others that has proven pivotal in saving TKE from the fate of other bookstores that have succumbed to chains and dot-coms—in

1978, a year after we opened, I bought the building that houses the store. The fact that I can lower the rent I collect from TKE in hard times has more than once been the factor that allowed us to squeeze through a tight spot accounting-wise, make it around an uncomfortable corner of our fiscal territory in one piece. While I'd like to say that I made the wisest move of my career out of some farseeing acumen, the truth is that my decision was based on matters of the heart rather than the head. Not that I bought the building out of love. On the contrary, I did it to get out of a date.

I was single back then, and my landlord was the kind of man who in theory I despise—a realtor who lavished his face and person with an excess of aftershave, adorned himself with an excess of jewelry, wore clothes cut with too much attention to flash. I particularly remember a gold chain that nestled not-so-discreetly in his thick chest hair, visible because the top two buttons of his mysteriously fibered shirt were (casually) unfastened. I had gone to Oberlin College during the late sixties, and I considered grunge (although we didn't call it that back then) much more attractive than polyester, valued books over money, VW vans over Porsches, The Beatles over Frank Sinatra. I was, in short, the worst sort of snob-in-reverse, a clueless one.

But, despite my snobbery, I sort of liked my landlord. He rented what is now the front room of TKE to some (very) old ladies who ran a beauty shop specializing in blue rinses, hennas, and tight perms for the over-sixty set, and he hadn't raised their rent in years. He didn't charge us much, either, and he paid for our window boxes, had them painted and planted with ivy. We chatted when we met in passing, and I could tell he liked me (probably in spite of himself—I doubt he admired my dirty Levi's any more than I did his leisure suits). He never actually asked me out on an official date but began inviting me to "help" him run errands for the building, offering his pool to my daughter, dropping by to show me a new plant he'd just bought for his office.

Although I enjoyed his company, I was a little frightened by my landlord. He clearly had a temper, for one thing. I had heard him rail at people in a voice that scared me—scared them, too, by the looks on their faces. And there were stories about his behavior with a woman he'd dated a while back, violent stories. Besides, he wasn't exactly my soul mate—he didn't read, garden, do anything I liked to do, and he was enamored of fast cars, televised football, condominiums. Frankly, not the man of my dreams (I'd already tried one of those and that hadn't worked either), my landlord was also manipulative; I could see myself getting boxed into a relationship without ever having agreed to one. But the more I withdrew, the closer he seemed to loom, and I was afraid to back away too abruptly, too obviously. He was my landlord, after all, TKE had only a one-year lease on the building, and I loved the bookstore with a passion equaled only by my love for my daughter. Should this man decide he was angry with me . . .

To understand what I did then and why, another small dose of personal history is necessary. I had been (or at least so I thought) very much in love with a fellow student during my sophomore year in college. The summer before what should have been my junior year, I discovered, to my horror, that my ardor had cooled. And because I genuinely liked this boy, didn't have a clue how to tell him that I was no longer in love with him, hated the thought of hurting his feelings, I left town. I checked out of school for a year, lived at home, worked at Sam Weller's Bookstore through the holidays, saved money and went off to Europe, not paying much heed to the consequences of my actions in terms of my own future, not even considering what haring off in the middle of college without good reason might do to my academic record. I wrote to him frequently at first, then let longer and longer periods elapse between letters, until finally we both stopped writing. When I came back to school the next fall, he was dating someone else.

Extreme manner of avoiding a painful conversation? You bet. To get out of a similar conversation with my landlord, I mortgaged my house. It was a scary thing to do, since my home was my only significant material possession, but I did it so that I could make an offer on a building that wasn't even for sale—the building that housed TKE—praying all the while that my landlord would admire my business acumen, find the money useful, and never discern my true motive. If he did guess, he never let on. He countered my offer, albeit half-heartedly, and I think by the end of our negotiations we were both relieved to come to a parting of the ways. I doubt I was any more my landlord's dream mate than he was mine—especially since I ended up raising the rent on the old parties who occupied the north end of the building.

Oh, I didn't raise it by much, and I hadn't much choice—or so I told myself when I finally looked squarely at the mortgage payment I'd committed to and realized that, as usual, I'd plunged ahead without thinking things through, that without an increase in rent to something at least approaching market value, the mortgage would eat up half the money my daughter and I lived on. I asked for as little as I could in order to earn enough for my own monthly payment, but it was too much for my elderly tenants. They moved on. And even though in the humdrum light of day I assure myself that my worst sin was merely one of omission—of my characteristic failure to look before leaping—in the dark hours of sleepless nights, when we all torture over our past actions, I think of the aging tenants, of the consequence they suffered for my heedlessness, and feel guilt.

SENSE AND SENSIBILITY

If a landlord's attentions and my own shortcomings motivated my purchase of the building in which TKE resides, that is only one of a hundred ways in which a hundred people have altered the store's course over the years, affecting all of us to a degree that couldn't have been prognosticated or planned for—unpredictability being the one constant across human behavior. Outside the confines of TKE, once a bond of friendship grows through shared experience or commonality of taste, I tend toward a blind acceptance. With staff, however, it is usually the opposite. I'm guarding, after all, the sacred portal—the front desk at TKE, where customers are greeted, smiled at, fawned over, and led toward that holiest of grails, the book that is perfect for them.

"Will she smile readily enough," I worry about a cheeky young woman, a graduate student, clearly knowledgeable, who is seeking part-time work that fits with her class schedule. "Does he read enough contemporary fiction," I wonder about a young man who is studying the Victorian novel. "Can you handle ringing phones, a computer, bumping hips with two other employees behind the desk, and still manage to smile at customers, be attentive to their needs?" I ask one applicant, a man who has been a customer for years and whom I consequently know to be as well-read as anyone I've met. He looks tired, as if he needs a haven from stress—I certainly hope he doesn't think he's going to find it at The King's English Bookshop, I think to myself.

"Pleasant, yes," I say to Barbara, after interviewing a lovely middle-aged woman with quiet eyes and an intelligent face. "And God knows well-read. But she seems shy—is she going to be able to reach out to people?"

The middle-aged woman turns out to be Kathy, employee for over fifteen years and the editor of our store newsletter, *The Inkslinger*, for ten of those years. More literate than I by far and much nicer to customers, as devoted to the store as anyone who has ever worked there, she was a gamble that paid off a thousand times over. Another, a strappy young redhead named Charlotte, a budding novelist, turned her Saturdays into virtual literary salons, so many people came in on purpose to visit with her over books. Yet another, Connie, with no book background, retired from job counseling, didn't seem particularly well-read; she not only had a gruff manner, but also was clearly someone who didn't suffer fools. Although I liked her on sight, I had my doubts about her PR abilities, not to mention the depth of her knowledge. Barbara knew her well, however, and was sure she'd work out, so misgivings notwithstanding, I agreed. Connie promptly read *all* (not just the ones in print, but all) the Booker Prize winners, and moved on to Pulitzers, National Book and Whitbread awardees, adding, when time allowed, smatterings of classics and classic contemporary novels she'd missed. She's now dabbling with Prix Goncourt winners (in translation, but I'm not taking anything for granted; she might take it into her head to read the French originals next) and is one of the best booksellers on the floor.

Then there was Henry, a lanky, raw-boned kid with a shy manner and a beatific face. Married to a Ph.D. student in English and at work on a novel himself, he seemed ideal—until he came to work, and it became obvious just how painfully shy he was. *Oh no*, I moaned, but Barbara counseled patience; sure enough, within six months he was a bookselling wonder, loping on Jimmy Stewart legs from shelf to shelf, book to book, customers in tow and in thrall, his knowledge of our stock so encyclopedic that he could find a tangential book to go along with any other book, however obscure. I swear, sales doubled when Henry was on the floor. And customers have seldom been so happy.

Nor have staff. We're mostly a bunch of middle-aged moms at TKE, and we took Henry to our collective bosoms with glee, advising and clucking over him like the mother hens we pretend not to be. We still cluck when he comes to visit. He left us when his wife got a position in New York and after a less-than-happy stint at a bookstore, he became the chief buyer at the Union Theological Seminary, a job he loved. He's now farming in Wisconsin, still working on that novel.

The middle-aged man whose multitasking skills I doubted? I was right. He can't juggle phones and cash registers, computers and people. He has to focus on one thing at a time so, when he's not working on our website, he walks the floor, checking inventory and shelving books—until a customer asks a question, at which time he unleashes a spate of recommendations, a font of knowledge that stretches from philosophy to fiction to poetry to art to physics. John has read, in slightly different fields, as much or more than Henry.

The dedication of these employees, and the sheer awe-inspiring knowledge some of them possess—not to mention their passion for books, for reading—would be amazing if they each were paid $100,000 a year. Need I say that none of us is paid a quarter of that? That we haven't made much more than that in net profits in twenty-seven years total? Yet they stay— and for every employee who is possessed of a passion for books and a willingness to work, there's a place at TKE. Staffing the front desk is largely a matter of mixing skills—of putting someone who knows stock inside out alongside someone possessed of good people skills, for instance, so that customers feel at once loved and well-served. Or pairing someone who knows children's books with someone knowledgeable in the store at large, so that all questions may be answered, whether the questioner be young or old. Or putting a good multitasker like the effervescent Jodie together with a focused type like John so that one can juggle and dance her heart out while the other plumbs the deepest recesses of his memory to come up with obscure titles in philosophy or Greek drama. Each of them pleases customers in one way or another, and together they please almost all customers, find the books customers want and those they didn't know they wanted when they entered. The King's English is defined by its staff, is, in fact (aside from the books—no small matter), the sum of all their parts.

A FEW BAD EGGS

I've doubted them all, though, at least initially. Well, not every one. Sometimes you can tell at first glance. And sometimes they trick you.

One plausibly bookish woman who devoured novels like candy also devoured cash, stealing it in dribs and drabs from the till until even I noticed that all was not right. We were trying to figure out how to verify our suspicions, when a lawyer in my husband's firm walked in, turned on her heel and walked right back out, called my husband and said, "Tell Betsy to fire her new employee. She's been in and out of jail all her life. She's a thief. Believe me, I know. She's my sister."

She wasn't our first thief however. That honor goes to a ten-year-old boy. In the days before we invested in a cash register, we'd leave the adding machine on the front desk at night, but hide the metal cash box under the bathroom scales (don't ask me why—maybe we thought we were being clever). Terry first applied for a job with us when he was nine. He would do anything, he said, he had to have some money. His dad was in jail and his mom needed help. He was a cute kid, he liked to read, and finally, after he pestered us for a while, we thought why not? He came twice a week to break down boxes, take them outside. He swept the back room (not very well), and we paid him generously by our standards ($4 per hour, which back then was above the minimum wage). He'd come banging in, beam at us, and we'd beam back, proud of his initiative, his good spirits, and his determination. By the time we realized he was stealing from us, our maternal instincts were in high gear. We probably should have fired him, but we both adored him, and despite his glib denials when we taxed him with the theft, we told him he needed to fess up. He finally did and even promised to pay us back, which he did, for a while. Then he quit, and we never saw him again. I wonder what happened to him and whether, finally, he went straight or not.

Another young man (this one nineteen rather than nine) who worked nights seemed ideal—until I walked into the children's room and saw that the "S" shelf had disappeared. This was the '80s when Shel Silverstein and Maurice Sendak sold as well (well, maybe not quite) as J. K. Rowling. The "S" shelf was a loss indeed—five or six boxes at a minimum. Next a raft of art books went missing, and before long the trickle turned into a torrent—twenty-six thousand dollars worth of books gone in less than a month. When I discovered the staggering dimensions of the problem, I knew we'd better do something fast. Not entirely convinced the theft was inside, unable to believe the young man in question would actually steal from us (despite the evidence of my eyes and my brain), we bought a security device.

Oh, we didn't do it immediately. First we tried to hire a private detective, but the reputable one told us it would cost more to pay him for the necessary waiting and watching than the store would ever recover if he caught the culprit. Next we tried amateurs, two college students out to make their fortune as modern-day Sam Spades. They had obviously watched too much noir TV, because from the minute they walked into the store, collars up, hat brims cocked (the hats were more in the manner of Indiana Jones than Sam Spade), it was painfully obvious that no self-respecting thief would slip a paperback into his pocket in the presence of our ersatz Pinkertons, let alone an armload of hardcover art books or children's picture books. Said Pinkertons must have deduced as much for themselves—they disappeared at the end of the second day and never asked for a check.

In the meanwhile, our Harper sales rep, John Zeck, told us he thought he knew what was happening to our missing books and who the culprit might be—a magazine shop downtown suddenly had quantities of Harper & Row mysteries on their shelves that he was positive hadn't been purchased from Harper or from a wholesaler. The reason he was so certain the books had been stolen from TKE was that ours was the only store in his entire territory to carry the missing titles (for once our taste in abstruse English detective fiction of the 1930s was paying off). I called my old friend Sam Weller to see what he knew about this magazine shop, and he said, "Nothing good." He agreed to help me catch them in the act, and the two of us went to reconnoiter the place, feeling a little like Nick and Nora Charles, sans Asta. We identified many titles we knew had come from TKE and enjoyed ourselves thoroughly in the process of loitering, but couldn't think of any way to actually prove that the books in question were TKE's. Finally, we had to retire in defeat; the proprietor was eyeing us as if we were the thieves.

We called the police since we knew where the books were going, thought it would be simple enough to set up a "sting" by marking books from our store in some fashion so that an officer could purchase the same books from the magazine shop, identify them, and arrest the proprietor for selling stolen goods. But the police refused. Such petty crime wasn't worth their time. "If someone stole over twenty grand from a bank, wouldn't you chase them?" I asked in fury. "That's different," they said.

Worse, our insurance company refused to cover our loss, echoing the police in calling the missing books "petty theft." "You call twenty-six thousand dollars *petty?*" I raged. But yelling didn't help. Unless someone broke into the store, took the books all at one time in a demonstrable robbery, complete with broken glass, the missing books were legally "slippage" and not covered under the terms of the contract. After racking our brains while another thousand dollars worth of books disappeared from the store, I called our alarm company and asked whether they had any suggestions.

CERBERUS FOR A DAY

The infernal device has been installed for two weeks and is a nightmare to deal with. For one thing, when the books are received each one has to have a magnetized strip inserted into the spine in order to set off the alarm in the unsightly gates that now stand sentinel at our door. Worse, said gates are hideous, and the customers hate them. I feel like Allen Funt in "Candid Camera" watching people catch sight of the dread devices for the first time, their shock apparent, their distaste palpable. I've taken to saying, "Smile, You're on Candid Camera," to ease the tension. They laugh, hoping it's all a bad joke.

It isn't. We'll be out of business in no time if this doesn't work. I've already borrowed $25,000 to cover our losses to date, and there isn't anything left to borrow. It isn't a joke to customers, either. The front door of their quaint and lovely bookstore now looks like the security entrance at a federal prison. The gates' bars are vertical, over six feet high, and broad. There is a pad on the floor that is clearly covering something technological, electrical, perhaps lethal. The gates themselves look as if they could single-handedly arrest and handcuff any thief that dares cross our portals, slay any miscreant attempting to depart through said portals with an unpaid-for book in hand. "We may not be pretty, but we're secure," we tell one another.

One day we're watching booksellers Gail and Marilyn prance in and out of the front door waving books bearing those magnetic strips while Cerberus chirps an accompanying chorus. We've been discussing with the other employees what we'd do if (as would inevitably occur, or so we believed) someone set Cerberus off for real, when I decide to try my own hand at shoplifting. I slip a book under my arm, as I imagine a thief would do, and pass through the portal. Our own personal Cerberus stands silently by. I try again, and again he fails, altogether, to roar. I pick up another book and put it in the same position under my arm. Out I go once more. Again, not a peep. Another book and, yet again, with feeling. Still nothing but silence from our techno-warden.

Tight-lipped with fury, I stalk into the back room and dial the alarm company, demand to speak with the owner (who sold me the damn thing). "Warren," I say, "we've got a little problem."

"Problem?" He's all innocence.

"Problem." My voice is grim. "I've just walked back and forth through your gate four or five times with a book—complete with strip—under my arm, and nothing happened. Nothing. I tried with another book, held it the same way. Again, nothing happened."

"How were you holding the book?"

"What difference does it make how I was holding the book?"

"Humor me. How were you holding it?"

"Under my arm. Like a thief would."

"Horizontally or vertically?"

"Pardon?"

"The book. Was it upright or tipped sideways?"

"Well, if you mean was it canted, the answer is no, of course not. It would *have* to be upright to be spirited out unnoticed by the people behind the desk. And that's the point, surely. To steal books without anyone noticing."

"Well," he says, sounding relieved. "If it was vertical, that explains it."

"Not to me it doesn't."

"Our machine, every security device I know of, has a window of vulnerability."

As he warms to his theme, his voice becomes condescending, as if he's the master, me the dim pupil. And maybe that does describe me, because I certainly was speechless by the time he had finished expounding on the complexities of security technology.

"Window of vulnerability?" I manage to squeak, after he has repeated this phrase for the fifth time, obviously enamored of its fulsome ring. "Are you trying to tell me that if you hold a book vertically and walk out the door of my bookshop, the damn machine doesn't do anything? Doesn't make a sound? And that you knew that when you sold it to us?"

I don't wait for him to answer, know by his silence what his answer is. "Since even in our store, where nobody's very observant, it's completely impossible to steal a book held horizontally, unlikely if it's at any sort of angle, then in practical terms, this machine doesn't work at all. Correct me if I'm wrong here, Warren . . . And the machine costs how much? No, don't answer that. Just come and get the damn thing. Now. And don't send me a bill."

"We have a legal contract. It's binding."

"Only based on your representation that this thing works."

"It does work."

"Except?"

"For the window of vulnerability," he repeats, sounding a wee bit uncertain now. "Most objects we deal with aren't quite so—uniform in, err, shape as books are, and er . . ."

"And that is whose problem? Did you disclose to me that such potential glitches existed in your system?" (It helps to be married to a lawyer—as I was then, am still—you pick up enough to see you through at least some of life's little bumps.)

The system was removed that day. The thief was never caught. But perhaps the dread device worked after all, despite its "window of vulnerability," because the theft stopped—and coincidentally, the young man in question, the one we thought the most likely culprit of an "inside job," made a move to distant lands. I hope he didn't go to work at another bookstore, wherever he ended up. Or maybe he wasn't the thief after all and the timing was coincidence—possible, but not very likely.

DOUBLE, DOUBLE, THEFT AND TROUBLE

I recently fired a graduate student, a wonderful bookseller and a bright, attractive young man. I liked him—and I trusted him. He stole several thousand dollars from the store, systematically and cold-bloodedly over two years—two years when he seemed an important part of a crew of people pulling together to keep the bookstore alive.

Why, in the almost thirty years of the store's existence, did these particular four people steal from us? Did they think we were easy prey? Dumb by definition? I hated firing X. Hated threatening him. But I did anyway. I did my best to scare the piss out of him in the process. I told him that he was headed for worse trouble than he could imagine. "Picture yourself, young, attractive, slight of build, in jail," I said to him. "You've got a good imagination. What do you think would happen to you?"

"You may think you're smart," Becky, our back-room manager and another longtime employee, told him. "But somebody is always smarter. You'll always get caught."

"I'm not calling the police," I said finally. "But I will sue you civilly if you don't give me a full and true accounting of what you've taken and a plan for restitution." He hung his head and cried.

With guilt? I wondered. Or relief? Is he sorry? Or just—as the cliché goes—sorry he's been caught?

He straightened up after a minute, and said, "I know I've behaved dishonestly, but I swear, I'm not dishonest."

"Pardon me?" I was nonplussed. "You've stolen money systematically, over time. More than enough to qualify for a felony conviction. You *are* dishonest. You committed a crime. Many crimes."

X promised to make restitution. I hope he does. I hope he's learned his lesson, but I can't kid myself that he really has. His statement that he's not dishonest echoes in my brain. That's denial.

But in over twenty-five years, over the hundreds of employees that have come and gone, the memories are mostly good ones.

LOVE AMONG THE RUINS

There have been all kinds of interesting tales involving the employees at TKE over the years, but perhaps the most intriguing, life being what it is, are the romantic ones. Eve Leonard (the PR maven who visited Harriet Doerr with me) remains the bookseller who had far and away the most cinematic romance at TKE. Oh, love blossomed more than once among the books: we saw it occur occasionally; watched customers appear coincidentally whenever a certain staffer worked, deliver flowers to this bookseller or that one; watched people trade night shifts in order to be together, trade again when passions paled—but Eve's romance was truly the stuff of Hollywood.

Eve had had an acrimonious divorce several years before, was raising three teenagers by herself, and, to supplement her meager bookstore income, was running book clubs as well as working the desk. She had had the brilliant idea of starting a single's club, and it was a wild success. The group read fiction, drama, poetry; attended plays and concerts; and generally filled the gaping voids Friday nights presented in a more-than-satisfactory fashion. One day, a newly single man, a bookaholic who happened to be an attorney, joined, and, although the antennae of more than one woman stiffened to attention, it was Eve that he focused on, Eve he watched, listened to, spoke with. His interest drew hers, and within minutes, the rest of the group could have disappeared for all the attention they paid to any but each other. It was love at first sight—or first listen, which is even better. They were married within a year, and the two of them live on Bainbridge Island now. At last report they were very happy.

I know firsthand about another romance that occurred at TKE—it was my own. It had actually begun a couple of years before the store opened, when Kit, my present husband, and I were "lined up" by friends. We fell in love—I thought him amazingly handsome, he was obviously kind, and aside from liking the same music (well, I could have done without the Rolling Stones, but we agreed on Croce and Mozart), we both liked to garden, walk, and best of all, he loved to read. We dated for a time, for a wonderful time. But due to circumstances that had more to do with our lives than with our feelings, we stopped seeing each other.

Salt Lake being the small place that it is, we ran into each other at parties occasionally, chatted awkwardly, but didn't have any real contact for over seven years. TKE opened, grew during that time, and one day Kit came in to buy some books. He was exhausted—he didn't need to say so, it was written in the dark circles under his eyes, that hollow look I remembered from when he had been involved in trials. In fact, he had just completed a grueling court case and was going on a vacation—to Tahiti, of all places, and he needed some books. He was traveling alone, he said, and wanted only to rest. Despite his fatigue, he looked good, and I wondered with a kindling hope if he had told me he wasn't traveling with a companion for any particular reason.

I have said Kit was a reader, but even better, he was a reader whose tastes coincided with my own, a man who liked good fiction, loved mysteries and thrillers as well, but who, like me, was made impatient by clichés, driven wild by bad writing, needed his books to be literate, thoughtful. I spent a long time helping him shop. We talked at length about John Le Carré, agreeing that his latest, *Smiley's People*, was one of the best books either of us had read. Kit had also devoured Nabokov, loved not just *Lolita*—the one everyone's read—but also *Pale Fire*, *Ada*. He liked classic mysteries: Dorothy Sayers, Michael Innes, P. D. James, and since there wasn't a Le Carré he hadn't read, I gave him the new P. D. James, *Innocent Blood*, along with a thriller I'd liked, *The Night Is the Time for Listening*, a couple of obscure novels new in paper I'd liked, *The Good Son* and *The Dogs of March*, and the magnificent *The Song of Solomon*, which I knew he'd love. He devours history, had just finished *The Path*

Between the Seas, so, amoral bookseller that I am, I sold him a hardcover—to take to the South Seas, of all places. It was a *good* hardcover, *Peter the Great*, and giddy with my success, I pressed *The Second Coming* by Walker Percy and *A Confederacy of Dunces* by the immortal John Kennedy Toole on my willing victim.

Handing Kit those books was an act of love. I'd put love into choosing them, and I suspect he'd put love into asking me for them (and certainly love into buying them—he spent a fortune). They re-forged a connection, though. I pictured him in the next weeks, lying on some island, reading the dialogue between the sanely mad protagonists in *The Second Coming*, contemplating the mother so like his own in *The Good Son*, laughing at the quirky environmental and ethical paradox presented in *The Dogs of March*, not to mention the glory and heartbreak of the book I still consider Toni Morrison's best, and the tortured madcap exuberance of Toole. I wondered if he would think of me while he read them (it turned out he was being swept into a coral reef by a tsunami, but that's another story). Although we didn't start to see each other again for some time, I remain convinced that it was those books that kept us linked, made our subsequent reconnection possible. As I thought carefully about which books would work best on his trip, which would work for *him*, I not only let him know I cared enough to consider him closely but also realized anew just how much we had in common. In addition, I learned a lesson: if someone shares your taste in books, chances are, you are compatible. It's certainly a better basis for romance than blue eyes, a wry smile, or a shared love of Chardonnay. When it comes right down to it, books are one of the best measures of people I know, be they customers, employees, or potential spouses.

INKSLINGERS FOR HIRE, INQUIRE WITHIN

I've already said she was wonderful, but what I haven't said about Kathy Ashton is that if there's one person at TKE who's made a profound difference—at a time when we most needed it—she is that person. By 1993, big-box retailers were on the rise, dot-coms had come online, and it was clear that the market was fragmenting. We needed to do something that only we could do—produce information that only people who read voraciously but with discrimination could produce and that other people who read voraciously but with discrimination could trust. We had no idea when we began (with the help of a knowledgeable advertising and layout person, Kathy Thomas) what publishing such a magazine as *The Inkslinger* actually involved.

But we waded right in, Kathy Ashton at the helm, interviewing Isabel Allende in the first issue, Mark Strand in the second, devoting a page in each issue to long reviews of a couple of books, edging each page with short reviews of the newest fiction and nonfiction, mysteries and children's books that were recently published or forthcoming. We added a poetry page, an art page written by a customer who is both an artist and an art scholar, penned an editorial about (what else?) the many benefits of buying locally, the loss to the community should chains drive local businesses out. Ann Cannon, a wonderful author of children's books, wrote a three-page children's section, and a friend who lives in Paris—someone who reads, travels, and has a divine sense of humor—Chris Papanikolas (the same Chris who attended my ill-fated dinner with Isabel), became our "foreign correspondent," reviewing books she purchased at The Village Voice on the Rue Princesse.

Here's how we write *The Inkslinger*. It's published twice a year (four times at first, but that was a pace too rigorous to maintain). Kathy (editor in chief), Barbara, and I meet at Kathy's house with a printout of all the books that, over the past season (we buy from publishers' reps well in advance of publication), we think seem promising. We divvy up the list, assign some out to staff (actually it's more that we bully, beg, and otherwise manipulate said staff into reviewing some), and we take the rest. We find bound galleys (those unjacketed paperback prerelease copies that booksellers in stores all over the country beg for, fight over) for the books we are assigned and start to read. We also begin to stalk the mail carrier, trying to get first dibs on those galleys by authors we love that for whatever reason have not yet been assigned, or galleys of first-time authors that look promising. We look for good omens on the covers of those galleys: a blurb (those sound-bite-sized comments on book jackets) by an author we respect (one of Ian McEwan's prompted me to pick up the galley of *The Curious Incident of the Dog in the Night-Time* by Mark Haddon, which I loved), an enthusiastic letter from an editor whose authors we know to be good, a blurb from a fellow bookseller whose store we know and like. Thanks to these galleys, we find new treasures continually for our *Inkslinger*—new authors to tout and gems by authors whom we already know are well worth raving about.

When books are assigned for which no galleys are available, we begin phoning our reps and the marketing departments of publishers, bullying, begging, manipulating (we do a lot of those three things, one way and another) to get the material we need. Then we read. And read. And read. Each time we encounter a book that we like, we write a blurb of between 75 and 150 words. Then we meet again in Kathy's living room, read the blurbs aloud, edit, and cut. Edit and cut. Edit and cut.

Meanwhile, someone (almost always Kathy) has interviewed an author, generally because he or she is slated to visit TKE. Because most of these authors live out of state, Kathy usually conducts these interviews by phone. She writes up the interview for the current issue, and we edit it, along with the children's book pages that Ann Cannon has produced. We then edit our editorial extensively (Barbara and I usually write these while on vacation in Montana, and often get carried away with our own rhetoric), our "foreign column," the poetry page, and whatever else we've cooked up to include. Pat Bagley, the political cartoonist sans peer from *The Salt Lake Tribune* always does an editorial cartoon for us, and we do Inkblots (long) and Inkspots and spatters (shorter and less vitriolic pans) for the books we don't like.

When all of this has been done and redone, we sit down one more time in Kathy's living room, read it all aloud yet again, then cut it into pieces and do a layout. We give all of this to Lynne Tempest (our original designer, Kathy Thomas, gave up on our living-room publishing group long ago), who has the eye of an artist and the patience of a saint. Lynne lays it out with professional skill, adds the ads (Lyn, one of our frontline booksellers, sells ad space locally for this), gives us a peek, and off it goes to the printer—who does a blue-line, lets us have one final look, and *voila*, as Chris, our foreign correspondent, would say. *C'est fini.*

We all have a part in this process, but it is Kathy who is its inspiration, its architect, its careful cultivator. An editor with a sharp eye, a sharper brain, a person possessed of culture, wit, and a passion for books unequaled by anyone I've met, Kathy makes *The Inkslinger* what it is. And it has served the purpose for which we intended it; people all over the country wait for it, shop from its pages, and call us with comments. People trail into the store with marked-up copies for months after each publication and thank us for it. Those thanks go, in large part, to Kathy Ashton.

HARD REMEDIES FOR HARD TIMES

Five employees make a family. Twenty-five make a dysfunctional family, or so it often seems in these days of chains and hard times. This one snipes at that one, he is jealous of her schedule, she says he . . . but never mind. Enough to say I, who loathe self-help as a genre, despise management books as a bunch of cheap devices and quick remedies, went to a management seminar given by the American Booksellers Association. It was taught by Ari Weinzweig, part-owner of Zingerman's Deli in Minnesota and of Zingtrain.

Ha! So he's not even a bookseller, for heaven's sake! I glower and gloom as he runs on about planning, training, communication. But then, when he asks us what we *do*, we owners and managers of bookstores from around the country, and hears us say over and over again that we sell books, he shakes his head. "No," he tells us, "your *employees* sell books. You manage employees. Or at least that's what you *should* be doing. And if you have problems with your staff, maybe it's because you are busy selling books instead of managing staff."

I stare at him, mouth open, and then lower my head into my hands. I would sob out loud if I were alone. Because I know he is right. My worst nightmare, I think. Me trying to make like some . . . some damned MBA, trained in people management, for God's sake. Me who would rather have my nose in a book or put a customer's face in one than breathe. I'm not a "people manager." I won't be.

Yeah, me and Peter Pan.

You'd think after twenty years it might have dawned on me. But it hadn't. Was it my fault the employees were dysfunctional? Mine and Barbara's? You bet, Ari said, when someone else in the room voiced the same concern. Think service. Think nurturing. Think of *them*. Treat them like your best customers. You're there to serve them. Not vice versa.

But, but, but, my mind screamed. I don't *want* to manage people. I want to sell books.

Tough, Ari answered the look on my face.

And Ari was right. *Is* right. I may think of myself as the frontline bookseller I used to be, but except occasionally on Saturdays—when the phone's quiet and the store's full of customers, short on staff—I'm not. I'm in the back room buying books from reps or trying to balance the checkbook. Or I'm poring over the schedule so this employee can take the weekend off, or that one can drop an evening shift. Or I'm interceding between employees over some territorial dispute (hard to believe in a store the size of TKE, but true). Or I'm over at Kathy's house editing *The Inkslinger* with her, or going over the books with Barbara, trying to figure out how to get through the next month without going on credit hold with the twelve publishers with whom we're too far behind. I'm not a bookseller at all. I'm a damned middle manager.

So, at once my sorest trial and my dearest friends, the staff at The King's English . . . dedicated, knowledgeable, generous, fractious, petty, easily hurt . . . It's not that I don't love them, I do. It's not that I don't respect them, I do, emphatically. It's just that my trying to manage people is a little like Lucy Locket trying to tame horses, Mike Tyson trying to tat doilies. We all have our strengths. And our weaknesses.

We had a meeting at TKE a couple of years ago. It was what Connie termed a "Come to Jesus" meeting. In part because of Ari's words—his advice to bring them the whole picture, show them the bottom line so they could participate on all levels—we bared our souls (or rather our balance sheets). It had been another in a line of bad years going back to the opening of the first Barnes & Noble (a topic for another chapter). We had been up 20 percent or more every year almost since our inception. That first "chained" year we struggled to stay level. The next year we lost ground. And money. So it had gone as chain after chain had come to town. Our taxes showed a net loss of $39,000. Barbara passed around the return and the room went still. All these people who had carped about weekend shifts and who had to clean the bathroom turned stunned faces toward us.

"Barbara and I have tried and tried to come up with answers. Now we're asking you. What do you think we should do?" What we were looking for was fresh ideas, new ways of looking at old problems. But these extraordinary people, some of whom can barely afford their rent (due to the low wages we can afford to pay them if we're to keep our doors open), looked at us, looked at one another, and as one voice volunteered to take pay cuts. "No," we said. And they came back with, "Then we're cutting our discount."

"But we only give you what Costco gives on bestsellers they stock."

"What you're giving us is everything you get. That means you're not even covering cost on things like postage. So you go further in the hole every time we buy a book."

Barbara and I nodded. It was true. It remains one of the things that has never made sense about the discounting chains and price clubs do. They claim they make their profit on volume, but if they're *losing* on every book even *with* the increased discount, surely increased volume only makes it worse? Or is my math flawed? (No, it's not, but this, too, is a subject for another chapter.)

"We'd rather lose some discount than lose the store," Connie says. The others nod.

And she has hit on the awful reality. The store would be gone already if I hadn't put money in when things got rough—put money in again and again over the past six years. They have their deep pockets, and I guess we have ours (although mine aren't all that deep if truth be told). It's crazy, this strange new reality, I think to myself, but as long as investors in the dot-coms and superstores are willing to take losses, we have to, too, to stay alive. And if we don't stay alive then the field is theirs. Anyway, The King's English is my life. I've put everything I know onto its shelves. So have all of them. I look around the room at all the attentive faces, look at Barbara who looks back at me, and all we can say is, "Thank you."

BOOK LIST
25 Self-Help Books Adapted to the Needs of Independent Bookstore Owners

1. *Driven to Distraction: Recognizing and Coping with Attention Deficit Disorder ~~from Childhood through Adulthood~~ in Bookstore Owners*
2. *I'm Okay, You're Okay [as Long as You Smile at the Customers]*
3. *Operating Instructions: A Journal of My ~~Son's~~ Store's First Year*
4. *Toxic ~~Parents~~ Partners*
5. *How to Talk So Your ~~Kids~~ Staff Will Listen and Listen So Your ~~Kids~~ Staff Will Talk*
6. *Getting Divorced [from Your Partner] without Ruining Your Life*
7. *~~Men~~ Booksellers Are from Mars, ~~Women~~ Accountants Are from Venus*
8. *All I Really Need to Know I Learned in ~~Kindergarten~~ Fiction*
9. *The Simple Living Guide: ~~A Sourcebook for Less Stressful, More Joyful Living~~ Read Books and Be Happy*
10. *Excuse Me Your ~~Life~~ Customer Is Waiting*
11. *Your ~~Child's~~ Bookseller's Self-Esteem*
12. *Do I Have to Give Up ~~Me~~ [My Vision of TKE] to Be Loved By You?*
13. *I Hate ~~You~~, [Your Taste in Books,] Don't Leave Me*
14. *Living with a Passive-Aggressive ~~Man~~ Bookseller*
15. *The Moral ~~Animal~~ Bookseller [never recommends a book she doesn't like]*
16. *Getting the Love You Want [from Your Staff and Your Customers]*
17. *Don't Sweat the Small Stuff—and ~~It's All~~ None of It Is Small Stuff*
18. *An Unfinished ~~Business~~ Partnership*
19. *The Art of Happiness: ~~A Handbook for Living~~ Read a Book a Day*
20. *The Good Girl's Guide to Bad ~~Sex~~ Books*
21. *How to Win ~~Friends~~ Customers and Influence ~~People~~ Reading Tastes*
22. *Developing the ~~Leader~~ Bookseller within You*
23. *The Art of Possibility: Transforming ~~Professional and Personal Life~~ Good Books into Bestsellers*
24. *This Is Your Life, Not a Dress Rehearsal [so turn off the TV and read some good books]*

25. *The 7 Habits of Highly Effective* ~~People~~ *Booksellers:*
    1. read
    2. smile at customers
    3. tell the truth
    4. read
    5. smile at customers
    6. tell the truth
    7. read, read, read

— Chapter Four —

D IS FOR DEATH

[*"I didn't realize Denver was so butt-ugly."*
— SUE GRAFTON, *TKE*, AUGUST 1989]

When Sue Grafton made the above uncharitable but funny comment on the way from the airport to TKE, Barbara and I were pretty sure we were going to like her—not because we hate Denver, but because we are disposed to love anyone as frank as she is. Later, en route to the store for the signing, Barbara asked her why she had started writing mysteries in the first place, and Grafton replied, "I used to spend an inordinate amount of time lying in bed at night dreaming up ways to kill my husband."

A woman after me own heart, I thought to myself, as she went on, "Ex-husband, now. And one of the plots seemed so good I wrote it down. That's actually how *A is for Alibi* was born."

"So murder pays, after all?" Barbara asked.

"At least on paper," Grafton agreed, laughing.

Oddly enough—and I hate to even think what this curious fact says about my character—murder (or the thought of it) has nestled somewhere close to my own heart for decades, been the place that I have gone for rescue when life has occasionally become unbearable. Like Sue Grafton, my preferred method of homicide was literary rather than literal, but in my case, in lieu of the actual commission of a first-degree felony after my divorce, I yellow-dotted my way through the downtown Salt Lake library (yellow dots on the spines connote the mystery category, or did back then). I actually wrote a mystery, years later, in order to make sense of the world my son lives in, and I still turn to mysteries the way an addict turns to crack whenever life threatens to overwhelm me. So does Barbara. So, for that matter, do many of our customers.

Although our personal tastes run most frequently to the thrillers, classical Brit whodunits, psychological suspense, and (often funny) American detective stories, we at TKE feel an obligation to stock our shelves with every type of printed meth necessary for blind immersion. Cutesy cozies and humdrum procedurals, the most inanely plotted cat mysteries and the darkest of the stalker/slashers can have a sick appeal when life seems hopeless and it's clear that a murder or two might serve to improve the situation. I have a friend, a very bright and well-educated woman, who actually picks up an old Nancy Drew from time to time when despair threatens. Whatever works, in other words—especially if the "whatever" is funny. Which brings me back to the subject at hand . . .

A DAME OF THE NEW SCHOOL

Sue Grafton came to TKE thanks in large part to yet another sales rep, Bill Maher. A book salesman of the old breed, educated, witty, urbane, and a man one might easily imagine behind a desk at the *New Yorker* or editing a manuscript at Knopf or some other large publisher, Bill worked on a commission basis for Henry Holt (among others), selling books to bookstores. And Holt was Sue Grafton's publisher, had been since her first book came out—unusual in these days of authors who switch from agent to agent, house to house, at the rap of an auction gavel. Because Ms. Grafton was loyal to Holt, loyal to her editor there, as the trickling sales of *A is for Alibi*, *B is for Burglar*, *C is for Corpse* gathered force, swelled into the rushing currents of *D is for Deadbeat* and *E is for Evidence*, became the bestselling performance of *F is for Fugitive*, she listened loyally to the suggestions of Holt's reps and went to the stores they suggested. Bill Maher knew of our proclivity for mysteries, our eagerness to host Sue Grafton. Since Holt had a shipping warehouse in Salt Lake at the time, we were on their radar anyway, so our small store was added to Grafton's schedule. We placed an order for (as had become our habit back then) 100 books.

Ms. Grafton, an attractive woman not nearly as casual (at least when on a publicity tour) as her protagonist Kinsey Mulhone, laughs her way through a phone interview, chats up customers, sends them away laughing, and signs seventy books in half an hour, still laughing. At first, Barbara and I laugh with her. But as we watch the pile of books dwindle, look at the hordes of people lined up out the door and down the street, our smiles grow stiff, our laughter brittle, until finally Barbara leans over to whisper, "We're not going to have enough books, are we?"

"We'll run out in fifteen minutes, at this rate."

"What can we do? It's after five o'clock. The warehouse won't be open and . . ."

"It can't hurt to try."

I dial the main number and get a recording. "This is Henry Holt and Company. Our hours are Monday through Friday, 8:00 a.m. to 5:00 p.m. If you reach this recording, leave a . . ."

Looking in the directory, I see other departments listed: shipping, customer service, ordering . . . I try them all. None of them answers.

Barbara finally says, "When you call county government after five, if you dial an *inside* number, your call bypasses the switchboard and rings into one office or another."

"But 'inside' means unlisted, right? Numbers not in the phone book. So what—"

"The unlisted numbers are usually off only one or two digits from the listed department numbers."

"It's worth a try . . ."

I spend the next several minutes dialing every conceivable combination of numbers the last digit of which is off one or two from the numbers listed in the phone book—with no luck whatsoever. I'm ready to give up, when an impatient voice interrupts the third ring of my seventeenth phone call.

"Yes?"

"Is this Henry Holt?"

"No, this is Tina Turner," comes the deadpan response.

"Henry Holt Publishing Company?"

"We're closed."

"But it *is* Henry Holt Publishing? Wait, don't hang up. This is an emergency."

"This is *shipping* at Henry Holt. And I can't imagine what kind of emergency I could possibly help you with at this time of day. UPS has come and gone. Shipping's over until tomorrow at 9:00 a.m."

"I'm calling from Salt Lake City, from The King's English. And we don't need UPS, we need you. Sue Grafton needs you. She's signing books at our store right now. But only for the next fifteen minutes. Then she'll have to stop signing, because she'll run out of books. Do you— could we come and get some from you? I know it's unusual to do this without an invoice, but . . ."

There's a silence. I'm tempted to beg, but (wisely) keep still.

He must hear the terror in my silence, the despair, because he says, "Twelve minutes should do it if I drive fast. How many do you want?"

"You mean *you'll* bring them here? To us?" I'm incredulous at our luck, and since Mother always told me not to look a gift horse in the face, I try not to be greedy. "Another hundred?" I venture.

"I'll bring a hundred and fifty to be on the safe side. If you don't need them all, you can return them in the morning."

Ms. Grafton is signing the second-to-last book when our warehouse wunderkind pulls up in front of the store. Later, after she has autographed books for the last happy customer, signed another fifty for stock, we introduce her to our hero of the hour, her hero of the hour. She signs books for him too, calls her editor in New York the next day and marvels at said wunderkind's deeds, tells us she'll never forget any of it, that she'll be back one day.

She did come back, three years later. And she was still just as feisty, as funny, as frank. A year before that, she had told the story of our last-minute rescue by the Holt warehouse to an audience at an American Booksellers Association convention; Barbara and I listened raptly, trying not to preen.

And that's the book business, or at least it was back then. Everyone, from publisher to shipping clerk, in it together.

A DAME BY ANY OTHER NAME

When Sara Paretsky came to TKE years later, we ordered 250 books, not ever again wanting to be caught out the way we had with Sue Grafton. And we sold 80. That, too, is the book business. Unpredictable. Unreasonable. Paretsky is easily as well known as Grafton. And *Hard Time* is one of her best books, a taut whodunit that explores the dark world of for-profit prisons. One of the things I most love about mysteries (besides their narcotic benefit) is the way they poke around in the dark corners of society, exposing ugly pockets to the light of day and questioning our complacence. No one does this better than Ms. Paretsky, and nowhere did *she* do it better than in *Hard Time*. Maybe customers were jaded by then, or perhaps the snow kept people away that icy November evening. Who knows? I certainly don't.

What I do know is that Sarah Paretsky was as impressive as her protagonist. While the smaller (5'8") P.I., V.I. Warshawski, emits a redhead's heat, Paretsky herself is long, lean, measured of movement, prowling the shelves of the bookstore, pouncing on this book or that one, quick and leonine. Responding to questions, she exuded a cool, steely intelligence, worrying the marrow of intention from the center of each query, answering thoughtfully, fully, with flashes of insight, of humor. We were honored to have her in our store, grateful that she feels such solidarity with Independents (which she does, emphatically), pleased to be able to tell her how much we admire her, how much pleasure her books have given us in times of greatest need.

A DAME ACROSS THE SEA

Elizabeth George is—no surprise to fans of the genre—an American who writes highly literate British mysteries in the classical style, mysteries that resemble those of P. D. James in tone, although they are in no way clones. Like those of James, and Sayers before her, George's continuing cast of characters form relationships that grow and change from book to book. Lynley is brilliant, aristocratic, ethical to a fault; Havers, defiantly blue-collar, sharp of tongue and thin of skin, bulldog-like in determination; Deborah, talented, hounded by memory, married (by mid-series, anyway) to St. James, who is a forensic pathologist, a friend and peer of Lynley's; and finally, Helen, who loves Lynley and has at last married him. If there is soap opera in the ongoing, ever-changing relationships between these characters, it is soap opera in the grand style, in the tradition of the Palliser novels of Anthony Trollope, John Galsworthy's *Forsyte Saga*—balm to the soul, each book leaving something to look forward to even after the last page is turned.

Elizabeth George visited TKE in 1991, skied in the same fashion as John Irving, and since it was during the era when autograph parties were still the common thing, she simply nodded to customers, murmured a few words to each as she put her signature on the title pages of their books, signed some of her latest, *Well Schooled in Murder*, for stock, and left, promising to return.

She did return, in 1994. "Superstores" were new and untarnished, independents dropping like flies, people's flirtation with dot-coms just around the corner. Business was down, debt on the rise, and fear was poisoning the atmosphere on our block like the smog that permeated the hundred-plus degree air in Happy Valley the day the call came. It was our Doubleday rep, Karen Hopkins—Elizabeth George was doing an author tour of the West, and TKE was on her schedule.

In honor of the Englishness that is at the heart of Ms. George's books, we decided to host a high tea for her: cucumber sandwiches (crustless, of course), tiny lemon muffins, tea—although in deference to the extraordinary temperatures, we opted for iced tea served in tall glasses rather than hot tea in cups. Because English dress of the formal sort seemed to be in order, we (then) partners three (a tale for the next chapter), hied off to the local costume shop along with *Inkslinger* editor Kathy Ashton, in search of tea gowns—something high-necked and pastel, refined. What they had in stock was distinctly funereal in color and design. How Freudian, I thought, ideal for our death throes. But I said only that black seemed apt for a mystery tea.

"It's apt for the state of our business, too," Barbara muttered, her thoughts matching mine as she regarded her black-clad image in the dressing room mirror.

The day of the tea dawns and we don our widows' weeds. On schedule, Ms. George—enseconced, appropriately, in a black stretch limo—pulls up to the curb with Karen Hopkins, the sales rep. Barbara, Carolyn, Kathy, and I move in unison toward the street, no doubt looking like members of some Black Sabbath brigade, and Karen rolls down the window in time for us to hear our author shriek from the depths of the limo, "My God, what are they? Witches or something?" Karen hastily rolls the window back up, but tells us later that when she assured Ms. George we were harmless, the mystery maven said, "Well they look pretty strange. This isn't some kind of a New Age event, is it?"

"Not at all," Karen told her. "The opposite, if anything. The fact is, they think they look English."

Recovering her aplomb, Ms. George emerges from her limo, pale but composed, shakes hands all around and delivers an absolutely chilling reading to the standing-room-only crowd at the bookstore. As she details the murder of one of England's premier cricket players and the subsequent investigation, her gloomy hosts lurk on the sidelines, afraid of the commotion their lace and taffeta will make if they even try to sit down. And perhaps our darkly hovering presence seems menacing to audience as well as author, because they nibble the food uneasily, barely sip their drinks, as if they have imaged our crone-hands spreading the sandwiches with rat poison, lacing the tea with tincture of cyanide.

Ms. George did sign a couple hundred copies of her mysteries and appeared pleased with TKE, despite the peculiar dress and demeanor of its proprietors. As her limousine disappeared down Fifteenth East, the partners three climbed into their separate cars, each with an autographed copy of *Playing for the Ashes* in hand, and went home to indulge in their favorite addiction. It helped, for a time.

THE RULES OF THE GAME

Literary snobs will tell you that mysteries are formulaic, even in the best of cases. And there is some truth to the accusation. But in defense of my drug of choice, *good* mysteries *are* good novels, even if the art and craft of writing the mystery are markedly different from that of other forms of fiction. Good novels can be plotless, or nearly so, and their narrative lines frequently wander in an ambiguity of circles. Characters in novels are sometimes insubstantial and can be, upon occasion, more a personification of an idea than of flesh and blood—as they are in *The Canterbury Tales* and *Tristram Shandy*, successful examples in classical literature, and, arguably, in *The English Patient* and *A Thousand Acres* in contemporary fiction.

The art of the mystery, on the other hand, resides almost entirely in plot and character (good writing and an overarching intelligence obviously help, too). Plot-wise, a mystery must have a beginning, a middle, and an end; must have a traditional narrative arc, a denouement; must not be open-ended. Indeed, it is vital that the end ravel up threads which some crime has frayed into a tangle of misperceived motives and miscalculated actions—and the raveling agent *must* be character; truth must spring inevitably from the who of each member of the cast. If it does not, if the solution to the mystery rests in some plot mechanism rather than the inevitability of character, the writer has cheated, and the reader has a right to be angry.

All of which is a long-winded explanation for the soothing effect which mysteries can have in times of tribulation. When life seems unjust, when people behave in unkind ways and suffer no punishment, when fate seems random and chaos reigns, what better solace than a dip into a universe which obeys laws, a just world in which truth prevails and cruel behavior results not in triumph but in punishment?

Perhaps, given Barbara's and my addiction to the genre, it was inevitable that TKE would develop, maintain, a mystery room. I first met Barbara when, a year after the store opened, a few fellow mystery addicts invited a few friends of similar taste to become members of a new club at TKE. We each contributed mysteries to a joint lending library, spent hours drinking wine and comparing our favorites and, in the fullness of time, actually wrote, produced, and directed our own mystery weekend.

THE MYSTERIOUS AFFAIR AT STEIN'S

In 1985, TKE's Mystery Club has been meeting for six years, and the endless discussions of the genre are beginning to pale, even in the eyes of the most fanatical among us. Susan Pixton, an attorney, has recently attended a mystery weekend back east somewhere, and when she describes the mechanics to us, we say as one voice, "We can do that!" We brainstorm a plot, assign scenes, begin to write dialogue.

As time and the play progress, tensions mount. It has become increasingly clear that some of us are doing more than others. Nevertheless, the dialogue accumulates posthaste, and two months into our mystery, we convince members of SLAC (Salt Lake Acting Company, the local cutting-edge theater group) to read from our burgeoning script. After a couple of read-throughs have occurred, we realize (duh) that what we are proposing to do is not only to write the play we have plotted out, but to produce and direct it as well—something which none of us is qualified to do. We are beyond the point where we can back out, however; we've put in so much time and effort that the thing has taken on a life of its own.

Rehearsals commence in earnest. Kate Woodworth, a good friend who has just landed a job doing PR for a plush ski resort in Park City, the Stein Eriksen Lodge at Deer Valley, asks us if we'd be interested in holding the affair there. Since it's the off-season, Stein's would be glad to accommodate us, she tells us, if we can generate publicity as well as participants who will pay to stay the weekend. We call the (then) three local TV stations, and two of them are interested. The date is set, and we have two weeks to polish the rough gem we have created.

Opening night commences with a reception in a foyer that has been closed off from the space adjoining it by French doors. One of them is slightly ajar and, as Mystery Club members and participants sip champagne and chat, voices from behind the door ratchet up in volume. Suddenly a young man erupts from the room. Flamboyant in his fury, strutting it before the stunned crowd in the foyer, he stalks toward our champagne table and grabs a bottle from the astonished waiter. He pours himself three glasses in swift succession, downing them one after another, barely pausing to swallow (to the consternation of the Mystery Club members, who are wondering how he'll ever deliver his lines dead drunk). Pouring one more for the road, he walks (lurches, more accurately) back into the adjoining room, leaving the door wide open in his wake.

As we gape at the now-visible owners of the voices we've been attempting to overhear, a satisfying cacophony of shouted accusations ensues, directing information our way; a complex but ferocious disagreement over water rights is afoot—three women and four men are hurling accusations at one another. Malice hovers in the air (convincingly done, we congratulate ourselves in whispers), and the weekend's participants goggle, eavesdrop avidly, shamelessly. At the center of this storm of ill will, buffeted but unbowed by the swirling hatred, stands a man with a shock of white hair and a contemptuous glare—a glare directed, over the next few minutes, at each person in the room.

Hap is the villain around which the plot turns. He is untruthful, manipulative, despised (according to our script, at least) by the other characters in the play—which means, of course, that each of them has a motive to do him in. Once murdered (he's poisoned during the dinner an hour later, expiring ungracefully, face-forward in a mound of mashed potatoes), Hap's sorry lot is to skulk around Stein's, concealing himself from all participants, since he's supposed to be dead.

Meanwhile, guests tail cast members around the hotel, searching the pockets of jackets left hanging on chair backs, lurking in the shadows to overhear damning conversations, meeting with one another to share evidence and to speculate on motive. One guest in particular, a fifteen-year-old girl who has come with her mother, is so involved in the spirit of the thing that she actually rifles two of the cast members' rooms, climbing in through balcony windows to conduct her search.

After that first satisfactory evening, the Mystery Club members are so exhausted that we stumble to our rooms without bothering to prepare for the morrow. Once in the privacy of our luxurious boudoirs, we soak our weary bones in the gigantic brass-fitted Jacuzzis and fall into bed. Still exhausted the next morning, we watch the scene that commences over breakfast through sleep-blurred eyes, depending on the actors to move our plot forward. They do, brilliantly, although a certain uneasiness permeates our fatigue when redheaded, electric Nancy Borgenicht, producer and driving force behind SLAC, peppers her dialogue with, "Fuck, fuck, fuck," repeating the words like a litany, in order, we suppose, to sustain her "hard-boiled" character. A concerned mother covers the alert ears of a grinning teenager more than once, but otherwise no one seems to mind.

Although the culprit was identified by one or two participants before our hard-boiled heroine revealed all, the "Mystery Weekend" was a wild success. We didn't do another, but none of us has ever forgotten a minute of the one we did. Just that small brush with "theater" made it clear to me why the SLAC members who participated are so smitten by acting. For a brief time a play is its own universe, its own *raison d'etre*, the cast a unified force adrenalized by a common purpose that is all-consuming.

As to our Mystery Club, we still meet in a sporadic fashion, and we still talk about mysteries. And read them, of course.

P.I. FOR HIRE

A perennial favorite of said mystery club these past years is Dennis Lehane. Patrick Kenzie, his wisecracking P.I., is competition for Robert Parker's Spenser on the mean streets of Boston. The sure-footed characterization, sarcastic humor, and dazzling prose of the four mysteries in this series have garnered rave reviews everywhere, deservedly. Lehane's first standalone, *Mystic River*, a harrowing novelistic tale of past sins revisited in the present, is stunning, both in terms of writing and characterization. It has taken him far past even the best of the "series" detective fiction he has written and into an arena in which the lines between literary and genre fiction disappear. It also took him into the world of movies when Clint Eastwood created a film from the book, coaxing harrowing performances from Sean Penn, Tim Robbins, and Kevin Bacon, among others.

Shutter Island confirms Lehane's dazzling reputation, stunning the reader with its action even as its characters' development makes said action inevitable. Set on an island in the Atlantic that houses an "institution for the criminally insane," as such establishments were labeled in the fifties, this mystery is so evocative of that era, so revelatory in terms of the psychiatric mores of the time, that it will become a classic, just as *Mystic River* has.

When he came to TKE, Dennis Lehane was just beginning to build the reputation that is coming to fruition with *Mystic River* and *Shutter Island*. He was in town to visit Chris Gleason, a grad student working at our store, and spent an afternoon on our patio. We had been fans of Lehane's from the moment we had read the wise-cracking, fast-paced *A Drink Before the War* and had sold it to every one of our mystery-loving customers. The book had substance—so did the sizzling *Darkness Take My Hand,* which came next, and when he read from it in the staccato rhythm that is his trademark, the audience sat rapt. Some among them were writers (novelist John DuFresne had accompanied Lehane from Florida), and the discussion that followed the reading was wide-ranging and intelligent—providing the sort of afternoon that makes booksellers feel like the game is worth the candle. Lehane spoke with passion about the art of writing (a passion reflected in the craftsmanship of his books), but he had a sense of humor, too, and he held the audience as spellbound as he does his readers.

Lehane's is a huge talent by anyone's standards, in or out of genre fiction. Clearly more interested in writing good books than he is in creating "bestsellers," he pens the stuff of true bestsellers—books that sell not because of publisher hype, or even because their stories are compelling, but because their themes are complex and interesting, their characters unforgettably and unforgivably human, their writing transcendent. He (along with Carol O'Connell) has always been an odds-on TKE favorite to become one of the towering names in the mystery field in the coming decades.

A LEGAL EAGLE, THE ORIGINAL OF THE BREED

What is it about Boston that is so attractive to writers of good mysteries? The blue-collar stew of Italian and Irish culture spiced with the hard-to-swallow flavor of rich Yank? Walter Walker's *A Dime to Dance By*, set just outside Boston, stars an ex-football-hero-turned-lawyer named Chuckie. Walker, like Lehane, deals with young men of that age when life's promise should begin to unfold, but doesn't—when, positive they know everything about everything, said sad young men begin to discover how shallow their knowledge actually is. Grisham, in his bestselling novels-that-are-movies, takes this type of character in one direction—that of the frustrated corporate lawyer; Walker, like Lehane takes it in another, probing the psyches of those young blue-collar know-it-alls as they grow into full-blown awareness of their ignorance.

A practicing attorney in San Francisco, Walter Walker wrote his first mystery well before John Grisham hit the big time with *The Firm* and, no disrespect intended, Walker is a far better writer than Grisham, his books meatier, his language more interesting. He had come to Utah to a writer's conference after his second book, *The Immediate Prospect of Being Hanged*, was published. Because we loved his books, we jumped at the chance to have him visit the store.

Remember Rule I, the admonition that under no circumstances should a book event be held near or on a holiday? Since I seldom if ever follow my own advice, I asked Walter Walker to visit TKE on Father's Day. It was an excellent idea, I informed my dubious partner Barbara.

Fathers have the right to do exactly as they please on Father's Day and, believe me, they'll come in droves. They'll bring their kids to browse in the children's room, their wives to browse in fiction, while they themselves sit on the patio chewing the fat with our, and their, favorite mystery writer.

As it turned out, we had Walter Walker to ourselves on Father's Day, to our humiliation and his. He was kind about it, didn't criticize us, perhaps because we were at once so sincerely (if desperately) complimentary and so abjectly apologetic. We truly do love his books. And unlike most attorneys I know (I have the right to be rude on the subject since I'm married to one of them, albeit a nice one), his ego is not swollen, his expectations not gargantuan—which was a good thing, under the circumstances. And I finally learned my own lesson; I haven't had an author on a holiday or holiday eve since.

P C OR NOT PC

Tony Hillerman packed them in both times he signed books at TKE. A large genial man, he doesn't make much of himself, doesn't wallow in the glory of his name, but bends his head to the task of signing with a good nature and a quick hand (or did until his arthritis made signings next to impossible). And rather than feeling used by the attention he pays them, the Navajo who flock to see him seem to appreciate that attention, perhaps because Hillerman is respectful—not to mention accurate—in his portrayal of their people. They drive in from all over the state to stand in line and chat a few minutes, buy a book, have it signed.

Sherman Alexie says that when whites write about people in any of the various tribes, they're just using Native Americans one more time in one more way. But he's wrong. If a man can convincingly portray a woman in a novel (which Alexie has done more than once), if a Navajo can portray an Ojibwa, a Zuni, a Ho-Chunk (all of whom have different customs, languages), then surely a white can portray a Navajo. Or vice versa. Alexie himself has, after all, portrayed whites. So why should he consider it such a staggering breech of decorum when the opposite occurs? In my view, the imagination of a writer can only be hampered by the limits of his or her knowledge. If a writer knows enough about a character to get inside her or his head or heart, then said writer knows enough to put what's in that head and heart on paper. *Knows* is, of course, the operative word.

Louise Erdrich said in an interview (*Atlantic*, January 17, 2001), when asked about non-Indian Ian Frazier's portrayal of the Oglalas, "if we all stopped to wonder if the people we were writing about wanted to be written about, half of us would not be writing."

I've loved all of Hillerman's mysteries over the years, adored the sagas of Jim Chee and Joe Leaphorn, the Four Corners landscape they dwell in. Not only are Hillerman's books accurately researched and well written in that understated journalistic style that comes so naturally to a former newspaper reporter, they are moving in human terms as well, seldom predictable or trite. Hillerman's were the first in a rash of mystery series using Native Americans as protagonists (Tom Perry, Louis Owens, Margaret Coel, Kirk Mitchell, and Peter Bowen are all latter-day but talented practitioners of the subgenre). Hillerman's were also the first of several series to successfully use the rural small-town West as backdrop and character (Jamie Harrison, James Crumley, Walter Satterthwaite, J. A. Jance, Sandra Prowell, and, of late, even James Lee Burke come to mind). Ironically, *Finding Moon*, which is set in Vietnam rather than the West, may be the single autobiographical book Hillerman has written, at least in terms of character. The protagonist, Moon Mathias, is a decent, well-intentioned but stubborn man, slow to rile but implacable once riled. Although Hillerman claims in his autobiography that the protagonist is patterned after a friend (and I'm sure he is), from the little I've seen of Tony Hillerman, Moon may be the character he has created who is closest to his own.

"SHUTTER" TO THINK

TKE and the Salt Lake City Library brought Hillerman to town not long ago—he came for the same gala which had occasioned my ill-fated dinner with Isabel, and he spoke in the library auditorium as our guest the day following Isabel's reading. Since we were hosting his appearance in Salt Lake, I made all the travel arrangements, and he and I exchanged several E-mails during this process. At some point, he requested a detailed itinerary, and I—never one for few words where many will do—provided him with a long-winded description of all that would transpire. In so doing I asked him if (since, due to arthritis, he had agreed to sign books only once, at the gala), he would sign spare copies of *Wailing Wind* at his leisure in his hotel room for us to sell at the reading—only instead of writing **Wailing** *Wind*, I wrote **Walking** *Wind.*

I blithely sent my message into cyberspace and forwarded a copy to TKE's publicist, who pointed out my misnomer by return E-mail. Embarrassed (who wouldn't be?) I fired another E-mail off to Tony, apologizing for the length of my last flatulent E-mail and for getting his book title wrong, saying that when I realized what I had done, it had made me "shutter" (yeah, I wrote "shutter," not "shudder"), but that at least I was less likely to misname the book title in my introduction the way I had once heard a Random House rep (*not* Ron Smith) do when, in introducing Wallace Stegner he said to the audience, "Ladies and Gentlemen, I give you the author of **Angel** *of Repose* . . ."

I fired that message off, reread it (after, not before I sent it), shuddered when I saw "shutter" and mailed off by way of postscript, "Dear Tony, that's shudder, not shutter."

He emailed back:

> *Betsy—Can I understand you getting a name wrong? I once introduced Marie as Mildred, after 29 years of marriage. Two years ago, at the MWA convention announcing we had elected Mary Higgins Clark as Grand Master, I had one of those senior moments and forgot her name. Mary had to rush up and snatch the award out of my grasp.*
>
> *Tony Hillerman*
>
> *(Anyway thanks for the information. Just what I wanted.) Tony*

I had known, after reading his often wonderfully funny memoir, *Seldom Disappointed,* that Tony Hillerman had a sense of humor, and I'd guessed at his kindness, watching him in action. But poking fun at himself to take the sting out of my own humiliation? What a guy!

He not only signed hundreds of books at the gala during his reading the next day, he also kept a huge audience in hysterics. Ginny McComber, one of the librarians, said, "He could have read recipe cards and I would have laughed." He signed a few hundred *more* books at the reading, arthritis notwithstanding. As gallant as he is funny, Hillerman is a man of great presence despite his humor (or maybe because of it). Neither Barbara nor I will ever forget him—or, for that matter, his wife, Marie.

THE WILDE WEST

If in the picture of Walter Satterthwait on tour (see page 126), his grin seems reminiscent of the one Toad of Toad Hall flashed when he first saw the "motor car" in *The Wind in the Willows*, it's because Satterthwait took the same perverse delight in his motor home. Outraged that his publisher wouldn't tour him, he used the proceeds from his last mystery, *Masquerade*, to buy the motorized monstrosity you see in the photograph and drove it from Florida to California, stopping at bookstores along the way. When he came to TKE, we were ready for him, knowing from various conversations and E-mails (not to mention his books) that he was wacky, off-beat, bound to be entertaining.

We packed the Framery (the art gallery next door, which we use for most readings when the weather doesn't cooperate), and to the crowd's delight, Satterthwait was every bit as funny in person as he is in his books. He had them all guffawing, and the more they laughed, the funnier he became. I wondered, as I wiped my eyes, if his publishers had any clue how good this man was on the road. *They* should have paid for the damn van, I told him later. And they should have. In fact, if they had any sense, they could make him a media star—he'd make a fortune for them.

But what do I know? I'm just an independent bookseller. Here, at any rate, is what I know about his books.

Satterthwait's first mysteries, a series of slightly zany and exceedingly well-written books, are set close to, if not quite in, Hillerman territory, in present-day Sante Fe, New Mexico. Satterthwait's Sante Fe is fertile ground for fiction and mysteries alike, peopled as it is by the sort-of-rich, the super-rich, the cloud-niners (high on new-age smoke), and the down-and-outers (low on cash). Although already avid fans after reading three or four of these mysteries, we had not been not prepared for *The Wilde West*. The tale of Oscar Wilde on a lecture tour of the Wild West, of a psychopathic killer, a drunken sheriff convinced that Wilde had "done the deed," and a cast of miners, hookers, and other quintessentially Western types, it is one of the funniest books I've ever read—a sort of frontier version of *Cold Comfort Farm* with a mystery (and Oscar) thrown in for good measure. This was the first in Satterthwait's series of historic mysteries, the rest straying from the West to such far-flung cities as London and Paris and featuring, along with a duo of Pinkerton detectives, various and sundry famous Europeans from Freud to Conan Doyle. Each is a witty, wonderful romp into history, mystery, and good humor but *The Wilde West* remains our favorite.

THE SOUND OF TRUMPETS

In 1995, when Salt Lake City made its ill-fated bid for the winter Olympics, the UK/UTAH Festival was also being planned. A PR idea dreamed up as a means of inciting local interest in things English, the festival was carried out jointly by Utah's governor and the British Consul General. Some official in the British consulate must have seen TKE's name in the Salt Lake phone book and thought we looked a likely festival prospect because one of them called one day, asking for the manager.

"This is the manager," I said with a sigh, expecting either an angry customer or a telephone solicitor (who else ever asks for the manager?).

A clipped British voice inquired whether as a bookstore we might be interested in joining in the year-long UK /UTAH Festival.

By now I knew the ring of potential profit when I heard it. "Delighted," I assured her, not having a clue what she was talking about but wanting to be signed on before she asked too many questions about our utility in her plans.

I was wondering how many authors she knew, just what clout she actually had with her government, how dedicated they might be to bringing things English to Utah, of all places, when she said, "I see from the Yellow Pages that you specialize in mysteries."

"And fiction," I added, visions of Muriel Spark and A. S. Byatt, Julian Barnes, and Ian McEwan dancing in my head.

"But mysteries are a strength?" Her tone informed me in that polite British way that brooks no argument that mysteries were the subject at hand.

"Absolutely," I assured her. "We love mysteries at The King's English. They are indeed a specialty." I thought as I said this that the "indeed" was a nice touch.

Perhaps she did too because she went on, "Do you carry many British mystery writers?"

"We have an entire room devoted to mysteries. And more than half are British."

"Oh?" She sounded intrigued now, a Rainbow trout circling under a bright hatch of mayflies.

"Living and dead," I went on. But when she didn't laugh I added hastily, "Among the living we carry John Le Carré's books, for example. And P. D. James's, Francis Fyfield's, Peter Dickinson's, Robert Barnard's, Colin Dexter's . . . and John Mortimer's, of course."

There was a silence and I prayed that, behind the tony accent, this British brain was hatching some scheme of its own—and that that scheme involved us.

"John Mortimer . . . Isn't he that Rumpole fellow?"

"The man who created him, yes. The man who wrote, among others, the books which have Rumpole as a main character."

"Ahhhh."

Ah, indeed.

Page forward six months. It is the dead of winter in the Salt Lake Valley. The wind is howling; snow crusted with ice and pocked with grit lies everywhere. There have been months of negotiations on both sides of the Atlantic: with the British Consul General's office; with Rachael Schnoll, Mortimer's publicist from Viking Penguin, his New York publisher; with KUED (our local public TV station); with attorneys here in town. Penguin had demanded that TKE buy Mortimer's plane ticket—first class, no less—From New York City to Utah. Since we couldn't afford to do so, we called in help, involved a lawyer we know, Ron Yengich, as a co-sponsor, made the entire affair a fund-raiser for KUED. Now all the efforts have paid off. John Mortimer is stepping off the plane right here in Salt Lake City.

As surely Rumpole as Leo McKern, who played the role to such wonderful effect on PBS, Mr. Mortimer's face splits with a sardonic grin as I gallop toward him, panting and red-faced, late as usual. Ignoring my all-too-apparent dishevelment, he conjures from behind him, rather like a magician producing a rabbit, Rachael Schnoll.

So this is the face that goes with that sharp New York voice I have been negotiating with on our side of the ocean. Petite and dark haired, she looks about twelve years old. But her youthful appearance belies her New York efficiency, and she has the two of us herded down the stairs and into the luggage area before we have time to so much as exchange greetings.

"Lovely flight," Mortimer says as we wait for his suitcases to decant. "Lovely champagne."

I wonder nervously whether, speaking of champagne, the expensive bottle we saved up two weeks' salary to buy him (Rachael had warned us on the phone that he prefers Dom Perignon) is safely on ice in his hotel room.

But there's his luggage—at least seven or eight times the weight of Isabel Allende's carpet bag (spare champagne? I wonder). And there's no more time left to fret. Out to the parking lot we stagger.

Since my own battered Subaru, whose heater works only sporadically and whose upholstery has seen better days, seemed inappropriate for ferrying such an august personage (and my husband's Toyota not much better), I had borrowed my mother's Audi Quattro for the two days during which I was to serve as author escort. I hadn't realized at the time how small the Quattro was, nor how large Mr. Mortimer.

Worse, I haven't driven the Audi before, and its front panels, however nicely burled, are a bewilderment of buttons and dials. But hey, I reason, I'm bright, and how hard can it be? Meeting the flight late, due to my failure to coax the key into the ignition for a heart-stopping ten minutes, should have served as warning. But like Odysseus, I don't heed the omens, to my sorrow (not to mention Mr. Mortimer's).

We're at the Audi now. Determined to do this right, I have managed to memorize, for once, the level on which I have parked and the correct coordinates for locating the appropriate row and space. Mortimer eyes the Audi, says, no doubt with irony intended (since he must by now have realized that he will need to get his considerable personage inside of it), "Lovely car."

Little did he guess.

I pop the trunk with aplomb and pile in the suitcases while Rachael climbs in the back, and Mortimer wedges himself in front. We exit the parking lot into a frenzy of snow, and when I flick on what I assume to be the wipers the storm continues to swirl at us unabated. I hear the persistent "click click click" of the blinker I have just activated and try another lever. The lights come on. I try yet another lever, then a dial. The road disappears behind a thickening screen of white while I'm turning one dial after another; I'm about to pull over when the wipers finally come to life. The windows clear and Mortimer clears his throat.

In silence we slog our way toward town, pulling up finally at the Peery, a hotel in which I've put up various authors over the years. As I open the door for Mortimer, I think with satisfaction of the Dom Perignon waiting on ice.

The room they've assigned Mr. Mortimer is miniscule. It is up a flight of stairs, and he doesn't do stairs easily. When he asks for a change of rooms, they are rude. Not uncooperative, but rude.

"Do you know who this *is*," I hiss at a young (too young) blank face behind the front desk. "It's John *Mortimer*, for God's sake."

The (too young) face remains blank.

"Rumpole of the Bailey?" I try.

Blankness is replaced by a sneer. Big deal, the sneer says.

Having overheard the end of this exchange (or lack thereof), Mortimer says, "We're leaving this—place. At once. I'm certain you must have some *nice* hotels in this city. Somewhere." A man of foresight, he has already grabbed a suitcase in one hand, the Dom Perignon in the other, and cradling the latter with care, he leads us forth once more into the maelstrom.

Exactly what *will* he consider nice? I wonder, whisking my guest through the driving snow, up one street and down another in search of inspiration. In desperation, I pull up at Little America. Dreadful flocked wallpaper is what I remember from the single time I visited a room there years before, so not the Ritz certainly, but still . . . large of scale and bound to have vacancies, its help well trained, its food decent . . . Many of the reps stay here, I know, liking the spaciousness of the rooms.

I pull in, ask my passengers to wait and charge inside. Yes, they do have rooms available. Yes, large rooms. Absolutely, there are vacant rooms near the elevators, more than one, within a few doors.

"We'll take two," I tell them. I give them a credit card, sign the receipt, scurry out to the car, and open the door. "You're all registered, why don't you go on inside, and I'll bring in the bags."

Oh, cruel optimism.

John Mortimer and Rachael Schnoll enter the lobby, while off-stage I sit still for a minute, mopping my brow. Then I pull the key from the ignition (with only a minimum of persuasion), climb from the car, go around to the trunk, insert the round key into the round lock, turn it to the right, and push the button. Nothing happens. I turn it the other way, push again. Still nothing. I turn it back. And forth. Wait. Try the button again. Look around for inspiration. Try yet again. And once more.

Then I stop. *Think*, Betsy, I tell myself.

"The trunk worked at the airport, why not now?" I ask this aloud, unaware of the bell-men watching. "I've got it," I tell the world at large. "I'll try the *inside* trunk latch. There has to be one." I insert myself back in the car, look around and sure enough, there's a second lever behind the gas tank latch. I pull it, and the car starts whooping as if it were a Nazi Klaxon announcing the eminent arrival of the SS. I make this comparison darkly, looking frantically at stray bellhops, then at the dash, searching for ways to shut the damn thing off and all the while praying Mortimer is safely in some room on the far side of the hotel.

Heads have turned, of course, and the bellmen are positively transfixed. Finally, one of them approaches, takes the keys from me without even asking and presses an insignificant black button on the ring-holder. Presto, the alarm stops. But not before my guests (who are *not* safely ensconced in twin rooms on the far side of the hotel but have remained in the lobby, peering out the glass doors) have witnessed most if not all of my futile and humiliating attempts at solving The Riddle of the Trunk Key. As they watch, I pull the truck latch again, and again the alarm whoops once, twice, before I press the button on the key ring to shut the damn thing up. Obediently, the alarm stops, but there is still no way I can see to release the trunk. I give the key back to the bellman, and he fiddles for a few more minutes but no luck. "Why don't you go in to your guests," he says kindly (if a bit grandly, a man of infinite skill). "And let me figure this out for you."

"There's been a problem with the luggage?" Mortimer asks as I face him in the lobby.

"You might say that," I hedge, thinking, If I were some naive young ingenue, all of this might be funny. *He* might think it funny. But I'm fifty, for God's sake, and I can't even work the trunk lock on the car I'm driving. "It's not my car," I tell him, feeling like a six-year-old confessing a grade-school crime. "It's my mother's."

"Yours not up to snuff? He asks this with kindness in his voice, and I choke on my answer.

"It's incomprehensible," I say after a minute. "I simply cannot figure out how to work the trunk latch. It took me fifteen minutes just to figure out how to start the silly car, and I've tried every way I can see to . . . I don't know if . . ." I'm dripping with sweat, despite the cold, and feel, horror of horrors, as if I'm about to cry.

But what's *he* feeling? I've seen his irritation when a hotel room was too small for his taste.

What's he going to say about this? Rachael, her eyes large with what appears to be fear, is no doubt wondering, too.

What he does is to whoop with laughter, whoop as loud as the car alarm. "Mum's car, is it? Mum's boot," he chortles, peering out the door again to where the Audi is waiting—in silence, at least.

"The boot of Mum's car," he repeats, guffawing now with an indecent glee. A sense of humor is a rare and wondrous thing. My tears evaporate before they've fallen, and I start to laugh, too.

"Why don't you go up and have some champagne," I suggest, "read a book or something, while I work on this, ugh, *boot* problem."

He nods, still laughing, and leads the way toward the elevator, Rachael in tow. Outside, I can see that the bellman hasn't had any luck, despite his assurances, so I get in, insert the key into the ignition (with some confidence now), start the car and drive a couple of blocks. Safely out of hearing distance of Little America, I park. Funny or not, if the damn alarm goes off one more time, John Mortimer is *not* going to hear it.

The manual, I think, and try to open the glove compartment. Unbelievably, that usually simple operation takes more than a few minutes; it is only after an inadvertent key-turn to the left, corrected to the upright, that a tentative button-push (my seventh or eighth) produces results. My God, I think, it's like Mission Impossible—never imagining at the time that herein might lie a clue. I reach in for the manual and leaf to the index, page from there to all references to trunks. To no avail. In this day of cell phones in every backpack, purse, and pocket, I could have called my mother, asked her how to open the damned trunk. I didn't have a cell phone, however. (But then why would I? I can't even open a car trunk.)

The next forty-five minutes are spent in close perusal of the Audi manual, accompanied by occasional bleats from the car alarm. Why can't people use their heads when they write manuals, I wonder aloud as I hunt desperately for any references to trunks, to locks, to alarms, to keys. "This is as bad as a damned computer manual," I yell at one point as I hit another blind alley, indexwise. "Failure to reference should be a felony."

I hunt and curse, curse and hunt, and finally, under some small-print sublisting which I had overlooked three times, the name of which is gone from my mind forever, I find the key (no pun intended). There's a sequence, very much like the one necessary to unlock the glove compartment, that goes like this, if memory serves me: Once the key has been turned to the right a half-turn, security is armed. After that, the button freezes and any attempt to open the trunk from the inside results (as I know all too well) in setting off the alarm. The key must be turned a half-turn to the left *twice*, and again to the upright position before the alarm is deactivated. Then, and only then, will the button work. It's a sequence that, to my mind at least, defies logic and is unlikely to occur to the average person, much less the mechanically challenged. I try it out, and *voila*! As at the airport, up pops the lid. The trunk, I reason, must have been off security at the airport. Inserting the key and giving it a half turn to the right at Little America was apparently the fatal move that doomed me to my subsequent humiliation at the hotel—to John Mortimer's vast entertainment.

Although I'm certain now how the thing works, I'm taking no chances. I drive back to the hotel with the trunk lid up, pull into the valet lane to the cheers of three bellmen, one doorman, and the concierge. I wipe snow off the valises, sweat off my brow, and arrive puffing at Mr. Mortimer's room just in time for the last of the Dom Perignon.

The events of the next three days have been planned in detail. After Ron Yengich and I brokered the trip and made all the arrangements, after Barbara and I dickered with Rachael Schnoll and KUED, sold tickets for the public television fund-raiser, and rented the hall at an exorbitant price, another attorney in town, who had met Mr. Mortimer at some bar (legal, not alcoholic) function and claimed acquaintance with him, got wind of his trip and called KUED (to which station his law firm had just given vast sums of money). He announced with the mix of self-importance and brashness that is so typical of corporate litigators that he'd like to be part of Mortimer's visit, that Mortimer would, he was certain, expect it. He said that he'd like to host a "legal" evening "in chambers," followed by a dinner, and would expect a couple of the front rows at *our* event to be reserved for the use of his friends and associates. He coerced Mortimer's phone number out of someone at the station, called Mr. Mortimer, reminded him that they had met, told him he and his firm and friends were to be included in the festivities, the schedule. Taken unawares, Mortimer agreed to the "legal" evening, at which point said attorney called back the TV station and announced the "new" schedule to one and all.

Barbara and I were furious. So was Ron Yengich. We had brought Mr. Mortimer to Salt

Lake City, after all, had paid hard-earned money and gone to a tremendous amount of work. We still had reams more to do. And this jackass attorney was simply waltzing in, stealing fully a quarter of our prospective audience for an event the night before, taking Mortimer off to dinner on the night *we* had planned to do so. We fussed and fumed, cursed and plotted, but in the end, short of murder (duly considered), there was nothing to be done. I called the attorney, who of course wasn't available, and when he finally did return my call two days later, it was to inform me (beneficently) that The King's English would be "allowed" to sell books at his in-chambers event.

It is Friday night. Attorneys and judges are milling around John Mortimer, and he is listening to first one, then the other, with a bemused smile on his face. Julie (TKE's PR person at that time) and I have set up a table outside the door to the courtroom where the famous barrister is to speak and are busy selling books. With customary refinement, attorneys are jostling and nudging, grabbing copies of mysteries, memoirs, novels to have signed, personalized, for themselves, for friends, for judges, making way for judges who want copies signed. Then it is time for the show. The take-charge attorney takes *his* star's arm (we watch Mortimer start to flinch, then restrain himself), ushers him into the courtroom and, as we start to fall in behind them, intending to sit in the back row where we can keep an eye on the books and hear Mortimer speak, the door slams in our face. Well, not quite in our faces, not quite a slam, but if actions were intentions . . .

Julie and I look at each other, jaws agape. "Well fuck that," I say, finally, and crack the door. Mortimer, in the midst of his comments, looks up and smiles at us, nods. Heads turn but we stand our ground defiantly. Surely we have a right to listen.

He is witty, articulate, blunt, impassioned. The considerable champagne he's imbibed might have been water for all the effect it has had on his tongue. He has the audience in stitches, in tears (no small matter with attorneys), in thrall. And then it is over, there is a tidal wave of applause and everyone has left for dinner at the New Yorker, a posh Salt Lake eatery. Everyone, that is, but us.

Despite my unflattering opinion of some lawyers, there are still some great people practicing law (my husband included), and Kit has friends who attended the dinner. They later regale us with tales of what occurred after we left that night. But none is so funny as Mortimer's description the following day of the attorney who hosted the affair, the man who had claimed such a special relationship with Mortimer. Characteristically, he attempted to dominate the conversation all night, and Mr. Mortimer's only comment to us is a question: "Who was that insufferable man?"

"Don't you *know* him?"

"Well I must have met him, I suppose, since he said I did, but . . ." He trails off, and takes another tack. "And who was that silly judge who kept putting his hand on my knee, grinning like . . . do you suppose he had feelings for me?" I start to laugh and try to explain the local culture, the back-slapping, knee-touching familiarity and the toothy smiles of good cheer that are so much a part of male bonding in this society.

At dinner, Mr. Mortimer doesn't eat, preferring to down a little of "the bubbly" before his speech. The rest of us don't eat much either. We are too busy laughing. Because with or without food, John Mortimer is *on*, every moment of the day and night. He tells story after story, but the one that still sticks in all of our minds is his bucolic saga of a farmer near Heathrow fornicating happily away with his sheep, oblivious to the international flight on approach above him, the passengers craning their necks, witness to romance as they'd never dreamed of it before, there on their pastoral British Isle.

The hall where he is to speak is the auditorium of one of Salt Lake's oldest high schools. It is vast—holds 1,100 people. They are beginning to trickle in while backstage there is the usual panic, this time occasioned not just by the potential for humiliation if the audience is small, but also by the resultant prospect of financial disaster. We watch nervously until the trickle becomes a river, the river a torrent of bodies in coats and scarves and gloves, people holding tickets, looking for seats. Soon the place is filled but for a scattering of empty chairs high in the balcony—and two rows in the front, empty rows, reserved by you-know-who for all his supposed attorney friends, few of whom have shown up.

I stand before the vast sea of faces and introduce Ron Yengich, who in turn delivers a feisty, funny, and perfectly wonderful introduction to John Mortimer. Who in turn delivers an hour's worth of howlingly funny, bitingly satirical, wrenchingly moving tales of life in the legal and literary trenches of Britain—from his own perspective and from Horace Rumpole's.

It is an evening to die for. It is memorable and too soon over. But it is not the end of our adventures with John Mortimer. Even though the next morning is a Sunday, KUED has scheduled an interview for 9:00 a.m. Mortimer's publicist has already warned him, but when I remind him that I'll need to pick him up at 8:30 the next morning, he is frankly and completely horrified.

"It's on your schedule, John," Rachael tells him in no uncertain terms, not one whit dismayed by his age or his fame. "It's been on your schedule for weeks."

How does she do it, this slip of a girl? I wonder, as Mortimer meekly nods his head. "Anyone for champagne?" he asks, but we both say no, and he climbs obediently into the dread Audi to return to the hotel for a woefully short night's sleep.

So there we are back in the snow on Sunday morning, back in Mum's car. We pull into the parking lot of the glittering new public television studio, but there are no lights to be seen, no cars in the lot. Still, we've promised, so I turn into the valet lane. "Why don't you two try the door," I tell them. "I'll park the car and be right behind you."

"Be careful with Mum's car now," he says grinning as he climbs laboriously out—and steps into a full six inches of icy water. He stands still for a moment, then gets back in the car. "It's past time for champagne," he says, firmly now, and I start the motor, drive off into the slanting snow, while even Rachael does not demur. Clearly, the interview was not meant to be.

My God, I think (oblivious to the irony), it's Sunday morning. Where am I going to find champagne on Sunday morning in Salt Lake City, Utah? We drive around for a while—aimlessly, although I'm pretending that I know where I'm going, and I finally take him to the Oyster Bar, a private club in Salt Lake (private clubs operate by different liquor laws than regular restaurants in Salt Lake). We arrive and are seated, but when Mortimer orders champagne, the waitress tells him that even in a private club no liquor may be served until noon.

"Champagne isn't liquor, it's ambrosia," he protests, but our waitress isn't swayed. We order oysters—a dozen, then another—and hunker down to wait out the law. During this caesura, Mortimer regales us with more tales of his dinner at the New Yorker the previous Friday, moving on to epic accounts of his own court cases, criminals he has defended, writers and playwrights he has known, sagas of the theater, actors, the glitterati of Britain. At last noon comes, and the champagne begins to flow. Before we know it, it is 2:00 p.m. and time to drop him at Ron Yengich's for a short visit, then on to the airport—where he watches with theatrical anxiety as I open the trunk (which I do with my own dramatic flourish). He thanks me then, and I him. I thank Rachael, too, while he looks on, and then as he turns to leave he adds, "I'll never forget Mum's car."

And he hasn't. Whenever I write to him, which I do occasionally, to ask for a quote for *The Inkslinger* or to urge him (futilely) to consider flying over one more time, he inquires after "Mum's car" with apparent glee. He recalls other parts of his trip fondly, too, taking special pride in the fact that he may well have been the first to utter the term "erection" before a public audience in downtown Salt Lake City. When we asked him the same *Inkslinger* question we had asked Margaret Atwood, the one about least-wanted holiday gifts and what one would trade them for, this was his response:

Least wants: "Any sort of machine which can be connected to the Internet."

Would trade it for: "I'd sell it at once and buy several cases of good champagne."

Growing old hasn't changed his sense of humor, either. This is how he begins his witty and wonderful memoir, *The Summer of the Dormouse: A Year of Growing Old Disgracefully*: "The time will come in your life, it will almost certainly come, when the voice of God will thunder at you from a cloud, 'From this day forth thou will not be able to put on thine own socks.'"

Sir John Mortimer (he was knighted the year after he visited Salt Lake City), like his countryman John Le Carré, another British writer I revere, is not just a genre writer. Both men are consummate craftsmen, the best examples I know of writers who transcend any genre to tell human truths. Both are men whose reputations (and books) will last long into future decades, probably longer than most other fiction writers of their generation—just as has Graham Greene's. Mortimer combines, in his person and his work, in his evident genius, the two traits I most admire: the courage of his convictions and a sense of humor.

Here's another of John Mortimer's quotes, something he said the night of the reading: "All fiction, all plays, all detective stories, all parables, all faerie stories, myths, and religions, are our attempts to provide an explanation for the haphazard events of our lives, or at least impose some order on them. . . . Fiction is our excuse to play God, to create characters and set them in motion, to make them act out, at our command, what

❈

we hope or believe, is the truth of existence." Reading it now, I find my faith in this whole enterprise confirmed.

One afterthought: I never did quite understand what the UK/Utah celebration that began the whole John Mortimer/King's English affair was in aid of. Oh, "things English" occurred: Salt Lake's arts establishment jumped on the UK bandwagon, performing English plays and symphonies on the stage, in theaters and concert halls citywide, and a few other notable Brits came to town (James Galway, for one). But what the entire undertaking was actually about I never could determine. Oh well, it probably doesn't matter. The important thing was, for us at TKE, at least, Sir John Mortimer.

❈

BOOK LISTS
Books Published During the First 25 Years of TKE in 3 Mysterious Categories

25 Mysteries to Die For

1. *Rumpole of the Bailey*, John Mortimer, 1978
2. *A Coat of Varnish*, C. P. Snow, 1979
3. *The Name of the Rose*, Umberto Eco, 1983
4. *A Dime to Dance by*, Walter Walker, 1983
5. *Always a Body to Trade*, K. C. Constantine, 1983
6. *Hindsight*, Peter Dickinson, 1983 (a vintage year)
7. *Duplicate Keys*, Jane Smiley, 1984
8. *A Thief of Time*, Tony Hillerman, 1988
9. *Time's Witness*, Michael Malone, 1989
10. *Well-Schooled in Murder*, Elizabeth George, 1990
11. *The Bootlegger's Daughter*, Margaret Maron, 1992
12. *Original Sin*, P. D. James, 1994
13. *Mallory's Oracle*, Carol O'Connell, 1994
14. *The Daughters of Cain*, Colin Dexter, 1994
15. *Coyote Wind*, Peter Bowen, 1994 (another vintage year)
16. *The Dark Room*, Minette Walters, 1996
17. *Going Local*, Jamie Harrison, 1996
18. *Aqua Alta*, Donna Leon, 1996
19. *Beat Not the Bones,* Charlotte Jay, 1996 (reissue of first Edgar Winner)
20. *Always Outnumbered, Always Outgunned*, Walter Mosely, 1997
21. *Blind Date*, Francis Fyfield, 1998
22. *In a Dry Season*, Peter Robinson, 1999
23. *Motherless Brooklyn*, Jonathan Lethem, 1999
24. *Mystic River*, Dennis Lehane, 2001
25. *Waking Raphael*, Leslie Forbes, 2004

25 Thrillers with Moral Heft

1. *Smiley's People*, John Le Carré, 1979
2. *A Spy from the Old School*, Julian Rathbone, 1980
3. *Gorky Park*, Martin Cruz Smith, 1981
4. *Murder at the Red October*, Anthony Olcott, 1981
5. *The Last Supper*, Charles McCarry, 1983
6. *Agents of Innocence*, David Ignatius, 1987
7. *Lies and Silence*, Brian Moore, 1990
8. *Spy Shadow*, Tim Sebastian, 1990
9. *The Flanders Panel*, Arturo Pérez-Reverte, 1990
10. *Dark Star*, Alan Furst, 1991
11. *Fatherland*, Robert Harris, 1992
12. *Smilla's Sense of Snow*, Peter Hoeg, 1993
13. *Headhunters*, Timothy Findley, 1993
14. *The Waterworks*, E. L. Doctorow, 1994
15. *Sacrifice of Isaac*, Neil Gordon, 1995
16. *The Statement*, Brian Moore, 1995
17. *The Dancer Upstairs*, Nicholas Shakespeare, 1997 (U.S.)
18. *The Art of Breaking Glass*, Matthew Hall, 1997
19. *A Small Death in Lisbon*, Robert Wilson, 1999
20. *In Her Defense*, Stephen Horn, 2000
21. *The Constant Gardener*, John Le Carré, 2000
22. *The Wall*, John Marks, 2001
23. *Canal House*, Mark Lee, 2003
24. *Bangkok 8*, John Burdett, 2003
25. *Due Preparation for The Plague*, Janette Turner Hospital, 2003

25 Mysteries for the Sheer Fun of It
1. *Thus Was Adonis Murdered*, Sarah Caudwell, 1981
2. *The Thin Woman*, Dorothy Cannell, 1984
3. *Dunn's Conundrum*, Stan Lee, 1985
4. *Skin Tight*, Carl Hiaasen, 1989
5. *Naked Once More*, Elizabeth Peters (or any Amelia Peabody mystery) 1989
6. *The Wilde West*, Walter Satterwaithe, 1991
7. *Bones of Coral*, James Hall, 1991
8. *After All These Years*, Susan Isaacs, 1993
9. *Gospel*, William Barnhardt, 1993
10. *One for the Money*, or anything else by Janet Evanovich, 1994
11. *What's a Girl Gotta Do?* Sparkle Hayter, 1994
12. *The Bad Samaritan*, Robert Barnard, 1995
13. *As She Rides By*, David Pierce, 1996
14. *What's the Worst Thing That Could Happen*, Donald Westlake, 1996
15. *The Death and Life of Bobby Z,* Don Winslow
16. *Felix in the Underworld*, John Mortimer, 1997
17. *Bad Chili*, Joe Lansdale, 1997
18. *A Long Finish*, Michael Dibdin, 1998
19. *Moghul Buffet*, Cheryl Benard, 1998
20. *Big Trouble*, Dave Barry, 1999
21. *The Hearse You Came in On*, Jim Cockey, 2000
22. *Monkewrench*, P. J. Tracy, 2002
23. *Skinny Dip*, Carl Hiaasen, 2004
24. *Drop Dead, My Lovely*, Ellis Weiner, 2004
25. *Live Bait*, P. J. Tracy, 2004

Chapter Five

PARTNER*S* IN HELL (AND HEAVEN): A ONE-SIDED DISCU*SS*ION

[
"A business partnership is like a marriage—without the fun of sex."

— ANN BERMAN, JULY 5, 1979
]

[
"Couldn't you all have just . . . calmed down?"

— SALMAN RUSHDIE, *The Moor's Last Sigh*
]

T he story of past and present partnerships at The King's English is a checkered one— so much so that if I didn't know better, I might think people find me hard to get along with. Ann Berman, my original partner, ostensibly left because of back surgery, dwindling finances (TKE seldom, if ever, helped anyone's bottom line), and a need for health insurance. But the truth is, there was trouble in paradise long before Ann's back went out. In the end, the breakup of our partnership was nearly as painful for both of us as our divorces had been— hence Ann's 1979 remark (above).

Ann and I actually tried therapy at one point, sat in chairs placed at equidistance from an aging female psychiatrist, and took turns casting aspersions at each other. Granted, said aspersions weren't very heinous in nature as aspersions go, but still.

HE SAID, SHE SAID

"Who does the receiving?" I ask, posing a "polite" question.

"You do." Ann is matter-of-fact.

"Who pays the bills?"

"Well, you most of the time but . . ."

"Who orders the books?"

"You do but—"

"Yes, I do. Often at home at night after Mandy goes to bed, since there's no time left in the day." Self-righteousness is reddening my cheeks and raising my voice to an inelegant squeal. "And who sees the reps?"

"You. But that's because we argue when we both do it."

"Yeah, because you think they're trying to trick you into buying too much."

"And you believe everything they tell you."

"But the point is, I do the buying, the unpacking, the receiving, the shelving, I reorder, pay bills . . ."

"I do lots of things."

"Like what?"

"I clean up after you, for one thing." There's a sting in Ann's voice for the first time. "I *organize* (the emphasis here serves as an effective reminder that I do not), and I'm terrific with customers, if I do say so."

True, I admit to myself, but then add silently (some might say sullenly), so you get to be the star while I'm off in the corner doing all the work? Is that the plan?

Ann, despite her gregarious personality, is far more passive than I am inside relationships; she positively hates confrontation. So I, of course, got in the last word (actually, almost all of the words). In retrospect, however, I have to admit that our problems were caused as much by me as by Ann. And after a few more failed stabs at partnerships, I can at least begin to imagine how the conversation might have gone if I had been the passive partner, she the assertive (she would have said "aggressive") one:

"Who keeps the store clean?"

"You do." Betsy is matter-of-fact.

"Who charms the customers and keeps them coming back?"

"Well, you, although I do my part."

"Who balances the checkbook?"

"You, most of the time. But we both pay the bills."

"Some of us more accurately than others. And do you really think it's best that you see the reps, which translates into spending money?"

"Yes, since you won't spend any."

"You make the mess, and I clean it up, is that the plan?"

When partnerships work smoothly the people involved, while different, admire each other's strengths, fill in the gaps left by each other's weaknesses. As friends, Ann's and my relationship worked that way—it still does. As partners, it did not. While I could see with perfect clarity the things Ann wasn't doing, I refused, absolutely, to acknowledge even to myself the things she was doing. Worse, the madder I got, the faster I worked (with ever more questionable results), while the madder Ann got, the more she balked.

The truth is that Ann and I both needed to grow up. We resented each other's short-comings rather than respecting each other's strengths, and as a result, we got in each other's way instead of smoothing our mutual path. I enumerated with exactitude all the things I was doing but utterly refused to acknowledge the fact that some of them were done sloppily, that my organizational skills were nonexistent, that I was (am) a slob, that she was a wonder with customers. With books. Which was, after all, the point. So we sat in our shrink's chairs sniping and posturing and didn't communicate much of consequence. Didn't save our partnership.

Ann left for back surgery. Was in bed for a year. Another year. And before she had recovered, we both realized we had come to a parting of the ways. Her alimony and child support, adequate when she divorced, had been eroded to nothing by the inflation of the late '70s. She needed a steady income—steadier than the bookstore was capable of providing. And the problems that had sent us to therapy were looming, certain to recur when she returned—if she returned.

In the end, Ann chose not to come back, and I bought her out with money I borrowed from my parents. She went to work at the library, but we continued to meet, to talk about books, and to write reviews and articles together. We managed, in the process, to salvage affection, and as our friendship reblossomed over books, writing, and gardening, hurt feelings receded on both our parts. We laugh now over the fact that she thought, when buying books from sales reps, that her job was to ignore their advice and buy less (in the book business we can return books for credit, so sales reps have little reason to load us up with books we don't need and every reason in the world to help us guess right). And I admit that my impulsive, untidy, damn-the-torpedoes style has driven more than one person around the bend over the years. We marvel in retrospect at the thought of the two of us—me on full throttle refusing to consider the danger of curves, Ann with feet pressed so firmly to the floor that the brakes howl in protest—both trying to arrive at the same destination.

A SUITABLE SOMEONE

Ann left TKE in 1981, and from then on, whatever time and energy I had left over from the mothering of my daughter, I poured into the bookstore. For a time, I ran it alone. Oh, I hired employees, first Judy (best and most faithful bookseller and friend), then Julie, Gail, Margaret, and, for the children's room, Lana, then Marilyn—wonderful booksellers, one and all. But for good or ill, I made the decisions myself. I continued to write but did so only sporadically, when work and family concerns weren't pressing.

Then in 1984, my life changed. I had married Kit two years before, and with my daughter hurtling her way toward adolescence (she seems to have acquired my hurtle genes), Kit and I had had misgivings about starting the whole glorious, fraught parenting passage anew. In the end, however, we decided to have another child.

Nick is, along with Mandy, the joy of our lives. Nick is, like Mandy, a hurtler. Severely brain damaged, he has an intractable seizure condition, and motherhood, never easy, became all-consuming, the bookstore my necessary anchor. Since Nick's seizures occur mostly at night, Kit and I sleep with him—one night Kit, me the next. We have for eighteen years. And when the sleepless nights of babyhood had bled into the sleepless nights of seizure alerts, when huge chunks of my time were devoted to organizing Nick's therapy, to serving on the boards that would help to change the system that is meant to support disabled children, I knew one thing: I needed a business partner.

It's one thing to sit down with a person and dream up a business, quite another to say one day, I need a partner, a mate—someone with whom I can spend eight hours a day six days a week, comfortably sharing the joys, pains, not to mention responsibilities, inherent in running a bookstore. I could have used the managerial mom in Vikram Seth's *A Suitable Boy* in my quest. Since my own mother is not (thank God) the managerial type, I began my quest by searching among my own friends. Two of them showed interest—until they looked at TKE's bottom line (just shy of red), our profit margin (one-half of one percent, when it existed at all), and the night and weekend hours we were (still are) open.

Since the other readers I knew well enough to consider were gainfully employed in jobs they liked, jobs that paid two to ten times what TKE did, I began putting out feelers in the book industry. And came up with Kristine.

EMMA ONE AND EMMA TWO

Kristine Kaufman was the buyer for the trade division of the University of Utah bookstore. She had years of experience buying and managing, a compendious knowledge of books, and was well liked and respected by reps and booksellers alike. We seemed an ideal match. Tired of putting all her knowledge and skill to work for others, she wanted a position of ownership, while I wanted someone with whom to share ownership. Better, we both knew the business and liked what little we knew of one another. Had Jane Austen been watching from the margins of our lives, her eyes would have twinkled at the sight of the two of us, both experienced and knowledgeable, both proud of that knowledge and experience, both headstrong . . .

Kristine has been in the store a couple of months. It has been agreed beforehand that she will work for a period of some weeks in a management position so we can both be certain of our compatibility. She has gathered up the reins with a will, organizing stock, learning and refining our "systems" for accounts payable and receivable, for payroll and employee training ("What systems?" I ask her when she brings up the latter subject). Meanwhile, her husband Tom, a carpenter, does some much-needed repair work. There have been a few rumblings and grumblings among the ranks about her managerial style, but since there have always been periodic bleats of outrage at my own chaotic—some say nonexistent—approach to management, I am not overly concerned. I tell myself that in time we'll learn to pull in tandem on these matters, that if she's a little headstrong in one area, me in another, so much the better (there's that silly, silly optimism at play again).

Now a publisher's rep is in town, the first one we've seen together. Reps from the various publishing houses come three or four times a year, each settling in with a bag of tricks (book jackets, catalogues, sample pages from children's, and/or big glossy books for the new season) ready to spend three or four hours selling their wares. During that time, they talk up the titles, which their editors have presented to them at sales conferences. In comes John Zeck, the rep from a company then called Harper and Row. John's an old and dear friend of mine whom I've known since the year after we opened. He's teased my daughter, Mandy, downed innumerable scotches with Kit, bobbled Nick on his knee. He greets Kristine and me with equal enthusiasm.

Somehow it has never occurred to me before that he will know Kristine as well as he does me, be as friendly and familiar with her as he is with me. "Grow up," I tell myself, as I recognize my jealousy for what it is.

After chatting, we all sit down and open our catalogues. Kristine has pen in hand—she is obviously assuming the job (customarily my own) of marking the catalogues. John tells us about a new novel that ordinarily might have inspired a "maybe" from me, and Kristine says, "That sounds intriguing, let's take a couple." Not to be outdone, when John hypes an academic title esoteric enough to elicit a "pass" from me in normal times, I say airily, "Oh, we should have at *least* two of those." And Kristine, on the next novel, "He's an excellent up-and-coming author. Let's get five." "Why not ten?" I ask, trying for irony, but Kristine only nods and changes her figures. Along comes a glossy art book we have no business getting more than one of, despite the fact that its text was written by a famous critic (we're buying books for the mid-summer season, emphatically *not* the time to sell $70.00 books), and I say two. Kristine raises the number to three. And so on.

John told me later that it was like watching two card sharks double-bluffing at Five Card Stud, upping the ante with each hand (read *book*) as if in the end one of us might break some enormous bank. The trouble was, it was The King's English's bank we were breaking.

Kristine and I competed on just about every front from bookselling to book-buying to personnel issues to accounting procedures. Looking back, I think she imagined at the outset that I was so overstressed and overburdened at home that what I wanted was for someone to relieve me of my burden at work, to sweep in and take TKE off my hands. I, on the other hand, told myself self-righteously that I had wanted a partnership in which two people would apply equal weight and pull together, each having time in the harness, time at home. Okay, so maybe I *did* want to lead, but after all, it was my store—or so this still small voice kept telling me. (Can the reader see the problem inherent in my attitude here?)

In any event, it didn't take the two of us long to discover that neither wanted to be employed by the other and to realize that working out something more equitable would, in all likelihood, prove more than merely difficult. It did, however, take several months for TKE to recover from our book-buying-as-a-duel binge.

A LONG CAME *SALLY* ("THE VISION THING")

I was back in the shrink's office, singing my by-now-old refrain about Nick and his seizures, about the scarcity of time and my inability to run the store alone, when my shrink said, "I've hesitated to mention this, but I have a friend, an English teacher and a voracious reader, who wants to be involved in a bookstore."

Sally was a reader, none better, and a schmoozer. A people person who could talk books with the best, make people feel at home, valued. She had vision too, and I thought, *at last*. She came to the store on the same terms as Kristine, wishing to try it out, make sure, before we did anything legal, that we would mesh, get along.

And we got along famously. We paid the bills together, which is harder than it sounds since there are hundreds of publishers to deal with every month, each with its own system, thousands of invoices to pay, every one (or so it seems) with problems. We bought from reps with admirable restraint and a minimum of conflict, and we worked the floor in harmony. Oh, we had some disagreements. For one thing, she envisioned the store as a potential haven for women, preferred the literature of women, while I (with my customary proclivity for understatement) insisted that literature, like life, should be a place of equality; that men shouldn't get top billing, but that neither should women; that an artist is an artist, regardless of gender or color; that to imagine otherwise was to do a disservice to women as well as to men. I thought we agreed to disagree—until she said, one day, a few months into the endeavor, "It's not working. Our visions don't coincide. I've decided to open my own store."

And she did, less than two miles to the east, in what I considered to be my territory. She called the store A Woman's Place, and in so doing, attracted many of the city's feminists, some of our best customers whom she had gotten to know during her time at TKE. Then she moved her store even closer.

Can you hear the hurt in my words? The outrage? Oh, Sally didn't take all our business. Just enough to deliver a nearly mortal wound (with a minute profit margin, even slight wounds can be mortal). She was all the rage, as new businesses can be in a community. Roz, who ran her book clubs, did a magnificent job, attracted hundreds to the store. Sally wooed reps, had them to dinner, met publicists, started to attract authors, while TKE floundered— until a dear friend of mine whispered in my ear the name of a dear friend of hers, a woman I had known slightly for years, a member of the mystery club that began at TKE in 1978. That name was Barbara Hoagland.

AN EQUAL MUSIC

Barbara is calm where I am chaotic, amused when I am missile-bent on God knows what, organized, tidy, ruly (I know, I know, *ruly* is not a word, but it ought to be, a divine opposite to "unruly," which might mean calm, collected, *measurable*, a known quantity). Maybe I'm just deluding myself, but after all these years together I do think Barbara and I both benefit from the relationship, our partnership. She harnesses and directs my willy-nilly

Top: *The King's English then (circa 1980).*

Bottom: *The King's English now (circa 2003).*

Top: *Ann Berman and Betsy Burton, 1977.*

Bottom: *Grand opening announcement.*

Top, left: *Isabel Allende signing at The King's English.*

Top, right: *Novelist John Irving and Poet Dave Smith on the infamous confessional bench.*

Bottom: *Betsy Burton, John Irving, and Ann Berman, 1978.*

(All photos this page by Christina Papanikolas.)

Clockwise from top left: *The West's best, Novelists Sherman Alexie, Ivan Doig, and Mark Spragg with Kent Haruf (photo by Michelle Macfarlane).*

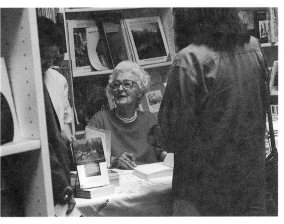

Counterclockwise from top right: Navigators of the Unknowable, Fiction writers Harriet Doerr, Jeannette Haien, Margaret Atwood (photo by Michelle Macfarlane), and Olive Ghiselin (pictured with husband, poet Brewster Ghiselin).

Top: *E. L. Doctorow (with Betsy Burton) signing copies of* City of God *(photo by Jon Caputo).*

Bottom:
Sir John Mortimer.

Top, from left to right: *The Black Sabbath Brigade: Barbara Hoagland, Kathy Ashton, Betsy Burton, Carolyn Ershler.*

Bottom, from left to right: *Mystery Mavens Elizabeth George and Sara Paretsky.*

Top: *On the road again: Walter Satterthwait (courtesy of Walter Satterthwait).*

Bottom, left: *Isabel Allende with Tony Hillerman at the Salt Lake City public library gala (photo by William Gordon).*

Bottom, right: *A younger Tony Hillerman at TKE.*

Clockwise from top left: *Lions of Poetry, Brewster Ghiselin, Mark Strand (photo by Rick Egan, courtesy of the* Salt Lake Tribune*), Larry Levis, and Joseph Brodsky, with Mark Strand in background (photo by Joe Marotta).*

Top, left: *Elizabeth Winthrop at one of her many signings at TKE.*

Top, right: *Guess how much we love you? Sam McBratney signs his best-selling book.*

Bottom: *Arnold Lobel signs books for Mandy Hansen (author's daughter, then age six), and her cousin Josh Bryan, among other fans.*

Top: *Running amok in the children's room with Jack Prelutsky (left) in full dragon regalia, and illustrator Peter Sis (right).*

Bottom: *Tomi de Paola with Betsy Burton and children's bookseller Marilyn Osborne-Butter.*

Top, left: *The "evil-eyed" Jon Scieszka with a few of his many fans.*

Top, right: *Storybook princess Jan Brett (photo by Debi Milligan).*

Bottom, left: *Brothers Tobias and Geoffrey Wolff on an ski break from their literary duties.*

Bottom, right: *Jan Brett's drawing.*

*Harry Potter day,
front and back doors
at TKE.*

Clockwise, from top left: *Ann Edwards Cannon (photo by Michelle Macfarlane). An equal music: Partners Barbara Hoagland and Betsy Burton. Jeannette Haien and Ann Edwards Cannon, two of my favorite people in all the world. A force of nature: Terry Tempest Williams (photo by Michelle Macfarlane).*

Top, left: *Avi signing at the TKE.*

Top, right: *Allen Say and Houghton Mifflin sales rep Michael Harrison.*

Bottom: *David Macaulay signs his name in concrete in TKE's parking lot. You can still see it today.*

Top: *Sue Grafton returns to TKE to sign books.*

Bottom: *Pat Bagley cartoon.*

energy, provides ballast to counteract the hot air of my loftier notions, while I contribute drive (or maybe "obsession" is a better word).

In 1987, Barbara brought TKE into the computer age, and with her husband Skip's help (he's a contractor), we doubled the size of TKE, made the store what it is today. It had already grown from three rooms to five, and I used the money Barbara paid me to buy the neighboring gas station. When Skip had finished connecting it to the existing bookstore, we had a huge new children's room; a lovely, light-struck space for nature, art, travel, and gardening books; and a badly needed office and receiving room.

Together, we reorganized the store, divided the buying, carved up other tasks according to our tastes, and began to lure back old customers, attract new ones. We really did pull together, and before long we returned to that annual 20 percent climb that had been customary B.S. (before Sally). Even while Sally was expanding her own store, opening a second, a third, we were solidifying, growing stronger. Thanks to Barbara, TKE was back on stable ground—and so was my life. If I felt a pang when Sally landed a major author, it was the jealousy of a business competitor and no longer felt personal. I came, however unwillingly, to regard her store as a part of the bookselling community of Salt Lake, just as was Sam Weller's, The Waking Owl (opened the same year as TKE and a literary store with whom we had much in common), The Golden Braid (New Age books), Deseret Book (Mormon books), the University Bookstore (affiliated with the University of Utah). I began to at least try to admit that she had a right to open a business wherever she pleased, compete in any way she pleased.

AND SHE KNEW SHE WAS RIGHT

Barbara and I purred along in tandem for the next few years. I've come to regard those as the glory years of TKE. Kathy Ashton came to work for us not long after Barbara bought in, and Kathy was a wonder on the floor, selling books. The three of us liked one another enormously, and still do. We worked well together and the business flourished. Before long, TKE was grossing well over eight hundred thousand dollars and with another 20 percent increase we would be at a million—not bad, we crowed, given the small size of our initial investments.

Never crow. One of life's lessons.

Rumors began to circulate—chains were on the move, expanding from city to city at an exponential pace. Even while these new chains billed themselves as "superstores," I, ever the foolish optimist, dismissed them as mere warehouses, discounted (no pun intended) their threat. We had, after all, prevailed over B. Dalton's and Waldenbooks, both on the book scene when we opened in 1977. Our customers didn't *like* chains; vast warehouses wouldn't appeal to them. They liked personality, intimacy. Anyway, these new big-box retailers were opening in *big* cities, in *eastern* cities. Why would they come to Salt Lake City, Utah?

Come they did. We have, along the Wasatch Front (the mountain range that lies to the east of Salt Lake), seven Barnes & Nobles, along with two Borders, two Media Plays (for a while there were more), and that's not to mention Amazon.com reaching out along the Internet. And when the first so-called superstore, a Barnes & Noble, came to town, we were by far the closest bookstore to theirs. Worse, when we went in to look them over, there was our mystery section (we were known across the city for the breadth and depth of the selection in our mystery room) almost title for title. It was as if someone had made a list of the authors whose books we stocked, missing not even those we imported from England. And maybe someone had, because Sam Weller said that he had actually seen people in his Western history section writing down titles (Sam is known throughout the West for the excellence of his regional history books, both new and used), and that his prize section had been replicated almost exactly at Barnes & Noble as well.

Our business, which had long since recovered from its tilt with Sally's, went flat again, and like a boat in a becalmed sea, was all but motionless. We held our breath, cut back our buying—and business went down ten percent. We cut back some more, out of fear and an inability to pay bills, but I started to protest. "We can't pull back any more. We're playing into their hands," I yowled at Barbara.

"We can't pay our bills, Betsy," Barbara said, inescapably logical, ignoring my outrage. "You do see the need to pay the publishers, don't you?"

"We have to fight back," I raged. "We can't just lie down and die."

That was when the three of us, Kathy, Barbara, and I, hit on the idea of *The Inkslinger*. We had always done a newsletter, but this was to be a magazine in the style of the *New York Times Book Review* (actually we got the idea from Elliott Bay Book Company in Seattle, to give credit where it's due). We poured time, effort, all our co-op dollars (the advertising allowance publishers give us, an allowance we had previously used for occasional newspaper ads and to help underwrite public radio) into *The Inkslinger*. Since Allende was making a return visit to the store, we headlined her in the first issue with both an interview and a review. We interviewed Mark Strand next, and then Harriet Doerr, Ivan Doig, Barry Lopez, Terry Tempest Williams. Kathy became editor in chief; all of us contributed.

And people responded. Business began to quicken—barely, but a start.

Then the second Barnes & Noble opened just a couple of miles north of us (the first was a mile to the south; Sally, remember, was a mile to the east). This was followed by a Borders downtown. Two Media Plays opened as well, and the book market in Salt Lake City was suddenly and completely saturated. There was no way *anyone* could survive—at least not without corporate or governmental subsidies. Costco and Price Savers clubs were selling books for less than we could buy them from the publishers; chains were discounting *all* books 10 percent, discounting *New York Times* bestsellers so that they retailed at the same wholesale price for which we *bought* books from publishers (they no longer do this; their stockholders must have finally grown tired of losing money). Full-page ads featuring chains were coming out in the paper, public radio was being underwritten by chains, public TV and radio's prices increased to the point that we couldn't afford to do as much underwriting to obtain the same exposure as we had before.

Rumor had it that each big-box retailer had to make a minimum of three million dollars a year just to break even, that no store could expect to do that for at least five years, but that they were being given the financial leeway necessary to discount because their investors believed that after five years of discounting they could drive us all out of business, corner the market. And somehow we had to hang on, hoping there would be a day of reckoning.

Hang on we did, but the going was rough, the seas of commerce roiling. Before long, we felt like the crew in *The Perfect Storm*, out alone on the ocean on a very small boat with minimal radar contact, nothing but knowledge of books and misplaced optimism to fuel us. Our debt increased, threatened to swamp us. We were on and off credit hold routinely (credit hold is that bleak situation in which publishers refuse to ship until the bills are paid), business was flat, then down, flat, then down, as one chain after another opened, launched an ad campaign, touted deep discounts. Patrick De Freitas of The Waking Owl told me privately that things were grim at his store, survival doubtful. I said I knew the feeling and borrowed money from my mom (thank God for Mom), from my best friend Chris, from Mom again to pay store bills. Then, one of our customers, a voracious reader whose buying habits we knew and respected, approached us with a proposal. She had just inherited some money and was interested in buying in. How much would it take?

Barbara and I conferred. One of the store's former employees already owned 10 percent (which I had given her years before, small recompense for her hard work and devotion), and if we each sold another 10, our prospective new partner, Carolyn, would have 20 percent, while we would each have 35. God knew we needed help, not just in terms of money, but also of time, employee hours. We had managed to stay alive thus far, despite the chains, not only because of our loyal customers and *The Inkslinger*, but also because we had increased floor staff and customer service. As a result of the latter, however, our payroll had ballooned. Carolyn knew books, would be good on the floor. Besides, she had been an accountant, could pay the bills quickly, easily.

Barbara and I did an inventory, determined the value of the books on the shelves minus the debt, calculated what 20 percent of that amount would be, and gave Carolyn the figures. Knowing that our bottom line was so shaky that it would be unreasonable to charge anything for the "blue sky" we would ordinarily have expected after nearly eighteen years in business, we made it clear to Carolyn just what a precarious position we were in, how uncertain our future, how threatened we were by the proliferation of chains. But she seemed determined, and we were glad.

Sadly, Carolyn and I were as mismatched as two people could possibly be. I'm direct, mouthy, impulsive, where she is indirect, a ditherer, a worrier. I'm a fighter, especially when I think I'm right (read *always*, Carolyn would say). I consider action, any action, better than stasis; Carolyn needs to study a problem from every side before she even begins to attempt a solution.

And Barbara (along with TKE) paid the price. Barbara, ever measured and thoughtful, understood Carolyn far better than I. But she understood me, too. As a result, she was well and truly caught in the middle as our mutual antipathy blossomed. I think that year almost killed her. I know it almost killed me, almost killed everyone else at the store, almost killed the store itself. I know Barbara was furious with both of us in the end. And I don't blame her a bit.

JUST IN TIME

Meanwhile, life with the "superstores" was getting bleaker by the day, and TKE was fairly foundering in debt. We had to return books to publishers in order to pay the bills, and the inventory was shrinking, slowly at first, then exponentially faster. We began to have some (depressing) discussions about the store's survival, and I began to have questions about my own survival. The store was no longer a refuge, but a battleground of bad feelings and seething resentment. Nick was on the cusp of adolescence, and his seizures, along with his fear and self-loathing (brought on by adolescence itself, of course, but also by his growing knowledge of his difference from others), were ratcheting up several notches. I lay awake nights, and when I wasn't worrying about Nick, I was stewing about the store's bills, wondering how we would pay them and whether another chain or dot-com was going to come along to finish us off. There was a rumor about a large space becoming available nearby, a space that would more than accommodate a big-box retailer.

"You're killing yourself," my husband said. My friends took me to lunch and listened to me pour out my despair over Carolyn, over the fate of the store, over my son's condition. And one of them, a friend since age six, did more than merely listen. Recently divorced and back in Salt Lake after seventeen years in New York, she was working part time in the store, had been since she'd returned. She offered to buy Carolyn out. "Are you sure?" I asked. "The store might go broke in the next year. Or the next month. How can you put money into it?"

"I'm sure," she said. "I want you to survive." I'm not certain whether Deon meant me or the store, but whatever she meant, she made Carolyn an offer based on the value of inventory at that time. Although obtained through the same formula we had used when Carolyn bought in, the price was far less than she had paid; the inventory had shrunk and debt had grown. But she accepted anyway, no doubt as miserable and heartsick at the way things had turned out as I was.

It took Barbara and me a long time to recapture our simpatico, took employees a long time to recover from the morale problems engendered by the great schism at TKE—a schism that couldn't have come at a worse time, a time when we were more vulnerable. But we survived it, thanks mostly to Barbara's forbearance and Deon's kindness. Our long-term survival is still in question, and so is the survival of every other independent bookstore in the country. But then, we have by now a long, honorable history of survival. We're tough, we independents.

A POCKET FULL OF WRY

I used to imagine, when I was suffocating on my own self-pity after my divorce thirty-odd years ago, that I was in an Agatha Christie novel—one character in a period-piece mystery from the thirties in which, yes, chaos reigned, but in the end peace and justice would prevail. As time passed, Christie failed to hold me, although I clung to the trick of literary disassociation. Now, at least in my more sane moments (in the darker ones, mysteries remain my salvation), I turn to Austen and Trollope, imagining myself in what is essentially a comedy of manners in which every human foible is at play, every base motive a part of the drama, but where to err is supremely human and often quite funny, if one can manage to achieve the proper perspective.

In that light, the whole debacle with Carolyn (not to mention the less-messy but still unfortunate problems with Kristine, Sally, Ann) is pretty funny in an awful way. Like Austen's Emma (I hope not Trollope's Louis Trevelyan), I set sail on some course or other, not even bothering to consult charts beforehand, sure I can steer by the stars, failing utterly to consider the fact that a cloud cover of bad feelings might conceal my path, or that ill winds might disrupt the journey.

The unfortunate truth is that I know where I want to go, where I think TKE should go, and head in that direction—God, partners, and the world at large be damned. I'm so obsessed by the initial vision of TKE, so single-minded in my determination that TKE survive, that I'd probably do anything to save it. (Well, maybe not embezzle—or murder. But that leaves me a lot of latitude.)

This is something I'm working to get past. Because Barbara is more important to me than the store. So is my family. And so are most of my employees—the ones who have been there a long time, given of themselves in terms of cheer, knowledge, expertise, and taken away such things as wisdom and humanity, learned from our customers and from the books themselves. I love most of them like I love my family, have abiding respect for them (although most of them probably wouldn't know it from my behavior). Still, the store, the books, the connection between what we all read and what we pass on to customers, is, in an important way, the highest good in my life, the thing that keeps me going—partnerships, friendships, and the rest of life notwithstanding. Bookselling in an independent bookstore is a little like a religion, a higher good complete with a set of tenets (customer relations; truth-telling about books; searching for truth and genius in books; passing it all along) that serves as dogma. It's not a bad religion, either, if one has to have one.

BOOK LIST

Psychology and Self-Help Books That I Haven't Read (on the theory that fiction can tell you more about life than facts) and **Fiction Dealing with Like Concerns** (not that any decent novel can be reduced to a single theme or concept)

1. *You Just Don't Understand*, Deborah Tannen's look at failure to communicate (or to understand one another) due to the lack of a common emotional language and/or perspective between the male and female of our species

    Pride and Prejudice, Jane Austen
    The Second Coming, Walker Percy
    Headhunter, Timothy Findley
    The Sparrow, Mary Doria Russell
    The Dogs of March, Ernst Hebert
    The Ambidextrist, Peter Rock

2. *Dance of Anger*, Harriet Lerner's book on the way anger controls and destroys lives—a theme with which I am all too familiar

    Great Expectations, Charles Dickens
    Cousin Bette, Emile Zola
    The Moor's Last Sigh, Salman Rushdie
    Fury, Salman Rushdie
    The Art of Breaking Glass, Matthew Hall
    Mallory's Oracle, Carol O'Connell

3. *Emotional Intelligence*, David Goleman's thesis on the importance of emotional IQ—or the lack thereof

    Northanger Abbey, Jane Austen
    Madame Bovary, Gustav Flaubert
    Ruin Creek, David Payne
    The Treatment, Daniel Meneker
    High Fidelity, Nicholas Hornby
    The Traveling Horn-Player, Barbara Trapido

4. *Controlling People,* Patricia Evans (there are many such, and this pot doesn't dare call any kettles black)

    Emma, Jane Austen

    And He Knew He Was Right, Anthony Trollope

    Crossing to Safety, Wallace Stegner

    The Good Son, Craig Nova

    The Summer at Gaglow, Esther Freud

    Poisonwood Bible, Barbara Kingsolver (societies that control or that foster controlling people are also a common theme, one present in the remainder of the books on this list)

    Penguin Island, Anatole France

    1984, George Orwell

    Handmaid's Tale, Margaret Atwood

    Not Wanted on the Voyage, Timothy Findley

    The Waterworks, E. L. Doctorow

    Ella Minnow Pea, Mark Dunn

    Name of the Rose, Umberto Eco

5. *Betrayed: Straight Talk about Betrayal,* Donna A. Bellafiore (a subject about which we all wish we knew less)

    Vanity Fair, William Makepeace Thackery

    The Perfect Spy, John Le Carré (or any other Le Carré)

    Lies and Silences, Brian Moore

    Headlong, Michael Frayn

    Not Wanted on the Voyage, Timothy Findley

    Sacrifice of Isaac, Neil Gordon

    The Twenty-Seventh City, Jonathan Franzen

6. *The Eight Stages of Life*, Erik Erickson's take on making choices over time that lead away from despair and toward fulfillment—my apologies to psychologists for the simplistic description
   A Dance to the Music of Time, Anthony Powell
   Light, Eva Figes
   The House of the Spirits, Isabel Allende
   On the Black Hills, Bruce Chatwin
   The Book of Ebenezer LePage, G. B. Edwards
   Love in the Time of Cholera, Gabriel Garcia Marquez
   Matters of Chance, Jeannette Haien
   Jayber Crow, Wendell Berry

7. *Necessary Losses*, Judith Viorst's look at recognizing what you need to give up, and doing so
   Human Croquet, Kate Atkinson
   Ruin Creek, David Payne
   Everything in the World, A. L. Kennedy
   Corrections, Jonathan Franzen
   Moon Tiger, Penelope Lively
   Private Altars, Katherine Mosby
   The Soloist, Mark Salzman

8. *Passages*, Gail Sheehey's seminal work on the life passages that are common to all of us—although any of the below-listed novelists would be horrified to have their books stuffed in such a simplistic niche
   Dancing at the Rascal Fair, Ivan Doig
   The Cunning Man, Robertson Davies
   Shipping News, E. Annie Proulx
   The Transit of Venus, Shirley Hazzard
   Being Dead, Jim Crace

9. *The Power of Empathy*, Arthur Ciaramicoli and Katherine Ketcham's book showing the importance of the ability to see the connections between one another rather than the difference
>   *Huckleberry Finn*, Mark Twain
>   *To Kill a Mockingbird*, Harper Lee
>   *A Fine Balance*, Rohinton Mistry
>   *The Constant Gardner*, John Le Carré

10. *Emotional Blackmail*, Susan Forward's look at emotional manipulation and how to counter it
>   *Tom Jones*, Henry Fielding
>   *The Good Son*, Craig Nova
>   *A Suitable Boy*, Vikrim Seth
>   *The God of Small Things*, Arundati Roy
>   *The Peppered Moth*, Margaret Drabble

11. *In a Different Voice*, Carol Gilligan's seminal work on the very different way women look at life (vive la difference)
>   *A Far Cry from Kensington*, Muriel Spark
>   *Splitting*, Fay Weldon
>   *Excellent Women*, Barara Pym
>   *The Lambs of God*, Marele Day

12. *Resiliency*, Tessa Albert Warshaw and Dee Barlow's look at what allows some people—like Faulkner's Dilsey—to endure
>   *Sound and the Fury*, William Faulkner
>   *Family Matters*, Rohinton Mistry
>   *The Book of Ebenezer LePage*, G. B. Edwards
>   *Smilla's Sense of Snow*, Peter Hoeg

13. *Pulling Your Own Strings*, Wayne Dyer's suggestions for taking control of one's own life
    Miss McKenzie, Anthony Trollope
    Consider This, Senora, Harriet Doerr
    Patchwork Planet, Ann Tyler
    Plainsong, Kent Haruff

14. *Feeling Good*, David Burns' remedy for depression through taking action in ways that make you feel better
    A Far Cry from Kensington, Muriel Spark
    Ladder of Years, Ann Tyler
    Moghul Buffet, Cheryl Benard
    Law of Gravity, Stephen Horn

And my own personal cure when all else fails is anything by Muriel Spark—or anything else that makes you laugh, from funny mysteries (Evanovich and Hiaassen rarely fail) to funny fiction to Dave Barry.

— Chapter Six —

A BLIZZARD OF ONE

[*"To be a poet is a condition rather than a profession."*   ]
— ROBERT GRAVES

Words that both nail us to the reality of our lives and allow us to hover outside and above those lives: the stuff of poetry.

Poets provide continuity between one generation and the next, one culture and another, between life, imagination, and memory. Poets matter. Poetry matters. It's scary stuff, though. Hard to get oneself around a good poem. One can pluck at its words; pull strands of meaning out of this phrase, that verse; but poetry resides in emotion as well as idea, and to paraphrase a poem destroys it. It's impossible to bottle ambiguity, to quantify magic.

The story of poetry at The King's English is by and large the story of Mark Strand—because he read here many times, and also because he brought nearly every famous poet alive in the past half-century to Salt Lake City at one time or another. But if poems, good poems, are terrifying (and they are, at least to me), poets are equally daunting—far harder to render than are the novelists, mystery mavens, essayists, and nature writers who've read at TKE. In terms of their presence at TKE (and at the University of Utah and Westminster College here in Salt Lake, where many of them have taught, read, or lectured), however, I'll do my best.

Mark Strand came to the University of Utah in 1981 as Distinguished Professor, and when he first arrived, I was invited to a luncheon in his honor at Fresco, the Italian restaurant that adjoins the bookstore. It was a good thing I was sitting down when he walked in, because he was (and remains) so classically handsome, so quintessentially the "great poet," that his students used to say Mark had "a face carved from the rock of poetry." Tall (over 6'2") and fit, he's square of jaw, high of cheekbone, has eyes that glimmer a hazel intensity, and a voice ideal for a poet—low, nuanced, with diction that polishes each word until it glows with surface meaning, hidden portent.

Mark is intelligent to a frightening degree. And he's deadly honest, sometimes past the point of politeness. His friend Jeannette Haien says it's because he can't wear a mask, can't breathe through the false nose. Which is just as well, since he's the only man of surpassing male beauty I've met in my lifetime whose talent measures up to his face. He *looks* the part of the great poet, he *sounds* the great poet, and he *is* the great poet. Even better, he has a sense of humor about *being* the great poet. (If you don't believe me, read his poem "The Great Poet Returns.")

Now why would I be intimidated by someone like that? Speechless during lunch, I spent my time chewing, swallowing, looking at my plate, hoping that he wouldn't mention the subject about which I felt so woefully ignorant. He didn't, at least to me, and mellowed by a decent Chianti, encouraged by the Northern Italian food, he wandered from the restaurant into TKE and headed for our poetry section, where he proclaimed himself pleasantly surprised by the depth and breadth of the stock. Gail Davern, our own resident poet, was on duty there, ready to talk poetry.

English by birth, bookseller by trade, and poet by vocation, Gail was a rule unto herself. A single mother of three, possessed of an idiosyncratic character, she was an uneasy student at the university (uneasy because she was more interested in poetry than in the criticism of it), was sharp of tongue, opinionated of taste, a wonder with the customers she liked and a terror with those she did not. It was Gail who had, almost single-handedly, made our poetry section the fine thing it was. We had always stocked the canon before she came to TKE, poets familiar to English majors whose primary interest was fiction rather than poetry—Donne, Dante, and Dickinson, Wordsworth and Whitman, Blake, the Brownings. We had Yeats, Auden, and Eliot, of course, and Wallace Stevens, Borges and Bishop, Lowell and Larkin, Millay and Moore. We also had some of the newer poets: Dave Smith and Robert Mezey, both of whom taught at the university, Leslie Norris who was at BYU, Jorie Graham and Louise Gluck, Richard Wilbur and Charles Wright. But we had never heard of Rita Dove (this was in her prelaureate days) or Stephen Dunn or Stephen Dobyns. Of Amy Clampitt or Adam Zagajewski or the great Anna Akhmatova. Or, for that matter, of Mark Strand.

Thanks to Gail, we had *all* of Mark's books when he walked in that day. I know that he was glad to see Wallace Stevens and Elizabeth Bishop in residence on our shelves. Reassured at the presence of Heaney, Hope, and Hollander, Fulton and Forché, Kumin and Kinnell. He mentioned some holes in the section, though, poets he liked that Gail didn't know, and she promised to stock their books.

Mark became a regular at TKE. And before long, he and Gail were hatching plans. Poetry plans. Gail had already conceived a poetry series, had gone to Scott Cairns, who taught poetry at Westminster College, and the two had launched a season of readings and lectures, all of which were open to both students and the public. Mark invited the University of Utah to participate, and the project became a three-way undertaking, in fact, if not in name. Westminster provided the space and some funding; the university more funding and (thanks to Mark) connections with countless poets; TKE publicity, the prize, some additional funding, and books. The happy triumvirate pitched in money from their respective institutions for honoraria (poets typically aren't well compensated for readings until they win some significant award), sent out invitations, and before long had the next year's roster of poets: Richard Howard, C. L. Rawlins, Donald Justice, Richard Kenny, Donald Hall, Janet Sylvester, Louise Gluck, and finally, Edward Hirsch.

Ed Hirsch turned out to be an interesting contrast to Mark. He was as tall, but in every other way Mark's opposite—outgoing, genial, possessed of a kindly intelligence but no discernable edge. I found myself talking to him, talking easily. And he talked back. So, after a time, did Mark, who takes people's measures slowly and is seldom quick to warm. Mark and I began a friendship of sorts. I was at long last reading poets other than those I had encountered in Modern Poetry 304 and I could carry on a conversation on at least a reasonable level—not elevated mind you, but still.

The series took on a life of its own, and everyone wanted to take part. The readings and lectures were packed, and people milled around afterwards, drinking wine and eating cheese, lining up to buy the books we were selling and again to get them signed. The poets often came to the store to sign as well, and we actually became used to seeing and talking to these wonderful literary luminaries on a regular basis. We were on such a roll it made us all heady; we had lined up such notables as Charles Wright, Carolyn Forché, Seamus Heaney, Paul Muldoon, Larry Levis, Heather McHugh, Stephen Dunn, Mary Jo Salter, Adam Zagajewski.

Creative, ever-impetuous, Gail was not content to rest on the collective laurels of the series. "Let's start a poetry contest," she said. "A national one. We can solicit poems from all over the country, advertise in *Field* and in *Poets and Writers*, offer a small prize (TKE contributed $250 the first year), and give the winner a forum at Westminster . . ." The ads were placed, and poems began to trickle in. Gail weeded through the submissions and came up with a stack of the best entries for May Swenson (the first judge); she chose one, and a winner was announced. Ed Hirsch became the next judge, Mark the one after that, and in that small world of aspiring poets, word spread. Submissions poured in.

Meanwhile, the poetry series was proceeding apace. David St. John, Gerald Stern, Kenneth Brewer, Cynthia McDonald, and W. S. Merwin came, and each read and signed books for sellout crowds; all were the subject of articles on the book pages of the local papers, were interviewed on the radio. Gail, Mark, and Scott had managed to bring a focus to poetry here in Salt Lake City that was new and exciting; they had created something that seemed, quite simply, ideal.

But life never is ideal (or at least not for long). In the third year, Scott Cairns left Westminster, and Gail's husband died not long after. She withdrew from pretty much everything for a time, and with Mark increasingly busy at the university and a new director at the helm at Westminster, the three organizations went their separate ways. The series continued, of course, under the capable hands of Katharine (Katie) Coles, and grew exponentially as she obtained additional funding in spectacular fashion. The tale of how this occurred is an interesting one, especially since the series has become the best-endowed poetry series in the country. The story goes thusly:

In 1995, when Katie was still new at Westminster, Steve Barr, the academic vice president, called her one day and requested that she record some poetry written by a nonagenarian alumnus of the college, Anne Newman Sutton Weeks. Katie replied that certainly she would if Barr would ask the ninety-nine-year-old alumnus for a donation for the now sorely under-funded poetry series. He simply laughed, saying that poetry was not something people gave money for. "They build buildings with their millions," he told her. "Or fountains. Structures that last for generations, with plaques attached bearing their names, for posterity. Or they endow chairs. Highly paid positions for prestigious scholars. With their names attached."

"But Anne Newman Sutton Weeks could have *her* name on the poetry series," Katie countered. "She's a poet herself, or you wouldn't be asking me to read her poetry. She'd probably love the idea."

When Barr still refused, so did Katie, whom no one has ever accused of cowardice.

A week later, Barr asked Katie once again and, once again, Katie requested that he approach Anne Newman Sutton Weeks for a poetry-specific donation. "She's a poet," Katie said. "A natural sponsor. She *likes* poetry."

Finally, he acquiesced, reiterating that it would do no good, but a few weeks later, a check arrived at the college. Made out to the Anne Newman Sutton Weeks Poetry Series, it was written in the amount of $250,000.

Several months passed, and one Saturday morning, Katie was at home in her pajamas, writing poetry, when the phone rang. It was a development officer at the college. Anne Newman Sutton Weeks' daughter was in town, and she wanted to meet Katie.

"When?" Katie asked.

"In fifteen minutes."

"It's a good thing my hair is short," Katie says, laughing at the memory. "I scrambled into something or other and managed to arrive on time, but barely. During the conversation that followed, I learned that both of Anne Newman Sutton Weeks' husbands—she had been widowed first by Sutton, then by Weeks—were geologists. I asked whether either of them might have known my grandfather, also a geologist, who practiced during the same era. When I named him, Marta [the daughter] said that she had recently seen my grandfather's name, that she'd been going through her father's papers and had come across a letter signed by a Walter Link—that evidently my grandfather and her father were good friends."

The two women spent a lovely hour talking about their respective families, and three weeks later, the Anne Newman Sutton Weeks Poetry series received yet another check—this one for $200,000. The poetry series, which had limped along for the first three years with a few thousand from the university, $1,500 from yours truly, and a few thousand from Westminster, was now endowed to the tune of $450,000. By poetry's standards—and almost anyone else's—a fortune.

THE CONTINUOUS LIFE

Anne Newman Sutton Weeks wasn't the only nonagenarian poet in Salt Lake at that time. Long before Mark Strand came to our university, we had on the faculty a poet well known by other poets and academicians across the country. His name was Brewster Ghiselin, and he not only wrote brilliant verse (which according to James Dickey was "entirely original in its fusion of landscape—particularly seascape and desertscape—with the human body . . . unexpected, evocative . . . Ghiselin is the truest of poets"), but also hobnobbed with the likes of D. H. Lawrence, Dylan Thomas, and William Carlos Williams. Like Mark, he was physically very much "The Great Poet" with his shock of snow-white hair, his stately bearing, his labyrinthine turns of phrase which, when unraveled, contained nuggets of sly humor, startling wisdom. Brewster, by bringing famous literati to our city and university for several decades, began the tradition of literary luminosity which Mark so nobly carried on by drawing a host of the nation's and the world's great poets (including five Nobelists) here to read and speak.

Mark's initial agenda in Utah was to bring new blood to the faculty, recommending to the committee academicians like Charles Berger and Rusty Brown from Yale, poets Robert Cassario and Jacqueline Osherow—all of whom came to teach in Salt Lake City during the years of his tenure. Richard Howard's off-and-on connection to the department (he was visiting poet at least twice during Mark's tenure and read there several times as well) was likewise due mostly to Mark, and his first hire among poets was Larry Levis.

Mark describes Larry Levis as a self-created outsider, a rebel of the James Dean school. Larry tore around our staid city on a motorcycle, *Easy Rider* personified, and rumors about his wild behavior were common. Studded out in riveted black jacket and boots, he befriended the "fringe students" and generally lived a '70s California lifestyle in Happy Valley. Perhaps surprising in our conservative community, he was well liked. He was a careful, attentive teacher, for one thing, with an affinity for youth (not to mention rebellion). From a bookseller's perspective he was a reader in the true sense of the word, a bookaholic, in other words (not all writers are), and a wonderful reader of his own work. He was also a fine poet whom Jill Maney, one of the three young poets on our staff at the time (the other two being Julianne Bassinger and Jennifer Ashton—we dubbed them the three musketeers of the poetry room), described as absolutely mesmerizing to listen to. Julianne said, "He had the classic romantic 'John Clare' view of himself and of poets in general, a view that included living on the extremities, of dying young." He died of heart failure when he was barely fifty years old, and his last book, *Widening Spell of Leaves*, has garnered such wide readership that it has become a sort of underground classic as has *Elegy*, a posthumous collection published a year later.

Jacqueline Osherow followed Larry to our fair university. A small woman with a wild mop of dark hair, a scintillating manner, and an enormous zest for life, Jackie is also a wonderful poet, one who combines storytelling ability, skilled craftsmanship, and Judaic twists of phrase with intriguing, often difficult topics and soaring language. Mark says she has a gift for *terza rima*, for keeping a poem going, for rhyme and meter. In writing about *With a Moon in Transit*, he calls her work irresistible and says, "I am always deeply absorbed when I read Osherow's work and I never fail to be exhilarated by its scope, its narrative ease, its good-natured and probing intelligence."

Jackie is, aside from a teacher and writer, the mother of three girls. Originally from New York, she has recently learned to drive a car and rushes from here to there and back again, flying into the store to buy books for a birthday party, or for a reading by a visiting poet, on her way to or from the university. She's also a self-described expert at the fine art of kvelling (kvetching's opposite, more or less). In fact, when Jennifer Ashton (our third marvelous on-staff poet) spoke here after getting her Ph.D., Jackie, Mark, and Barry Weller, another formidably knowledgeable professor from the U, all sat in the second row busily kvelling about their prize student.

Jackie has read at the store twice, once from *Looking for Angels in New York*, once from *With a Moon in Transit*, and she signed here when *Dead Men's Praise* was new. Her readings are nothing short of miraculous. She has a cantor's voice and can invoke tears and laughter almost simultaneously, even while she has the listener entwined, entranced by the sheer narrative pull of her poems.

THE DELIRIUM WALTZ

During Mark's twelve-year tenure at the University of Utah, he read at TKE, at the University of Utah, at Westminster College, downtown at Symphony Hall and the Gallivan Center—read any number of times around the city over the years. Maybe it was because I hadn't heard him read from this volume before, but when his *Selected Poems* was republished by Knopf and he appeared in the restaurant adjacent to the store, it was an achingly poignant afternoon. He read, among other things, "Elegy for My Father," read it in that low throbbing voice that seemed to bounce sorrow off the Italian tiles, and I heard a stifled sob behind me, another down the row to my left.

Yet there was no self-conscious drama in the reading. The words seemed quite simply to come from the heart—or perhaps more accurately, the gut. One need only read his poetry, listen to it, to see that, for all the grace and elegance of his style, the lurking humor, he hones and shapes until he reaches some absolute core of purity in terms of language, its meaning, so that his words speak directly to the heart. A rare talent, the ability to speak to the heart, to be *unafraid* to speak to the heart (perhaps because one is constitutionally unable to do anything else, unable to wear a mask).

There were many other memorable Strand readings as well. "The Continuous Life" remains a favorite poem of mine, so simply and absolutely true. He read that and much of the volume *The Continuous Life* in a TKE event held at the Framery next door to the store. Along with his darkly funny ballad (number 3 from "Grotesques") about the couple coupling (sorry) on the train tracks, he read "The End," and was subsequently asked to recite it at the funeral of a friend. He did so, movingly, and that poem has now become part of the funereal lexicon of non-Mormon Salt Lake, recited at more than a few of the funerals I've attended since.

Mark read from and signed that brilliant and ground-breaking long poem, *Dark Harbor*, too, and before that he and Red Grooms had a signing for *Rembrandt Takes a Walk*. When his book on Edward Hopper came out, he also did a slide show for us that none of us will ever forget. It was not one of my finer moments.

A mechanically minded employee sets up the projector and the mike for Mark, checks the lights, and departs. The wind picks up, the crowd flows in, and as our techno-employee disappears into the gathering gloom, the power goes off.

Everyone waits patiently in stifling darkness while the temperature and humidity climb and thunder crashes around us—until finally Mark begins to read (or more exactly, to recite, since there's no way to see the words on the page). And there's an eerie aptness to those words, spoken in the dying light, evoking Hopper's images.

But then the power comes back on, and we all (Mark included) assume it is at last show time. The projector disagrees, and Mark asks *me* to see to the infernal machine. I do, in my fashion. Assuming the air of invincibility required of the person in charge, I take out the tray and fiddle with it, trying to instill confidence in the rustling crowd with an air of assurance that is entirely false. When, thanks to my tinkering, some slides slide out, I hurriedly replace them and, after further futile fiddling, I reinsert the tray, monkey with the lens here, a switch there—

Light suddenly bathes the screen, images begin to waltz across it, and Mark begins his narration. The staccato dance of Hopper's figures is difficult to follow, however, as one lonely creation after another lurches across the screen's white surface, some hopping sideways in decidedly un-Hopper-like fashion, some upended, disappearing vertically down the screen as if falling into a Dantesque vision of Purgatory. While Mark talks, images careen, collide, bob up, bobble down, are turned upside-down, backwards—it is Hopper as he's never been seen before. Or since, I'm sure.

Mark (thank God) thinks the whole thing is funny and finally allows in his driest tone that on the whole he preferred it when the power was out.

Mark Strand was instrumental in bringing so many poets to Salt Lake City (and to TKE) that the university's reputation as a mecca for writers became almost legend. Poets from all over the country came to study here, and readings became commonplace. Despite their increasing frequency, however, they continued to be well and enthusiastically attended. Julianne, who left Salt Lake and now lives in Virginia, says, "In the East it's common to go to a literary reading where attendance is next to zero—I went to see Richard Howard, and there were only five or six students listening to him. But in Utah he *packed* the lecture hall where he spoke. And the audience was so enthusiastic. When Octavio Paz came, people were snaking through the entire bookstore waiting in line for his autograph—think of that many people waiting for the autograph of a *poet*. During those years at the store, the focus on poetry was amazing. We pulled in the literary community, not just from the university, but from all over the city. *Everyone* was interested."

And how could they not be? We had at the store during those years Jorie Graham, Robert Pinsky, Carolyn Forché, Louise Gluck, Mary Jo Salter, Ed Hirsch, Alice Fulton, Richard Howard, John Hollander, Stephen Dunn, Stephen Dobyns, Larry Levis, Jane Hirshfield, Donald Hall, W. S. Merwin, Mary Oliver, Roberts Haas, Alison Hawthorne Deming, Sharon Bryan, James Galvin (pre-*The Meadow*), Bei Dao, Charles Simic, along with such notable "local" poets as Larry Levis, Jackie Osherow, Katie Coles, Mark Strand, Leslie Norris, David Lee, Lisa Bickmore, and Agha Shahid Ali (who had been hired and was intending to stay until, seriously ill after one semester, he left for New York, where he later passed away). We sold books after readings by Richard Wilbur, Amy Clampitt, Anthony Hecht, Linda Gregerson, Stanley Kunitz, Czeslaw Milosz, Adam Zagajewski, Heather McHugh, Derek Walcott, John Ashbery, Seamus Heaney, Charles Wright, Galway Kinnell . . .

Even after Mark left, the poets kept on coming. Charles Wright (again), Adrienne Rich, Charles Simic (again), Derek Walcott (again), Stanley Plumley, Ai, C. D. Wright, Maxine Kumin, Tomaz Salamun, Craig Arnold, Yusef Komunyakaa, and Sandra Cisneros, along with such stunning local talent as Judy Jordan (the year she won the National Book Circle Critic's Award), Mark Doty (he's since moved on), Natasha Saje, and Joel Long.

It was as if Mark Strand left us a legacy of possibilities, one that persists to this day—a "Delirium Waltz" of poets, in fact, to borrow a phrase from him, including, along with many of the nation's laureates, all but one (Wislawa Szymborska) of the world's living poet-Nobelists:

Octavio Paz, Joseph Brodsky, Czeslaw Milosz, Seamus Heaney, Derek Walcott . . . And, incredibly, two of them came to read at almost the exact point in time they received the Nobel Prize for Literature.

Octavio Paz came to the university in late autumn, within weeks of receiving the Nobel Prize, and on the heels (or perhaps wings, more accurately) of the publication of his *Collected Poems*. He read some of his poetry in Spanish while Mark, who had translated those same poems, read alongside him, in English. Imagine them there, two of the world's great poets, their voices floating out over the auditorium, reading in counterpoint, transfixing the audience . . . Julianne, who knew Paz's work in Spanish *and* in translation, said, "It was like hearing Keats, like having the canon, the poems I'd studied and loved, materialize right there before my eyes. I'll never forget that night."

Neither will any of us. A small, compact man, Paz was beautifully turned out in a tailored suit of deepest navy. His manner was grave, often humorous, sometimes passionate. The applause was extravagant, adulatory. As it finally subsided, Mark made the announcement that there would be a signing at TKE. It was November, close to the holidays, and Paz was a newly decorated Nobel laureate. Within half an hour he was ensconced at the store, bent over newly minted copies of his *Collected Poems*, pen in hand, autographing while lines wound around the store and out into the street, people wanting two, three, five copies to give as gifts. (If there's anything better, from a bookseller's point of view, than having a Nobelist sign books in the store, it's having a Nobelist sign books in the store a month before the holidays.)

We also sold books when Seamus Heaney and Derek Walcott read at the university, and their appearances were equally memorable. Heaney's voice had a rich, peaty flavor (ahh, the power of Irish suggestion), and he was often quite funny in a cynical way, while Walcott was by comparison more distanced, measured in delivery, despite his lilting Caribbean diction. It is Joseph Brodsky, however, who sticks in all our minds as the most memorable of all the Nobel laureates.

In the book world (as in any other), new celebrity is more noteworthy than old—when you're hot, you're hot, to put it crudely. And in November of 1987, no one was hotter in literary circles than Joseph Brodsky. He had been awarded the Nobel Prize for Literature just *days* before his arrival in Salt Lake, his *To Urania* had just been published, and the media frenzy that surrounded his coming was more customary for a Hollywood star than for a poet. Like Paz, he read at the university and, also like Paz, he ended the evening standing side by side with Mark.

It is the reading of a lifetime, Brodsky speaking in Russian, the cadenced rhythm of his voice strong, the audience swaying to its music, while Mark renders the meaning in words that are a translation, yes, but from poetry *into* poetry, Brodsky's own translation, delivered in Mark's liquid voice, a voice as astonishing as Brodsky's own. Side by side they stand, Brodsky the bemused poet, glasses askew, eyes closed, tie crooked, jacket rumpled, probably longing for a cigarette but grinning hugely, while Mark, all tall elegance, grins just as hugely, caught up in the sheer poetry of the moment. Then they are finished, the stunned silence has broken into wave after wave of applause, people have yelled themselves hoarse standing in the aisles, shouting hosannas, until Mark finally puts up a hand to stop the commotion, announces that Joseph Brodsky will be signing books at The King's English in ten minutes.

Twenty minutes pass and it's a mob scene at TKE. People are lined up around the store, out the door and down the sidewalk, are milling, murmuring, drinking wine, watching, as the great Nobelist signs books. Customers stack up more and more copies of Brodsky's *To Urania, Less Than One, A Part of Speech*, each one of them wishing to speak to him, ask a question, praise his work, connect with him. The poet bears it all with patience and courtesy, nodding, smiling, exchanging pleasantries. But as time wears on and the line doesn't diminish, I see him glance at Mark. Neither of them has eaten and it's late.

We begin to prowl the line, limiting copies to be autographed to one per customer, promising that Brodsky will sign for stock before he leaves town, that we'll have autographed copies available the next day. The line gradually shrinks; there are only a few people left— two, one . . .

The last woman in line seems slightly disheveled, but there's not really anything in her appearance to alert us as she leans toward Brodsky, book in hand. He reaches out, then draws back his own hand, a question plain on his face. "This is not my book," he says in careful English.

She doesn't reply, just stares silently at him. He stares back until, as though given a cue from someone behind him, she begins to speak, in English, but with an accent that sounds very much like his own. She asks him in a kind of growl how he can abide the barbarity that goes on in his country, has gone on in his country, how he can live under a government responsible for so much death, work under a state that has killed her aunts, her uncles, her grandmothers on both sides, her cousins and their parents.

At first I believe in her. Even after she invokes "The Motherland" in melodramatic fashion, I speculate that she must be some sort of displaced nobility, an Anastasia whose aristocratic family has been slain. And indeed, everyone still there is puzzling over her identity, just as I am. Only Brodsky does not appear surprised when her accent begins to soften, slur and to sound, suddenly, more drugged than foreign. Which is when it finally occurs to me, to the room at large, that what's in question here is her own "altered state," rather than "crimes of the state," that it is the booze we can suddenly smell wafting from the table (Brodsky looks as if *he* could use a drink, but I know he hasn't had one) rather than any state atrocities that are loosening her tongue, giving it that Slavic passion.

Barbara and I look at each other and walk toward the table, assuming our bouncer stance (we may not look threatening but we are). Each of us takes an arm (Why didn't I tumble earlier to the fact that's she's blind drunk? I wonder silently, she *reeks* of booze), and we tell our "Russian" princess as nicely as we know how that the store is closing, that it's time to go home (I keep thinking of that dumb song, "I'm tired and I want to go home/I'm tired and I want to go to bed/I had a little drink . . .").

Brodsky maintains a poker face, kind to the end, as our visitor winds down. His courtesy seems to allow her to hang on to the illusion that she is some lost princess, he some forgiving czar, until finally we urge and coddle her out the door and someone who knows her (*now* they tell us) offers to give her a ride home. Brodsky is clearly famished, exhausted, and after signing the extra stock, he and Mark vanish into the night, arm in arm. We imagine the two of them, heads bent over dinner, over the wine of the one, the whiskey of the other, voices murmuring into the night.

Our poetry musketeer Jill Meaney, who says Joseph Brodsky was not only an extraordinary poet but an extraordinary teacher as well, has one more poignant memory of his reading, one I had forgotten. In teaching his poetry workshop, Brodsky was known for insisting that his students memorize a minimum of 1,500 lines of poetry. And when, during that long ago evening in Salt Lake, a student familiar with Brodsky's requirement of such prodigious feats of memory, asked whether he himself was capable of a like performance, Brodsky's answer was to shut his eyes and declaim with both fluency and a grand passion Auden's entire poem, "In Memory of W. B. Yeats."

REASONS FOR MOVING

Back at the university, Mark Strand was, in addition to his teaching, writing on every topic under the sun (or at least those of interest to him). His work over the next decade would span not only genres, as he moved between poetry and translation, fiction and children's books, but other disciplines as well. He produced books, articles, lectures, and essays on such disparate subjects as literature, art, travel, wine, food, and "style." He wrote two wondrous volumes of poetry, *The Continuous Life* and *Dark Harbor*; books on two artists he admired, *William Bailey* and *Edward Hopper*, along with the fabulous *Art of the Real*; three whimsical children's books, *Rembrandt Takes a Walk* (with artist Red Grooms), *The Planet of Lost Things*, and *The Night Book*; and the quirky wonderful story collection *Mr. and Mrs. Baby*. He also translated poetry (he works in Spanish, Portuguese, and Italian), edited the *Golden Ecco Anthology: 100 Great Poems of the English Language*, and penned the text for a photography book on the country's national parks, *These Rare Lands*. Mark was awarded a prestigious MacArthur fellowship (a "genius grant") and was then named our nation's poet laureate, in which capacity he served for two years. Not bad work for a decade. In 1999, five years after leaving Utah, he was awarded the Pulitzer for *A Blizzard of One*.

Mark Strand is a sort of one-man unified theory, an Einstein of poetry, concerned with the relation of the particular to the universal, the real to the metaphoric, the word to the in-describable. And it is his extraordinary awareness of the world, his unique gift for language, for transcription (transubstantiation, more accurately), his full and complex understanding of his own experience, which Mark brings to bear on each poem. Ultimately, the process is magical rather than rational. He told Wally Shawn in an interview in *The Paris Review*, "I think that what happens in my poems is that language takes over and I follow it. It just sounds right. And I trust the implication of what I'm saying even though I'm not *sure* what I'm saying . . . It's this 'beyondness,' that depth that you reach in a poem that keeps you returning to it."

It is no doubt accurate to say that Mark's intense interiority tends to isolate him. Although he has a host of friends around the globe, I sometimes see him as one of those solitary light-struck floating islands he began engraving three or four years ago (art was Mark's first love—and his first degree from Yale), an island that is well and truly stranded, however light-struck, in a grey ocean—as he himself is stranded by his own poetic sensibility.

A SUITE OF APPEARANCE*S*

Mark is a formidable teacher as well as a great poet. Jill says this of him, "I think I learned more about how to write poetry from Mark than from anyone. Mark was a prosody nut—very interested in the formal workings of meter in English, and a stickler about doing serious apprentice work in forms. You wouldn't necessarily think that from reading his poetry. I remember looking at a draft of one of his poems one time and exclaiming, 'Hey, this is in iambic pentameter!' He was really embarrassed, took it away from me, and rather sheepishly said, 'That's the way it comes out. I'll rough it up later.'"

The last reading Mark gave in Salt Lake (actually, the first reading he returned to give, once he'd left) was, fittingly, at Westminster College, where the poetry series began. He read from *A Blizzard of One*, and while he stood there, reading from "The Great Poet Returns" and "Delirium Waltz," there was delirium in the very atmosphere as the throngs of family, friends, colleagues from his poem waltzed through the air above our heads, through the cadences of his voice, his memory, remaining in *our* memories for weeks, years, thereafter. It seemed such a grand leave-taking. Mark will, like his good friends Joseph Brodsky and Octavio Paz, win the Nobel Prize one day, if there is any justice in the world of poetry.

THE LATE HOUR

Mark is in Illinois now, where he's teaching at the School for Social Thought at the University of Chicago. He's published five books in the past two years alone, and has five more slated, including a novel. He never stops writing poetry, of course, and he was in a movie not long ago at which time he said of his new career (in *The New Yorker*), tongue firmly in cheek, and ever the poet, "I think I'd make a good president or ambassador. If they dressed me right. I'd like to do such roles. The Dignified Older Gentleman. I'm so much the opposite, I feel. A little clumsy, a little disheveled. I wear good jackets, but that's the extent of it."

The gift Mark has given TKE is one of memory—an astonishing collective memory of the time when poetry, our store, the academic community, the community at large were intertwined, all-of-a-piece, connected by language and the love of it which he inspired in us. The voices of the poets he brought to us echo off the walls, the shelves; the poets themselves still inhabit those shelves, speaking to us whenever we pick up a book of Mark Strand's or of Joseph Brodsky's, of Louise Gluck's or Jorie Graham's. The voices amplify each time we suggest a new poet to a customer, whenever a young poet comes to the store to read for the first time, or when one poet quotes or refers to another. Mark says, "Poetry is always building these connections. It's not showing off. It's the verbalization of the internal life of man. And each poet forges a link in the chain, so that it can go on."

And on. And on.

Book List
35 Favorite Poetry Books from TKE's First 25 Years

1. *Bells in Winter*, Czeslaw Milosz, 1978
2. *An Explanation of America*, Robert Pinsky, 1979
3. *Venetian Vespers*, Anthony Hecht, 1979
4. *Windrose*, Brewster Ghiselin, 1980
5. *Changing Light at Sandover*, James Merrill, 1982
6. *The Complete Poems 1927-1979*, Elizabeth Bishop, 1983
7. *Collected Poems*, Derek Wolcott, 1986
8. *Dream Work*, Mary Oliver, 1986
9. *Collected Poems*, Octavio Paz, 1987
10. *The End of Beauty*, Jorie Graham, 1987
11. *Collected Poems*, Phillip Larkin, 1988
12. *To Urania*, Joseph Brodsky, 1988
13. *Book of Gods and Devils*, Charles Simic, 1990
14. *Complete Poems*, Anna Akhmatova (trans. Judith Hemschemeyer), 1990
15. *The World and Ten Thousand Things: Poems 1980-1990*, Charles Wright, 1990
16. *Outside History: Selected Poems, 1980-1990*, Eavan Boland, 1990
17. *Atlas of the Difficult World*, Adrienne Rich, 1991
18. *Flow Chart*, John Ashbery, 1991
19. *Wild Iris*, Louise Gluck, 1992
20. *Man with Night Sweats*, Thom Gunn, 1992
21. *Life Work*, Donald Hall, 1993
22. *View with a Grain of Sand*, Wislawa Szymborska, 1993
23. *New and Selected Poems*, Donald Justice, 1995
24. *Sun Under Wood*, Robert Hass, 1996
25. *Collected Poems*, Odysseus Elytis, 1997
26. *Selected Poems 1960-1990*, Maxine Kumin, 1997
27. *Collected Poems*, Amy Clampitt, 1997
28. *On Love*, Edward Hirsch, 1998

29. *Opened Ground: Selected Poems 1966-96*, Seamus Heaney, 1998
30. *The Bird Catcher*, Marie Ponsot, 1998
31. *A Blizzard of One*, Mark Strand, 1998
32. *Elegy for Departure and Other Poems*, Zbigniew Herbert, 1999
33. *Daily Mirror*, David Lehman, 2000
34. *Collected Poems*, Joseph Brodsky, 2000
35. *Without End: New and Selected Poems*, Adam Zagajewski, 2002

Chapter Seven

KEEPER*S* AT THE GATE

[
"We live in fascinating times . . .
fascinating sharing the same root as fascism."
]

— A. L. KENNEDY, *Everything in the World*

❖

[
"A bookstore is a house of ideas."
]

— JOYCE MESKIK, THE TATTERED COVER, FROM *Bookselling This Week*, NOV. 13, 2000

❖

[
"Nobody is more dangerous than he who imagines himself
pure in heart, for his purity by definition is unassailable."
]

— JAMES BALDWIN

If, as John Mortimer asserts, the telling of stories, in whatever form, is an attempt to act out, impose order on, explain the truth of our existence, then the interruption of that narrative flow, or any attempt to control its content, may surely be seen as an attempt to distort that truth. To strike a serious (even self-important) note, one thing we booksellers do is to keep the bridge over the moat open, stories flowing in and out of the keep. We, along with universities, colleges, libraries, and the media, are not only participants in the free flow of ideas but also protectors of the right, which the First Amendment guarantees to all of us, to disseminate those ideas.

REGARDS TO THE CZAR

There are good things about living in Happy Valley. The mountains are nothing short of miraculous, and the wide streets make getting around fairly easy (Brigham Young had vision in more ways than one, it would seem). Also, the Mormons take care of their own, physically as well as spiritually. They have a sophisticated welfare system, complete with communal farms, food banks, canneries and bakeries, and the bishop of every ward has a responsibility to make sure each member of his flock (the male pronoun is entirely appropriate here) is fed, clothed, and housed. Even nonpracticing Mormons are eligible for this kind of aid, so long as they've been baptized, and overflow from church coffers goes to help local churches of different denominations and third-world countries.

More than a few Mormons have bad traits along with their good ones, however, at least from a "gentile" perspective. One of the worst is the propensity to believe that what is good for them must, a priori, be good for everyone else. It's not an uncommon failing: Many Catholics believe their truth is God's truth, and so do most Baptists and Hare Krishna. Liberals and feminists are just as guilty—they (myself included) may leave God out of the equation, but they're often every bit as single-minded, as convinced that life is a closed system and that there is "one way" to live it. Anyone fixated on a belief, be it religious, philosophic, ethical, or scientific, is in love with the idea of spinning all-encompassing constructs out of the straw of a single tenet of Truth—of "quack, quacking quacking" (preaching, in other words) to bolster that construct, just the way I am.

The same attempt to codify, simplify, *unify*, has recurred on a regular basis since time immemorial. If E. O. Wilson's recent book *Consilience* bears overarching resemblance to the tenets of medieval scholasticism, where's the surprise? One purports to be a scientific system, at least presumably based on experience, experiment, the other a theological system, embracing science, yes, but religious at base, a system which works from the general rather than the particular. Still, both systems work at fitting knowledge *into* some construct. Neither one attempts to eliminate knowledge that doesn't fit, as Hitler, the Inquisition, Salem's Puritans, and extreme fundamentalist Muslims have tried to do, as the so-called "Moral Majority" tries to do, as fundamentalists everywhere try to do, as some ultraconservative Mormons try to do.

THE PORN CZAR

There must be an inherent conviction shared by a large proportion of the human race concerning the abnormality of anyone who sees the world through a different prism, because throughout history, there has been wave after wave of attempts to monitor, expurgate, banish, blast out of existence one belief or another, this practice or that one, all in the name of whatever religion, state, or community organization happens to be (or is trying to be) in control.

And although it's true that odd things do happen in the name of God, religion, and/or "morality" here in Utah with alarming frequency, so do they all across this fair land. My brother-in-law, who left Salt Lake because he couldn't bear the dominance of the LDS culture, has found Colorado Springs, where he teaches college, to be a less tolerant and far more difficult place to live. A dear friend who left us for Chicago says Wheaton, Illinois, makes Salt Lake look like a liberal bastion, while Idaho and Montana are home to more than one survivalist and neo-Nazi group. And we've all heard stories about the South, the intolerance and racial bigotry that are still part of the fabric of some towns and cities there.

One has only to look at the list of banned books at the end of this chapter, view the websites for Banned Books and Censorship and Banned Books Online (an American Library Association website) to see how widespread censorship is in the book world, how much of the country is or has been embroiled in censorship issues. In a local brouhaha, a student association invited Michael Moore to speak at Utah Valley State College, arousing a firestorm of protest in the community (one parent actually offered $25,000 to the school to cancel the appearance and subsequently sued); the administration "countered" Moore's influence by bringing in Sean Hannity. An almost identical situation existed in Florida, where Utah's Terry Tempest Williams was invited to speak at the freshman convocation, then *un*invited after the university president read *The Open Space of Democracy*, the opinions of which he, a Bush supporter, disapproved. Some of the students no doubt disapproved of the sentiments as well, but not of their own right to hear them; Young Republicans joined with Young Democrats to offer Terry Tempest Williams an opportunity to speak, just as the student body in Utah stuck to their guns and insisted that Michael Moore be allowed to appear. Students, it would seem—in Utah and Florida alike—are more tolerant than their elders, more curious about other points of view besides their own. A good thing, too, in a country that is cross-hatched with pockets of those who believe they know what is right, not just for themselves but for everyone else as well—a dangerous sentiment that makes glaringly obvious the wisdom of our forefathers when they ratified the Bill of Rights.

Getting back to my own neck of the woods, yet another attempt at censorship (well, more than one, honestly) occurred right here in Happy Valley a while back: the proud appointment, by Utah state government, of our very own porn czar. (Perhaps "czarina" would be a better term, especially since she's a self-proclaimed virgin to boot, a fact that she declared with apparent pride in *The Salt Lake Tribune* in an interview on Sunday, February 11, 2001.) Her name was Paula Houston.

Ms. Houston, apparently not realizing logic would dictate that, far from being a qualification for the job, her virginal state should have been a *dis*qualification, insisted that her innocence in no way impaired her ability to know porn when she saw it. Nor did her Mormonism skew her judgment about what porn was and was not.

Her job? According to *The Salt Lake Tribune*, "To ferret out and prosecute those who violate obscenity laws and to help communities write their own." Said Houston, "[Porn] is foul sleaze that makes its exploiters wealthy, its victims impoverished. It will become an obsession. It will destroy your home life. It will destroy your marriage."

Ye gads. All of that. One could only hope that Ms. Houston herself didn't fall victim to its addictive attractions after viewing a satiety (no pun intended) of the material—as her job description surely required her to do. When asked by *The Salt Lake Tribune* if she saw this as a danger of her occupation, whether pornography's "foul" effects might pollute her in some damaging way, she said that she spent her time away from work on "wholesome activities," like going to Disney movies.

The stuff of satire? Yes. But terrifying, too. Because I don't even want to guess what someone who has never engaged in a meaningful and loving sexual act, someone who takes her clues about life and how to live it from Disney movies, might construe to be pornographic.

This issue of censorship is, of course, far more complicated than it might at first appear, especially when coupled with pornography—a subject with which it is frequently paired in books and movies, since porn is something many dislike (with good reason). Indeed, many liberals for whom censorship used to be anathema are split on the topic, feminists so at war with pornography on the grounds that it demeans women (which it often does), is brutal (which it often is), that they invoke censorship rather than fighting it. An intriguing book addressing this question is, oddly enough, a mystery—one written by Marianne Wesson, a law professor at the University of Colorado. *Chilling Effect* takes on the worst type of porn, that involving children, throws in the concept of snuff films, and places both issues squarely in the context of the First Amendment. Hard questions are posed about such issues as the drawing of lines between erotic and pornographic, where those lines should be drawn, who should draw them and under what legal standards, and what effects the resultant limits will have on society and on the Constitution.

For a more thorough examination of the issue, Chris Finan, head of American Booksellers Foundation for Freedom of Expression, is hard at work on a book about censorship, *The Fight for Free Speech*. One chapter of this book looks at the feminist battle against porn and the legal ramifications of that battle. As a whole, Finan's book addresses almost every aspect of censorship—I can't wait to get my hands on the entire manuscript when it's finished. It's due out in 2007 from Beacon Press.

OF VICE AND SIN

History has a way of repeating itself. In 1977, when we were the new kids on the block, a feminist bookstore had also opened in town. It was located in the Avenues, a residential mix of Mormon and Gentile, rich and poor, which was (and remains) a perfect place for a business that serves alternative lifestyles. The Open Book had a large selection of books on the politics of feminism, along with some feminist fiction, some books on lesbian issues, and a small children's section which included books from small presses dealing with one-parent families,

families with same-sex parents, the need for tolerance of people's differences. Most titles were not available in other stores in town, many of the books were better in terms of child development, feminism, gay issues, and sexuality than the "standards" on the subject, and the store was an enormous resource to the community.

Until it was closed down. Apparently, someone (probably more than one someone) considered it a den of inequity and sent the vice squad in to prove that this was the case. What the vice squad found, if memory serves, was *The Joy of Lesbian Sex*. Not shocking in this day and age, but in 1978, enough "evidence" to charge the store's owner and to prosecute her. The owner could not afford to pay the lawyers enough for an adequate defense; bookstores (as you have heard in these pages ad tedium) do not afford much in the way of a living—certainly not enough to hire lawyers, finance a major court case. The store closed its doors, and the case was subsequently dropped.

The vice squad actually came to TKE not long after this—or at least we think they did. Are almost positive they did . . .

A pair of large crew-cut heads atop thick necks descend into grey suits that bulge here from a gun, there from a well-developed muscle clump. The two men to whom the heads belong are hard to miss among the kids and moms, hippie students and busy professionals on power breaks from power lunches. The darling duo, as Ann dubs them, pluck first this book and then that one off the shelf, leafing through each as if it were some coded Sanskrit document which no doubt would prove interesting if only they could decipher its contents. They gravitate slowly but surely to the photography section, drawn there by the pictures, no doubt, or perhaps (Ann whispers to me) merely the comforting absence of those confounding words that comprise the sentences that comprise the pages of the books in the rest of the store.

This is years before Mapplethorpe and the NEA brouhaha, and in any event, we have long since discovered that in a small personal bookshop such as ours anything graphic is far too embarrassing to buy from the middle-aged women at the desk and either sits on the shelf (often well-thumbed in place, but never purchased) or is stolen. As a result, the most shocking thing our desperately seeking twosome discovers at TKE is an attenuated nude in a volume of Edward Weston's photographs, another, more fulsome female torso photographed by

Margaret Bourke-White, a misshapen rear-end as seen in the viewfinder of Diane Arbus. Tame stuff, even by the standards of bygone years.

The pair spends a long ten minutes scrutinizing the work of Arbus and Weston, hunting for prurient details. They finally give up and move on to the feminist section where, lips moving busily (just kidding), they pore over paragraphs, whole pages, until sweat darkens their armpits, glistens on their foreheads. Judy Chicago's *Dinner Party* is not in stock that day, thank God, so all they manage to unearth is a rant about patriarchy and abuse. Although this stiffens their spines into angry columns, it doesn't give them much ammunition for prosecution, since even in this benighted state in those unenlightened times, to be feminist is not, strictly speaking, illegal.

This was TKE's first brush with censorship but not its last by any means. Censorship is an issue every bookseller deals with almost daily in one way or another. School teachers and librarians, counselors and parole officers question the age-appropriateness of this title or that one constantly, since one person's standards of "age appropriate" material can vary so radically from another's in terms of both language and subject matter. Parents question books, too. A story one parent feels to be an ideal vehicle for dealing with a difficult matter—race relations, for example, or divorce, or something as dark as child abuse or the holocaust—will horrify another. And although we have never suggested that it is our job to be the arbiter of such decisions, we do feel, strongly, that it is not only our job but also our duty to make choice available, provide knowledge of the various choices, so that responsible parents and teachers can make informed decisions. What we at TKE hate and fear, what all booksellers hate and fear, is the attempt to limit choice, or, God forbid, eliminate it.

Although there are moral "majorities" everywhere that attempt to assert control over what the rest of us read, think, to whom we pray, whether we pray, they are not usually the majority at all. Indeed, *within* any given group, including Mormons, it is most often the rabid but vocal few, not the many, who are guilty of attempts at suppression, *re*pression. Most of us, Mormon and non-Mormon alike, relish the freedom to make choices, even if there are occasional mistakes as a result. We don't like czars or czarinas making them for us. And we don't believe that just because a group of people has proclaimed itself the "moral majority," its members really do live on some higher moral plain where the views are unimpeded by the steamy air of temptation, of (gasp) sex. Nor do we think that just because this parent or that one deems a book inappropriate for his or her child, it is necessarily inappropriate for another's. There are, if the news stories are to be believed, scores, perhaps hundreds of angry parents in this country convinced that the Harry Potter books are evil, that they traffic with the devil (although millions disagree). There are also parents who believe *Huckleberry Finn* is racist rather than a book that decries racism, that *To Kill a Mockingbird* is as well. Surely, the fact that some parents hold such opinions does not mean that all parents must abide by them. If it did, where would free will be? How are our children ever going to be arbiters of their (and our) destinies if they grow up believing that what they know will hurt them—that to keep people in ignorance somehow protects them?

TATTERED FREEDOM

The most interesting, high-profile example of all this as it pertains to the book business involves, surprisingly enough, not pornography but the drug wars. Denver's Tattered Cover, one of the country's largest and best bookstores, independent or otherwise, is run by one of our country's most courageous booksellers, Joyce Meskis. During the bust of a methamphetamine lab in Denver several years ago, police found an empty Tattered Cover mailing envelope and copies of two books: *The Construction and Operation of Clandestine Drug Laboratories* and *Advanced Techniques of Psychedelic and Amphetamine Manufacture*. Never mind that heretofore the most frequent purchasers of these books had been law enforcement officers, the police were convinced that if the sales of these *particular* copies could be tied to the suspects, little other evidence would be necessary to convict said suspects of the manufacture of illegal substances. Instead of pursuing other evidentiary avenues, police fastened on the acquisition of Tattered Cover's sales records as the single best method of proving guilt.

When law enforcement asked for bookstore receipts, Joyce refused to produce them, saying that the buying records of her customers were protected by the First Amendment. The police then obtained a search warrant, which normally compels the recipient to immediately turn over what is sought. Joyce and her attorney were able to convince the district attorney to let the store challenge the warrant in court, and the police withdrew without obtaining the information they were seeking. When Joyce appealed the warrant to the state district court, Judge J. Stephen Phillips upheld it (although narrowing the warrant's scope from all records involving the suspects to only those involving the receipts in question) and ordered Tattered Cover to comply; Joyce again declined to do so, appealing the district court's ruling to the state supreme court.

Before this case was appealed, precedent for Meskis' resistance was established quite publicly when Kenneth Starr attempted to procure Monica Lewinsky's book-buying records. Although Ms. Lewinsky ultimately agreed to turn over her records in return for immunity, thereby halting the court case, still a federal district court judge, Morna Holloway Johnson, declared that prosecutors must weigh the chilling effect of their demand for bookstore records and that, "Therefore the First Amendment is indeed implicated by the subpoenas."

Said Meskis in reference to her own actions, "If we turn over this information, our customers will start wondering if we would ever do the same to them. It will undermine their confidence that we will do everything we can to protect the privacy of their purchases and make them afraid to buy controversial titles. That would be a tragedy for us, for them—and for free speech." Meskis and her attorney argued (quite logically in my view, the view of most booksellers I know) that since reading a book is not a crime, the reading of a book on the manufacture of drugs is not proof positive that the reader is a manufacturer of drugs. Chris Finan, president of the American Booksellers Association Foundation for Free Expression, said, "If the First Amendment means anything it means we have the right to purchase books without fear that government will inquire into our reading habits." Added Meskis, on the argument of the chilling effect of the subpoena, "I strongly believe that they would immediately discontinue making purchases from my store if they learned that the Tattered Cover did not treat their purchases as private and constitutionally protected." (Press release from American Booksellers Foundation for Free Expression [ABFFE], April 13, 2000.)

"Chilling" is a good word to describe what occurs when government attempts to control, or even to examine, what people are reading—which books they buy, which papers they subscribe to, which magazines they read. The image of the vice squad making their lumpy way into our small bookstore twenty years ago, perusing the photography books with an eye toward evidence gathering, may have had its funny side, but it remains a chilling memory. On a local level, it is one that took on a new reality with the coronation of our "czarina." Because for a small (as in TKE) or large (as in Tattered Cover) business, the intimidation inherent in the mere *act* of examination, investigation, could be enough to keep certain titles off shelves, limit choice, freedom. The question that must always be asked when government attempts to infringe on people's rights for prosecutorial, or indeed any reasons, is, which is worse: the violence thereby done to the Constitution or the crime in question? Is, for example, an explicitly photographed love affair on videotape or a meth lab in full swing *really* important enough to warrant the abrogation of a citizen's right to privacy; the abrogation of a bookseller's right to shelve a book without fear of search, seizure, prosecution; the abrogation of a customer's right to buy without fear?

In the end, the Colorado Supreme Court agreed with Joyce Meskis (and with the federal judge). In April of 2002, it refused to force the Tattered Cover Bookstore to turn over its sales records. In a 6-0 opinion, the court said the ruling doesn't preclude law enforcement from ever getting the records, but that before such records are ordered, turned over, police must "demonstrate a compelling governmental need" for the records. Also, bookstores will be entitled to a hearing to challenge any request for records.

In other words (this according to Dani Eyer, Utah director, ACLU), "the court raised the standards for the government before they can intrude into bookseller records and customer information. The general rule set forth is that except in the rare instance where police can show that the information is absolutely essential and cannot be obtained in any other way, police cannot have access to book-buying information. The bar was set higher for obtaining a search warrant."

Said the court: "We recognize that both the United States and Colorado constitutions protect an individual's fundamental right to purchase books anonymously, free from governmental interference. Bookstores are places where a citizen can explore ideas, receive information, and discover the myriad perspectives on every topic imaginable. When a person buys a book at a bookstore, he engages in activity protected by the First Amendment because he is exercising his right to read and receive ideas and information."

In an ironic footnote, some months later, Joyce Meskis, with the permission of the defendant in the Denver case, released to the media the *actual* title purchased by that defendant at her store. The title in question? *Guide to Remembering Japanese Characters*, a book on Japanese calligraphy.

IN THE BUFF

It isn't just books that suffer from the "iron rod" of moral control here in Happy Valley. Movies, perhaps because they are easier for vice squads to critique, are far easier to censor. We used to have a local chain of film rental stores along the Wasatch Front called Movie Buffs. And Movie Buffs had, along with a goodly variety of family films (including shelf after shelf of Disney movies), a "blue room." Clearly marked "Adults Only" and separated from the rest of the store by a curtain, this was a space in which men would spend a few minutes (if women did, I never saw them), then exit with two or three tapes, checking to make sure no one they knew was watching before they took said tapes to the counter. They would often grab a couple of Disney movies on the way by, no doubt as camouflage—or maybe to watch with their kids in the early hours, before midnight and (horrors) adult sex . . .

I liked to go to Movie Buffs—not for the porn (what I've seen of the stuff strikes me as, among other things, deadly boring), but because the clerks, pimpled young men and women with intense eyes and passionate opinions, loved to recommend movies. They *watched* movies, thought about them intelligently—unlike the employees at the chains in town that I've been forced to frequent for reasons that are about to become clear.

A Movie Buffs store was prosecuted by local government on pornography charges. The store was located in Provo, home of Brigham Young University, and a town that is well over 90 percent LDS. In Salt Lake City, which is less than 50 percent LDS, government is endlessly influenced by the Mormon Church. In Provo that influence is exponentially stronger, and much of the local population had never approved of Movie Buffs. Needless to say, the "community standards" that are the measure of what constitutes legality and illegality in terms of pornography are stricter there than in most communities, and police were certain that Movie Buffs' inventory was in violation of those standards. Not only did they slap pornography charges on Movie Buffs, but they seized—not subpoenaed, but seized—Movie Buffs' customer records. The records detailed, of course, the titles of movies rented, along with the names of the customers who had rented these films. Police seized the records because they (along with city government, one assumes) were convinced that most offenders were not local citizens, but nasty Salt Lakers—business commuters, students, and other nonlocal riffraff.

Movie Buffs' attorneys, roundly seconded by the ACLU, protested the seizure of what were arguably confidential records—records which turned out to show that, for the most part, the renters of these nefarious videos were not depraved Salt Lakers at all but homegrown Provoans. These locals emphatically did not want their movie-watching habits made public, not to the courts, the media, or anyone else.

Movie Buffs won its case. Not only was the seizure of records declared illegal, but it also turned out that the worst of the movies rented from the "blue room" were no more "pornographic" than the so-called soft porn being shown in rooms at the local Marriott. Movie Buffs is gone, however. It couldn't afford the lawsuit, declared bankruptcy midway through the trial. Now, with only a couple of small exceptions, the only shops left in Salt Lake City that sell and rent movies are chains. And in Provo there are no exceptions. End of story.

TO EVERY RULE . . .

A colleague of mine, Linda Brummett, runs the trade department of the Brigham Young University Bookstore in Provo. She's a woman of great moral conviction, but her convictions are not entirely in line with those of the stereotypic Provoan. She believes in free choice, at least on the subject of books, and when customers complain about this book or that one, claiming indecency or apostasy, she says this to them: "Please remember that our religion has a long and painful history of persecution in this country [Mormons were driven from Palmyra, New York, then from Nauvoo, Illinois, and even here in Utah were hounded and persecuted by the federal government]. Also keep in mind that when censorship is legally embraced by a government, religion is always the first thing to be censored."

Wise words from a wise woman. People like Linda Brummett and Joyce Meskis make me proud to be a bookseller. And people—Mormon people—like Linda Brummert and Ann Edwards Cannon (whom you'll meet in three minutes if you don't take a coffee break) remind me of the serial dangers of generalizing. Doing so makes me guilty of the very thing

I decry, since within any group of people, the full spectrum of human virtue and peccability are bound to be represented—your choice how each is defined. All of which is a long-winded way of warning the reader (and myself) to avoid that most heinous of sins literary: stereotyping.

*S*ATANIC HEAR*S*E*S*

The censorship that occurred around Salman Rushdie's *Satanic Verses* is famous, no, infamous, around the world. It is the censorship of terror, pure and simple. Rushdie is arguably one of the best novelists writing today, but ironically *Satanic Verses* was by no means his best book and probably wouldn't have sold well were it not for the ayatollah. But when said imam pronounced the death sentence on Rushdie, that act ensured sales above any the author had known before. The good ayatollah's intent was, of course, the opposite. When the Muslim moral mafia first issued its *fatwa*, it included as targets not just Rushdie but also those who published and sold his book: His Japanese translator was stabbed to death, and attempts were made on the lives of his Italian translator and his Norwegian publisher. In America, Barnes & Noble and Borders took the books from their shelves—the censorship of terror responded to by the politics of the corporation.

The King's English, along with independent booksellers across the country, put *Satanic Verses* in its front windows. We didn't call each other, plan a response. We did it independently, instinctively. Not out of disrespect for Islam but out of respect for the First Amendment. Seldom in our memories had our prized freedom been so viciously threatened (at least until John Ashcroft came to power). So we stacked Rushdie's book deep, faced it out in every window pane—except, at TKE, not in the center pane. There we placed a toy gun with a black X taped across it. Shame, we were telling customers, passersby. Shame on anyone who tries to tell others what they can and cannot read, threatens to shoot people (authors, translators, booksellers, and publishers alike) who make certain books available.

Since independent stores all across the country did the same thing, didn't just carry the book but displayed it prominently, collectively we made the same statement: we will not be intimidated. The fact that some chains did the opposite, not wanting to give offense or take a risk, raises the specter of "censorship of the bottom line"—something that, in my opinion, corporations are guilty of on a daily basis anyway. But today national chains don't (thank

God) completely control the industry. The question is, what would happen if they did? If we're gone, we independent booksellers, who will protect your right of access to books that might be unpopular or even dangerous to carry? The chains? Not if the example of *Satanic Verses* is any measure.

It is the unfettered (at least before 9/11) and unruly independent booksellers who care passionately enough about freedom of expression, about continuity, and about diversity to take risks, to ignore the bottom line (not to mention their own safety), and to do what's right. If that sounds self-righteous, that just proves what I've said all along: that people's propensity to think they know best, to limit others' access to information according to their own beliefs, is the single most compelling argument for protecting the First Amendment. When some "system," be it political or religious, denies the right to information, history tells us that evil is not far behind, sniffing at the heels of any deviants from "right thinking," unleashing the dogs of tyranny on all of us in the process.

LATE-BREAKING NEWS FROM THE HOME FRONT

Here's the latest from the Utah State Legislature:

A law stating that teachers cannot actually *talk* about sex in their sex education classes. The occasional exception, should it be deemed necessary, must be conducted *one-on-one* (a little weird, and I'm not even going to speculate about the reasons behind something that could conceivably result in the single truly frightening thing that every parent and educator wishes to avoid).

A law making gun safety mandatory in churches and schools (guns are okay for kids, sex taboo?), followed by a law guaranteeing every citizen's right to carry concealed weapons in churches, schools, and all other public buildings.

And . . . a young woman, a student at the University of Utah who was majoring in drama, is suing the university and the state because she was "forced" to swear (as in curse) while reciting her lines in a play. Basing her suit on the fact that she was made to say naughty words against her conscience, she seems oblivious to the fact that her decision *not* to say the lines as they were written infringes on the rights of the playwright, audience, cast—as do expurgated inventories in Provo video shops.

LATE-BREAKING NEWS FROM CITY HALL

Salt Lake Mayor Rocky Anderson decided a citywide book club might be in order in this place where the community is so evenly divided along religious lines, reasoning that such a club might help to provide a bridge across what many would label a chasm of misunderstanding. He named the club Salt Lake City Reads Together. Mindful of the pitfalls involved in choosing books the entire community might embrace, he appointed a committee of people who live their lives around books and—perhaps even more importantly—live and work in this community and have a professional obligation to respect the rights of all its members. Along with a representative from his office, one from the Humanities Council, and a student representative, the committee consisted almost entirely of librarians, educators, and booksellers. The books this committee chose were in three different categories

Fiction: *The Curious Incident of the Dog in the Night-Time* by Mark Haddon

Nonfiction: *The Blood Runs Like a River through My Dreams* by Nasdijj

Children's: *Mrs. Frisby and the Rats of NIMH* by Robert C. O'Brien

Each choice was viewed by the committee as a book that might help readers see other points of view besides their own, vicariously experience realities besides their own—something we all hoped would foster that ability citywide. A website was created, a press conference called, enthusiasm and interest were generated, and all seemed well . . . until a city council member received an E-mail reporting the number of times the "f-word" and the "s-word" appeared in Mark Haddon's novel. The council member, Eric Jergensen, expressed his outrage in the press, on radio and TV, challenging the choice of such a book in strong terms, questioning the makeup of the committee. The city staff and committee members responded and another firestorm was begun. Angry letters were exchanged in the press on a daily basis; I wrote an editorial, so did a number of other people, and the liberals I knew went around shaking their heads in weary resignation. "This state . . ." they'd say, finding no need to finish the sentence.

Then, wonder of wonders, Councilman Jergensen read the book in question. Liked the books. Was brave enough to say so in public.

At least part of the magic of books lies in their ability to reach across chasms, heal rifts. I haven't spoken with a single person who read *The Curious Incident of the Dog in the Night-Time* who didn't like it. Wasn't moved by it. Didn't learn from it. And if the sales in my bookstore are any measure, Salt Lake City Reads Together really *is* turning into a citywide book club.

WHAT ARE YOU REALLY AFRAID OF?

More than one school district in the Salt Lake Valley has published an "approved" reading list and allows teachers to assign books only from this list to their classes; a teacher we know who was attempting to impart to her class the concept of utopias couldn't find a single book on the list that addressed the subject. Various districts use an "accelerated reading" list, supposedly to hone the students' reading abilities; teachers complain that such lists narrow the scope of children's interests and limit their choices in harmful ways.

Not long ago, the superintendent of the Nebo School District (in Utah County) banned as pornographic the Newbury Honor Book *The Watsons go to Birmingham, 1963*, written by Christopher Paul Curtis. The sin described in the book's lustful pages? While reaching for the radio dial in a car en route to Birmingham, Alabama, the hand of one of the characters grazes (gasp) his wife's breast.

Now don't blame the Mormons as you're reading this. Remember the dangers of stereotyping. Because Ann Edwards Cannon, an accomplished children's author and a practicing Mormon who writes weekly columns for the *Deseret News*, the "Mormon" newspaper, got so incensed over the book banning in question that she lost her sense of humor (well, not really) and wrote a rant for the paper. Her editor, Chris Hicks, said, "Come on, Ann. You've lost perspective here. You're not a reporter, and you don't have all the facts, I'm willing to bet. I'm turning this over to our education specialist down in Utah County [read *Provo*]."

The Hollywood ending to this anecdote, given that this is a chapter on censorship, would be that the *story* of the book banning was then buried somewhere in the back pages of the paper by the obvious bad guys—"those bigoted Mormons down in Provo." But guess what? The Mormons weren't the bad guys in any real sense. While the *two*, I repeat, two parents (that damn vocal minority) whose initial complaints caused the books to be pulled from the school curriculum may have been Mormon, they were just two among many who did *not* object to the books. And far from burying the story, the papers gave it full front-page coverage. Here is what Ann Edwards Cannon said on the subject of that particular example of censorship:

> We once lived in a small WASPY village called Tuxedo Park just off Route 17 in New York State. It was surrounded by a gray stone wall, and the only way you could get inside is if you lived there or knew someone who did. We lived there because my husband worked in New York City for a year.

The "Park," as it is called by the residents, is forty-five miles northwest of the city. Not a great commute, but not a bad one either—especially by East Coast standards. We landed in the Park because we have friends who live there, and they were kind enough to find us a place to rent.

We arrived early one evening in August driving a U-Haul, and I will never forget how exotic the village seemed to me in the dying summer sunlight with its elegant, out-sized houses surrounded by manicured green lawns that bled into dark woods which were filled with fireflies and the perfect music of cicadas.

"This must be where the Great Gatsby lives," I breathed to my husband, and even though we were not on Long Island he agreed. It was such an unlikely spot for someone like me to land—a Utah County Mormon girl with serious populist leanings, a member of a huge and mostly blue-collar extended family, the daughter of a former tiara-toting rodeo queen. I soon earned a reputation for myself in the village as the woman with "five children and no help." The guard at the gate assumed I was the Cannon family nanny, and I never said anything to correct his misperception.

By day I sat in sandboxes with real nannies from western places like Rock Springs who were wild with homesickness, disappointed as they were by the false promise of the East. The nannies and I wore blue jeans and talked. Or I should say they talked while I listened to stories about affluent employers who expected them to be at once invisible and omnipresent. Meanwhile, babies crawled over us like puppies. When night came I put on hose and heels and went to functions where I talked with the nannies' employers. Or I should say they talked while I listened to stories about sullen young western girls who didn't appreciate the opportunities being handed to them. They told me these stories while casually dangling wine glasses from their hands and fingering strands of pearls wrapped around their lovely white necks. It was an odd time for me. I felt like someone with walking pneumonia, only in my case it was walking schizophrenia. I was two people inhabiting two worlds. The upstairs world and the downstairs one, too.

One of the things both the Upstairs and the Downstairs people said to me was how safe they felt in the Park. I was always intrigued by this comment, which I heard many times, because the desire to feel safe is not something that drives me particularly. I say this, of course, with the innocent arrogance of a person who has mostly been safe. So I began to wonder what it was that felt so threatening to people. Big bad New York City maybe? But that was miles, as well as light years, away from Tuxedo Park.

Then one day I heard two older women talking. They were country club women, filling their days with rounds of golf and rubbers of bridge, and they were talking about the shady characters that hung around the entrance of the little pharmacy in Sloatsburg—a tiny working-class town down the road from the Park. Both women rapidly agreed that they were very lucky to live behind iron gates that kept that element out.

Well I knew who these ladies were talking about. I'd seen them myself on jaunts to the pharmacy. They were teenage boys, mildly grungy, with a few piercings. Nothing serious. Just ordinary kids trying to look a little bit badass. The kind of neighborhood kids who used to show up at our house in Salt Lake to make nachos for themselves in our kitchen where they joked with me and each other. Suddenly I understood what the fear was all about there in the Park. It was a fear of people who were different. People from different places. People with different lives and different stories. And living behind a gate only intensified that fear. I was different, to be sure, but I was acceptably different because I was well-spoken, and when I put on hose and heels I looked just like a rich lady from Tuxedo Park. Not like those trashy boys in front of the pharmacy in Sloatsburg.

I tell you all this because of some information I recently received from a friend named Wendy Lamb who lives in New York City. She works as an editor of children's books for Random House, and one of her authors is Newbery Award winner Christopher Paul Curtis who wrote a fine first novel for kids called *The Watsons Go to Birmingham— 1963*. It's a story about an African-American family (dad, mom, three kids—a real Dr. Laura nuclear unit) from Michigan who take a road trip to Alabama to visit relatives, arriving there during the summer of Birmingham's discontent, when four little girls were killed by a bomb while singing in church.

I admire this novel for its humanity and its humor and finally for the way it subtly yet powerfully evokes the evil people do to each other in the name of a cause. I used it when I taught Children's Literature at Westminster College in Salt Lake City, and I urged my students (most of them aspiring teachers) to use it in their future classrooms as well.

This book was recently removed from a middle school classroom in Utah County (hello! my family seat!) because two parents (count 'em) objected to some of its content, including a quick sentence which mentions that the book's father "accidentally on purpose" brushes his arm across the breast of his wife. Not his girlfriend. Not his mistress. His wife. Whom he loves. These parents were not satisfied with the teacher's willingness to delete allegedly offensive passages or to give their children alternative choices. They wanted complete removal of the novel from the classroom.

And, baby, they finally got what they wanted. Probably felt all righteous about it, too. Probably felt like they not only rescued their own kids, but everybody else's kids as well. My friend Wendy (who edited the novel) is livid. And that's why she wrote me. I haven't responded to Wendy yet, but when I do I will tell her I think a parent is within his or her rights to question a teacher's choice and to demand an alternative for his or her child, if necessary. I am a parent myself, and I think that parents who do not monitor the movies, music, books, and television programs their children consume are fools. And I have precious little use for this kind of fool. But I will also tell Wendy that I am within my rights to shout down the person who makes a move to censor a good book so that an entire classroom of kids is denied access to it. Especially when I know that books are chosen with care before they can be used in a public school setting, and especially when I know from personal experience that the public here is sensible and often more moderate than we are given credit for. Understand me. You challenge a worthwhile novel and you have stepped onto my turf as a teacher, a writer, and especially as a mother. Now watch me call you out.

Bottom line. Censorship is about fear. Fear of people who are different. Fear of people with different lives and different stories. So you two parents down there in Utah County where I grew up and which I will always think of as my true home, filled as it is with the best people I know. Come on. Tell me. What are you really afraid of? And why are you afraid of it?

On the other hand, the Utah Legislature still maintains its vigilant stance here, reminding us all that openness is not always the local state of mind, despite the efforts of the likes of Ann Cannon and Linda Brummett. Examples? Condoms were removed from safe-sex brochures set to be distributed at the 2002 Olympics in Salt Lake City, and a beer ad featuring polygamy as a theme was banned from local billboards (would that the city banned *all* billboards instead of excluding only the ones of which they disapprove).

And so it goes, here in the land of Zion.

LATE-BREAKING NEWS FROM THE NATIONAL FRONT

And so it goes in the U. S. of A. since the so-called Patriot Act was passed (although in view of the fact that that act is allowing our "patriotic" government to dismantle our democracy, "unpatriotic" would be a far more accurate description). According to Dani Eyer, executive director of the ACLU in Utah:

Section 215 allows the FBI to obtain records (and other "tangible things") from libraries, bookstores, universities, and really any entity, on anyone whom the FBI chooses to claim is involved in "clandestine intelligence activities." *There is no require-ment of probable cause that the target of the surveillance is engaged in criminal activity.* [emphasis mine].

The ACLU finds this provision to be extremely problematic in its sweep and lack of judicial oversight.

Section 215 also includes a gag provision that prohibits those served with orders from disclosing to anyone else, *including the target of the surveillance* [emphasis mine], that the FBI has asked for information.

Constitutional Concerns

Section 215 probably violates the Fourth Amendment by authorizing searches not based upon probable cause.

The provision might be used to obtain information about the exercise of First Amendment rights.

The provision violates the First Amendment by prohibiting those served with Section 215 orders from disclosing that fact to others. Essentially, the provision penalizes the publication of lawfully acquired, truthful information about a matter of public concern.

The provision violates the Fourth and Fifth Amendments by failing to require that a person who is the subject of a Section 215 order be afforded notice and an opportunity to be heard.

TKE had a tangential brush with the mentality behind this act, the use of the fear of terror to abrogate civil liberties—or rather an author we had invited to the store did . . .

It began like this: Ron Smith, the Random rep, was selling books to me and mentioned in passing that Rohinton Mistry had a new novel due out in the fall.

"Fall?" I asked, stiffening to point. "As in September? We're having a birthday in September. Our 25th. It's a huge milestone and we're looking for an author who *means* something to us. Someone we've sold with passion. You know how we feel about Rohinton Mistry. About *A Fine Balance*. Is there any chance at all . . . ?"

"I doubt it. His tour is limited and he's unlikely to be stopping here. I don't even think he's going to the Tattered Cover."

"We'd do anything, Ron. He'd be so perfect. We found *A Fine Balance* before almost any other bookstore did. We hand-sold bushels full before Oprah had ever heard of him."

"How many copies have you sold, anyway?"

"Let me look . . ."

The answer was several hundred copies, and the upshot of the conversation (with a huge dose of Ron Smith's help) was a request from publicity that I justify TKE's invitation for Rohinton Mistry's appearance via E-mail. Which I did. With passion. Which, apparently, was persuasive, because we received a call from publicity not long after this saying Rohinton Mistry was coming to TKE. Not in September as requested but in November.

"That'll give us not one but two *Inkslinger*s to advertise in—the birthday edition and the usual winter edition," I said with glee.

It's early October, and we've done everything right, for once. We've all read Mistry's new book, *Family Matters*, and I've written a glowing review (not hard to do—the book is not only brilliant, but moving, involving, and gloriously, if sadly, true to life) for the front page of *The Inkslinger*, along with a radio review for our local NPR station, KUER. Anne, our new publicist, has talked up interviews with both papers, and with the same NPR station which ran my review. Dennis Lythgoe, the book editor at *The Deseret News*, is thrilled at the prospect of interviewing Mistry, and although Brandon Griggs, the longtime arts editor for *The Salt Lake Tribune*, has been transferred to the news department, his replacement, Christy Karras, sounds interested as well. We arrange for an auditorium that seats six hundred people, paper the university with fliers, stuff customers' bags with announcements, give tickets to people who buy *Family Matters*, sell tickets, promising to donate the proceeds to the Utah Food Bank . . . books and tickets start flying out the door. People begin calling. "Is it true Rohinton Mistry is coming?" they ask. "Yes," we say, bursting with pride. "He is."

All is in place, the momentum building, literarily speaking. This will be a truly memorable evening in TKE's history, we crow to one another a week before the event. And the articles and interviews haven't even appeared yet.

It's a Thursday morning at the end of October. We have a managers' meeting every Thursday at 8:30 a.m. Talking over the upcoming events, we center, of course, on Mistry. I ask Anne whether she's heard from the publicist yet concerning dinner—we had invited Mr. Mistry to dine with us, and we also wanted to know whether he might need a ride from the airport. "I haven't heard from her yet," Anne tells me, "and I can't understand it. I've E-mailed her twice, called her three times, and there hasn't been any response. I'll go down and check my E-mail right now and call her again if there's nothing there."

"You aren't going to believe this." It's Anne, her face grim. We all look up.

"He's not coming."

"What do you mean he's not coming? How can he not come? He's due this Monday."

"I don't know how. I just know he's not coming. The publicist's E-mail said he's been harassed in airports and that he's cancelled his tour."

"We're all harassed in airports." I can't remember who said this, but one of us did. 9/11 had come and gone but its scars were still fresh.

"I'll call Ron," I say finally, "try and get some details."

I go downstairs and start to pick up the phone, but it rings before I get the chance. It's my husband, Kit. His sister has lung cancer, he tells me. It appears to be inoperable—the tumor is sitting too close to a nerve bundle for surgery to be feasible. We're going to Colorado Springs next week.

I start to cry, tell myself to get a grip, it's *his* sister, I need to be strong. I say all I can think of by way of comfort and tell him I've got a small crisis to take care of at work, and then I'll be right home.

Crisis is a bit of an understatement, I think, and I dwell (selfishly) on the debacle we're facing at TKE. I have to bring things into some sort of order before leaving, but how exactly do you call off an event for which you've sold 120 tickets before any major publicity has even begun? An event for which we've planned on filling up a six-hundred-seat auditorium? An event to which the radio is about to give huge coverage. Not to mention the pap—

"The papers," I say out loud, panic in my voice. It's Thursday, and both papers put the Sunday art section to bed on Thursday. It might be too late already. I grab the phone, call the Tribune, ask for Christy Karras. She answers, and I tell her Rohinton Mistry has cancelled.

Why? she wants to know.

Why indeed, I wonder, thinking about the tickets, the auditorium, the book clubs and customers and fans we need to somehow contact.

"He was hassled at airports," I tell her and take a breath, ready to elaborate. Instead I burst into tears. Get a grip, I tell myself for the second time that morning, but I can't. The reality of the news about my sister-in-law, coupled with the catastrophe of the Mistry cancellation, has undone me. Vicki hands me a Kleenex, I wipe my nose and apologize, so mad at myself for losing control, so angry at our helplessness in the face of the mess, that I could spit. I try to tell Christy what I know, but I'm not very coherent. After getting (somehow) through the conversation, I call Dennis Lythgoe at *The Deseret News*, leave a message on his phone (thank God he's not there, I think. At least I don't have to make a fool of myself all over again).

I blow my nose once more and breathe deeply for a few minutes, then call Ron Smith, and this is what he knows: that Rohinton Mistry has been profiled at U.S. airports, as have all Canadian citizens of foreign birth of late, that he and his wife have been searched at *every* departure gate (since he's been flying once and sometimes twice a day, that's a lot of departure gates) and have been humiliated over and over again in the process. NPR has just done a story on the profiling, and the Canadian government has actually protested the practice. Ron says that Random House and Mr. Mistry feel badly about the cancellation, and that they will send us signed copies to replace the ones already sold to disappointed customers.

The idea of systemized racial profiling throws the whole thing into a different light, and the NPR story gives validity to the version Ron has heard. This is not some thin-skinned author backing out of responsibility because he was incommoded. This is wrong, is outrageous behavior on the part of our government. Righteous anger assuaging my angst, I sit down and bang out a statement. Here it is:

The King's English Bookshop is devastated to announce that Rohinton Mistry, three-time Booker Prize short-listed author of *A Fine Balance* and of the new novel *Family Matters* is canceling his appearance in Salt Lake City which was to have occurred on Monday, November 4, 7:00 p.m. at the Rowland Hall Middle School. Mr. Mistry, halfway through his national tour, has been so badly treated in U.S. airports that he has flown home to Canada. His publicist said, "as a person of color he was stopped repeatedly and rudely at each airport along the way—to the point where the humiliation to him and his wife (with whom he has been traveling) has become unbearable."

Mr. Mistry is one of the great novelists at work in the world today and the fact that he has been treated this way in a country predicated on individual liberty is shocking, to say the least. On behalf of all those who believe in freedom and in basic human decency, we wish to extend our deepest apologies to Mr. Mistry and to his wife for the barbaric treatment they have suffered. We will continue to read and sell his wonderful books with the same fervor as always.

All of you who purchased tickets and wish a refund may collect one at TKE. All money left over will go, of course, to the Utah Food Bank as originally promised. Those who obtained tickets by purchasing *Family Matters* may return books plus tickets (necessary as proof of purchase at our store) to TKE any time in the next two weeks and receive in exchange a signed copy of *Family Matters* as soon as we receive them from Canada. Mr. Mistry and his publisher, Random House, have agreed to arrange for these copies to be sent to us as soon as possible and extend their apologies for the cancellation as do all of us at TKE.

Betsy Burton, The King's English

I call Christy Karras and read the statement to her message machine. It has been only a short time since I last spoke with her (sobbed at her, really), so I feel comfortable that she will get it in time for the story, will quote me as being in sympathy with Mistry, appalled at his treatment. I call Dennis Lythgoe, but all I get is another answering machine. I leave another message with him and go home to my husband.

I am talking to Kit about his sister when the phone rings. It's the store. *The Globe and Mail* has called from Toronto. A reporter there wants me to call him back. Apparently he just has "a couple of questions," and is pushed for deadline.

"Go ahead and call," Kit says. "You've already written a statement, you might as well give it to him."

But do I stick to my statement? Of course not. In my defense, I'm not used to the press. Oh sure, I've talked to book page editors, done radio interviews in which I've spoken about authors, about small business. And I've done dozens of book reviews on the air. But I've never dealt with real controversy in the press before, and when the reporter asks me how I feel, I tell him.

After all, I rationalize, we're talking racial profiling here, and it's wrong. Whatever our provocation, we in the U.S. can't behave as if everyone on the earth with a skin that's darker than ours is a prospective criminal. We can't make enemies of the entire world because of 9/11. "If that's really what our government is up to," I say, "if there is actually racial profiling going on, people being humiliated, it's wrong and it makes me ashamed. We shouldn't be treating Canadian citizens—who are our friends and neighbors—like this, much less world-famous authors."

My voice rings with fervor, and when it finally stops echoing in my adrenalized brain, all I hear is silence—the sort of silence that occurs at the end of a performance just before wild applause break out, the sort of silence that precedes the roar of an avalanche.

Then the reporter asks another question, one completely off the subject at hand—to deflect me, I realize now in hindsight. He didn't want me to alter one delicious syllable of what I'd just said, especially the part about being ashamed of my country. I mean, *what* a sound (or rather, print) bite!

And that, of course, is exactly what he prints—with very little of the context of our conversation to soften it.

Oh well, I think, after I get on the website, read what I supposedly said (did say, even if it was out of context and, consequently, more unequivocal than I had meant it to be, containing none of my "ifs"), it's a Canadian paper. No one here will see it. When *The Toronto Star* calls the next day I'm more measured, stick more closely to my printed statement. And think, good, that's over.

Until the next day when Doug calls from the store and tells me about the hate mail.

"Hate mail?" I ask.

"I'll forward it," he tells me, and does.

"YOU FUCKING BITCH I HOPE YOUR BOOKSTORE BURNS DOWN," I read (this is but one of a dozen E-mail messages of hate). One of the respondents, the sole supporter of my position, has kindly attached the article that occasioned this outpouring of hatred. The BBC, paragon of responsible journalism, has picked up from the already-out-of-context quote I gave *The Globe and Mail*, the simple fact that a U.S. bookseller is ashamed of her country—not bothering to give that bald statement any context at all.

"But I never spoke with anyone from the BBC," I say to Kit after reading my pithy words on world news. "And I never said that. At least not the way they made it sound."

"Sound bites," Kit tells me. "Taken out of context or not, they make great headlines. And that's what the news business is all about these days."

"Maybe I could get a job in PR. What do you think?"

We both laugh, but it isn't really funny.

Meanwhile, back in Salt Lake City, *The Salt Lake Tribune* goes to press. On Sunday morning, I go sleepily downstairs, pick up the paper and begin to read the Mistry article. It opens with a description of the way we convinced Random House to send Mistry to us, talks about the cancellation, and then quotes me as saying something about the little guys always taking it in the shorts.

"I didn't say that," I tell Kit, outraged.

"I mean, I couldn't have said that, could I? I don't *talk* about taking it in the shorts. I don't wear shorts. I wear panties, for God's sake!"

The sad truth is, I don't know what I said between sobs on the phone that day. Vicki and Anne were in the office with me when I supposedly uttered those fateful words, and they tell me I didn't speak them, but as for me, I couldn't swear to anything. I mean I do swear, frequently. But, "Take it in the shorts"? "Fuck" would be more elegant. More eloquent. As I stare at the hard reality of my printed words, think about people reading my petty, mean-spirited reaction, I writhe, literally. PR indeed.

The rest of the article's nice. But it doesn't help.

Oh well, I think, trying (and failing dismally) to shrug it off, humiliation is good for the character. Although the irony of being maligned on the World Wide Web and the BBC for being unpatriotic, while being featured at home as the most whiny and self-involved of capitalists doesn't escape me. Anyway, I console myself, outside of Salt Lake, no one will ever know I uttered those stirring phrases. And people do forget stuff like this quickly. Soon it will all be over.

That is, other than an evening spent in front of the rented auditorium telling people who haven't received news of the cancellation that Mistry isn't, in fact, in town, that he is in Canada, having been treated horribly in every airport in every U.S. city he visited. A few people are miffed, saying they too have been searched ad nauseum. Every time you fly? I query? Treated rudely every single time? No, they all say. Not every time. And not rudely. Keep my money for the food bank.

Despite my fondest wishes, however, it isn't quite over. On the plus side, a gentleman from *The Times of India* calls my home that same evening. He wants to know more about Mistry as an author than about racial profiling, more about TKE as an independent bookstore than about politics, and we talk mainly about books. It's exhilarating this time, not scary, and I don't say anything untoward (or if I do, he has the kindness to keep it to himself).

On the minus side, the BBC calls wanting to do a half-hour interview on the radio.

"Live?" I ask wildly, thinking, Not on your life. If I can do this much damage with a couple of sound bites, think what I could accomplish in half an hour of live radio. "I have a statement I'd be happy to fax you," I tell the reporter.

Just before Kit and I leave for Colorado, Ron Smith calls me. I've already told him about *The Globe and Mail* and BBC fiascos, but I've kept mum about *The Salt Lake Tribune*, ashamed to even think of him seeing it. Ron tells me he has been engaged in a telesales conference with the entire sales force of Random House and that, en masse, they have visited—you guessed it, *The Salt Lake Tribune* website—where they have had a joint peek at my immortal whine about the little guys always taking it in the shorts. All I can hope now is that Mistry himself hasn't done likewise. I am afraid to ask Ron. I don't want to know.

On the way home from Colorado (where, it turns out, Kit's sister had lymphoma, not lung cancer—not that that was exactly good news), he and I hear the postponed interview that Mistry had agreed to do with Doug Fabrizio on our local NPR station. It is a wonderful interview. Mistry is obviously a kind and a dignified man. He has refused any national interviews regarding his trip cancellation, preferring to make a private rather than a public statement, and is clearly not the self-aggrandizing sort. He talks about his new book, his work, his life. I admire him more ardently than ever, and hope more fervently than ever that he has not been privy to the media storm I have, however unwittingly, created in his name.

Not long after this, he sends us a check for $300.00 to be forwarded to the Utah Food Bank.

Lessons learned (one would hope) in a business sense?
(1) Never talk to a reporter if you're feeling:
    (a) upset,
    (b) self-righteous, or
    (c) sorry for yourself.
Better still, never talk to a reporter, period—just issue written statements.
(2) If you break rule #1, whether for reasons of business or ego, speak only in sound bites, since that's all that will find their way into print anyway.
(3) If you break rule #2, be prepared for anything (and make sure your business, not to mention your loved ones, are prepared too).

Lessons learned in a broader sense?
(1) Since none of this would have occurred in the first place had not such a climate of fear existed in our country, it is important to note that when fear (whatever its cause)

is used to override civil liberties, the very fabric of our nation can be threatened, arguably doing more damage than *any* outside enemy possibly could.

(2) However irresponsible reporters may sometimes seem, they are one of the major safeguards against erosion of liberty (so long as they themselves are not too frightened to print what they see and hear). Even sound bites are better than silence.

(3) Under the so-called Patriot Act, libraries and bookstores no longer have the legal right to maintain confidentiality regarding people's reading habits. Chilling? *Terrifying* would be a better word. Patriot Act indeed. The founding fathers must be turning over in their graves.

In hindsight I'm thankful my statement *was* taken out of context, since a bald statement of outrage was, absolutely, called for. Who could have guessed, three years ago, that our individual liberties would be eroded to such a degree—that we could travel so far down the road toward censorship and away from individual liberty? Who could have envisioned in 2001 that the FBI would *ever* have unlimited power to search the bookstore and library records of our readers without even having to show probable cause? Who could have guessed they (the FBI, Homeland Security—who knows who else "they" might include) would be able to do so in complete secrecy, thanks to the gag provisions of that ironically named bill?

Oliphant summed it up best in a recent cartoon in which two shadowy figures stand in a doorway, the wife saying to her husband (who is immersed in a fat tome and has his back turned to the door), "Farnsworth, The Patriot Act people are here to ask why you borrowed *War and Peace* from the library."

It's too chilling to be funny.

ON THE OTHER HAND

Irony of ironies, a small rural Utah town made these headlines in *The Salt Lake Tribune*: "Utah Town Bristles at Patriot Act."

The article goes on to say that "convinced that the federal Patriot Act threatens civil liberties, the mayor and Town Council [of Castle Valley, Utah] have unanimously affirmed support for The Bill of Rights." Castle Valley is, apparently, part of a growing grass-roots movement across the country in which "cities and towns from Vermont to Oregon have signed such resolutions in response to sections of the Patriot Act, the Homeland Security Act and a series of executive orders issued by President Bush and Attorney General John Ashcroft." The mayor of Castle Valley is quoted as saying, "This is not just an issue of radical left or radical right politics . . . If people really read what the Patriot Act says—not just the rhetoric that's put out about it—they'll see, as we did, that it's a 180 degrees from what this country is supposed to be founded on," (*The Salt Lake Tribune*, March 11, 2003).

And, in early March 2003, Rep. Bernie Sanders (I-VT) introduced the Freedom to Read Protection Act (H.R. 1157), federal legislation that would remove a threat to the privacy of bookstore and library records posed by Section 215 of the USA Patriot Act, and urged booksellers to rally behind H.R. 1157 so that more members of the House would support the bill.

Rally we did. The American Booksellers Association sent petitions to all independent bookstores around the country in support of the Campaign for Readers' Privacy. Since we put that petition on our counter, literally thousands of our customers signed it—not only signed it, but thanked us for *doing* something about this erosion of our rights, for allowing *them* to do something. Other bookstores around the country had the same experience. One hundred and eighty thousand readers across America signed that same petition, and it was presented to Congress on September 29, 2004, by, among others, Bernie Sanders, Salman Rushdie, and Pat Schroeder.

Gives one faith—in Utah, *and* the U. S. of A.

Book Lists

An Incomplete and Unscientific but Nonetheless Shocking List of Books Challenged or Censored by Bookstores, Libraries, and Schools

NATIONAL

All Quiet on the Western Front, Erich Maria Remarque

Animal Farm, George Orwell

1984, George Orwell

Song of Solomon, Toni Morrison

Bluest Eye, Toni Morrison

July's People, Nadine Gordimer

Burger's Daughter, Nadine Gordimer

Children of the Alley, Naguib Mafouz

Candide, Voltaire

The Decameron, Giovanni Boccaccio

The Group, Mary McCarthy

Jude the Obscure, Thomas Hardy

Lady Chatterley's Lover, D. H. Lawrence

Ulysses, James Joyce

Madame Bovary, Gustave Flaubert

Sanctuary, William Faulkner

Tropic of Cancer, Henry Miller

The Bell Jar, Sylvia Plath

Diary of a Young Girl, Anne Frank

Black Like Me, John Howard Griffin

Clockwork Orange, Anthony Burgess

Satanic Verses, Salman Rushdie

Last Temptation of Christ, Nikos Kazantzakis

Doctor Zhivago, Boris Pasternak

The Grapes of Wrath, John Steinbeck

The Gulug Archipelago, Aleksander Solzhenitsyn

In the Spirit of Crazy Horse, Peter Matthiessen
The Prince, Niccolo Machiavelli
The Rights of Man, Thomas Paine
The Ugly American, William J. Lederer and Eugene Burdick
Oliver Twist, Charles Dickens
The Red and the Black, Stendhal
Sorrows of Young Werther, Johann Wolfgang von Goethe
Catch 22, Joseph Heller
To Kill a Mockingbird, Harper Lee
Manchild in the Promised Land, Claude Brown
The Scarlet Letter, Nathaniel Hawthorne
Of Mice and Men, John Steinbeck
One Flew Over the Cuckoo's Nest, Ken Kesey
Matilda, Roald Dahl
In the Night Kitchen, Maurice Sendak
The Stupids (series) Allards
Little House on the Prairie, Laura Ingalls Wilder
The Amazing Bone, William Steig
Anastasia Krupnik, Lois Lowry
Julie of the Wolves, Jean Craighead George
Harry Potter (series), J. K. Rowling
The Giver, Lois Lowry
Jump Ship to Freedom, James Collier
Where's Waldo?, Martin Handford
The Watsons Go to Birmingham—1963, Christopher Paul Curtis
Bridge to Teribithia, Katherine Paterson
Scary Stories to Tell in the Dark, Alvin Schwartz
How to Eat Fried Worms, Thomas Rockwell
View from the Cherry Tree, Willo Davis Roberts
A Light in the Attic, Shel Silverstein
I Am the Cheese, Robert Cormier

The Outsiders, S. E. Hinton

The Boy Who Lost His Face, Lois Sacher

Roll of Thunder, Hear My Cry, Mildred Taylor

Complete Fairy Tales of the Brothers Grimm

Indian in the Cupboard, Lynne Reid Banks

A Day No Pigs Would Die, Robert Newton Peck

Forever, Judy Blume

The Martian Chronicles, Ray Bradbury

Farenheit 451, Ray Bradbury

Ordinary People, Judith Guest

Catcher in the Rye, J. D. Salinger

Go Ask Alice, Anonymous

I Know Why the Caged Bird Sings, Maya Angelou

July's People, Nadine Gordimer

Brave New World, Aldous Huxley

Slaughterhouse Five, Kurt Vonnegut

The Color Purple, Alice Walker

On the Origin of Species, Charles Darwin

The Canterbury Tales, Geoffrey Chaucer

Bible, King James Version

Koran

Talmud

On a lighter note, Marilou Sorenson, an educator who served on Caldicott and Newbery award committees and who has worked locally and nationally to protect literature for children, has many stories of censorship to tell. Among them:

- *Bridge to Terabithia* was challenged because a character used the phrase, "Oh, Lord."
- *Sylvester and the Magic Pebble* was challenged because pigs were dressed as policemen.
- A woman stole all copies from a public library of *In the Night Kitchen*, drew jockey shorts where she deemed them appropriate, then returned the copies.
- *The Rabbits' Wedding* was challenged because it featured integrated bunnies.

UTAH

These lists are smaller and strictly anecdotal due to the fact that no "official" list is kept here. Also, because of the strict supervision of curriculum, few controversial books are allowed in the classroom in the first place.

Americana, John De Lillo (our sales skyrocketed the day this book was challenged in the Bountiful library)

Fifty Years of the New York City Ballet, Lynn Garafola (who can guess?)

Beethoven: His Life Work and World, H. C. Landon (ditto)

Elementary School

Mommy Laid an Egg, Babbit Cole

Clifford Goes to Hollywood, Norman Bridwell

In the Night Kitchen, Maurice Sendak

The Watsons Go to Birmingham—1963, Christopher Paul Curtis

One Hundred and One Ways to Bug Your Parents, Lee Wardlaw

Bridge to Terabithia, Katherine Patterson

Julie of the Wolves, Jean Craighead George

Middle and Upper School, or Public Library

The House of the Spirits, Isabel Allende

Show Me the Evidence, Alane Ferguson

Go Ask Alice, Anonymous

Forever, Judy Blume

Grendel, John Gardner

I Never Promised You a Rose Garden, Joanne Greenberg

The Girl, Robbie Branscum

Chancers, Gerald Vizenor

The Boy Who Lost His Face, Lois Sacher

The Crucible, Arthur Miller

Invisible Man, Ralph Ellison

The Sun Also Rises, Ernest Hemingway
The Grapes of Wrath, John Steinbeck
Huckleberry Finn, Mark Twain
The Scarlet Letter, Nathaniel Hawthorne
Beloved, Toni Morrison
Hawaii, James Michener
The Great Gatsby, F. Scott Fitzgerald
Black Like Me, John Howard Griffin

Finally, Jerry Sorbin, an English teacher at East High in Salt Lake City, said: "I wanted to teach the *Canterbury Tales* but when I called the school board they told me I had to disclose to the students ahead of time which tales contained objectionable content, then let them choose which ten they wished to read. The result, of course, was that 98 percent of the students read the ten that I had identified as containing objectionable material."

Chapter Eight

A *SENSE* OF PLACE

[
*"Industrial America turned out to have a vast appetite
for the romance of Nature, for the adventure of creatures,
human or animal, unmediated by civilization."*
]

— E. L. DOCTOROW, *Jack London, Hemingway and
the Constitution: Selected Essays*, 1977-1992

❊

[
*"A Gentile in the New Jerusalem: certainly I was.
Salt Lake City is a divided concept, a complex idea.
To the devout it is more than a place; it is a way of life, a
corner of the materially-realizable heaven; its soil is held together
by the roots of the family and the cornerstones of the temple.
In this sense Salt Lake City is forever foreign to me, as to any
non-Mormon. But in spite of being a Gentile I discover that much
of my youth is there, and a surprising lot of my heart."*
]

— WALLACE STEGNER, *Hometown Revisited* (*Tomorrow Magazine*), 1950

❊

[
*"The Mormon habitat has always been a vortex of
legend and lie. Even today, as the state settles down to gray hairs,
there lingers something wonderful and outrageous about
Utah, a flavor of the mysterious and strange."*
]

— DALE L. MORGAN, *Utah, A Guide to the Sate*, WPA PROJECT, 1941

[
"It's a simple equation: place + people = politics."
]

— TERRY TEMPEST WILLIAMS, *Red: Passion and Patience in the Desert*

One thing that all of us who live in this valley share, Mormon and non-, literary and non-, environmentalist and non-, is a love of its beauty. True, we all have our different takes on our landscape, treat it, according to our various proclivities, as a dumping ground for everything from old tires to nuclear waste, as a commodity to be sold, a playground, a sacred shrine, a treasure to be guarded. But none here would deny the fact that physically, the Salt Lake Valley is a marvel of a place. We are a city ringed by spectacular mountains: the Wasatch Range, pine cloaked, granite tipped, runs along Salt Lake's eastern perimeter, while the Oquirrhs fall away to the west, their vastness broken only by the city's namesake lake which gleams its way out to Antelope Island and beyond. Usually, these mountains seem comforting, motherly, a bastion against outside forces (too true, I think, in my darker moments). But when it snows hard, or we are beset by one of those Wagnerian thunderstorms for which the Mountain West is famous, the female metaphor turns on us, and we remember that with a single twitch of her hips she might flick us into oblivion, harridan that she can be. This is, after all, earthquake country, a place where plates shift, mountains crack, topple, moving along currents none of us fully understands. Garish, voluble, the West keeps us in a continual state of awareness as it jolts us through its four seasons in high dramatic fashion, blowing, flinging snow, sleet, blistering us, thundering, singing, soughing, at us, to us, tarted up in vivid orange and ochre and mauve, shawled in green, or in purest white—I mean, who needs religion with all of *that* going on right before our eyes on a daily basis?

These green mountains, the deserts, the red rock of the canyon walls and mesa tops, the gorges, gullies, gulches, the arroyos and dry washes, creeks, streams, and rivers, the synclines, inclines, and basins in our territory have been an indelible part of our nation's literature and culture for a long time, a gaudy, larger-than-life, hard-to-believe part. And while the outsized sublimity of our native terrain may seem in keeping with the larger-than-life villains and heroes of western mythology, it is an implausible backdrop for an ordinary life—too lofty to be *real* in a day-to-day way.

All of that is changing. The West is no longer the territory of Zane Gray and Louis L'Amour, of Jack Schaefer and Owen Wister, no longer high-voltage backdrop to adventure, drama, melodrama à la John Ford, but rather, a fascinating character in its own right, integral to the lives of its inhabitants—the land of Wallace Stegner, Ivan Doig, and Kent Haruf. Of Terry Tempest Williams, Mark Spragg, and Jon Krakauer.

A Sense of Place, Erotics of Place: *Place Last Seen, The Big Sky, Land of Little Rain, Heart Earth, Land of Enchantment* . . . The West is a land that feeds literature, feeds its finest fiction practitioners from A. B. Gutherie and Willa Cather down through Wallace Stegner to Harriet Doerr, E. Annie Proulx, Barbara Kingsolver, Judith Freeman, Jim Harrison, Brady Udall, and Sherman Alexie. Even the mystery genre is on fire out here in the West, and in nonfiction, John Muir passed his clear-eyed version of landscape on to Mary Austin, Wallace Stegner, and Ed Abbey; it continued from them to Terry Tempest Williams, Barry Lopez, Gretel Erlich, Nasdijj, Gary Paul Nabham, and Ellen Meloy. Bernard Devoto, Juanita Brooks, Fawn Brodie, and David Lavendar passed their passion for the history of this place and its people to Patricia Limerick, Leonard Arrington, Will Bagley, D. Michal Quinn, and Jon Krakauer.

The land informs, suffuses the fiction of its writers, is at the heart, the soul (and I use that word advisedly) of their nonfiction. Their West gives, then as easily takes back, gold, oil, uranium, water, fir, lumber, crops, grass for cattle, life itself. Common themes addressed by fiction and nonfiction alike are the availability and profligate use of the above; the ability to live in, live with the land's rhythms or the failure to do so; the respect for, renewal by wilderness, or the destruction of (or by) wilderness.

The vein of literary ore being struck out here is vast—so vast, so barely tapped that it makes me think of a pair of books that sat on my parents' shelves during my childhood, a fat two-volume set by Van Wyck Brookes. They were reddish in color and boxed in beige, as I remember, and one of the titles was *The Flowering of New England*. If flowering then seemed an apt metaphor for that green part of the world, it is even more so now for this arid quarter of our country. The land may be harsh out here, and it's true that we don't have much water, but under our 12,000-foot mountains, within the walls of granite, of sandstone and schist, something is happening—a literary coming of age is breaking apart stereotypes, blasting out tired clichés (and creating new ones in the process).

The past decade alone has unleashed fiction in the West that is as good as any in our country, nonfiction equal or better, even while an entirely new art form, creative nonfiction, particularly that involving nature, is influencing literature everywhere. Its best practitioners are nearly all Western and are so focused on land, sky, water, that the West is pure character, not backdrop but active participant. Out here, it is as if the two art forms, fiction and nonfiction, are merging, becoming something else, maybe something better than either was before.

THE MONKEY WRENCH GANG

The Cosmic Aeroplane was an iconoclastic bookstore/head shop disliked by the vice squad far more than was TKE. Run by Ken Sanders, Bruce Roberts, and Steve Jones, it was known for (aside from its paraphernalia) its edgy fiction, its science fiction, the wild side of Utah's history, and more than anything else, its books on the wilderness. Ed Abbey was an icon at Cosmic, and he returned their fierce loyalty in full measure. He came to TKE once or twice to visit and to sign stock, but most of his events were held at Cosmic. We admired him for his writing, for his love of the land we live in, and for his fierceness, his loyalty.

Indeed, if people who love wilderness regard one man as God the father, leader of a whole environmental movement in the West, a new way of life with wilderness as its center, that man *is* Edward Abbey. Abbey came of age under the tutelage of Wallace Stegner, and of John Muir before him, but carried their words and ideas further, radicalizing them. He worshiped at the shrine of desert beauty but did so with violence, both in his fiction and (if local lore is to be believed) his actions, clubbing, spiking, and sabotaging, as a way of insisting that the land be protected. In *An Unspoken Hunger: Stories from the Field,* Terry Tempest Williams quotes these words of Abbey's: "What we need now are heroes and heroines, a million of them, one brave act is worth a thousand books." Abbey may have been the first eco-terrorist, in fact, and was certainly the first to gain notoriety. He was the first to use words to advocate violence as a way to protect the wilderness and, if his own words are any measure, the first to use it himself in order to protect our natural world from abuse, from destruction in the name of corporate development. All of which gives me a sick but fascinating idea. If eco-terrorism is so effective in fighting corporations' unquenchable thirst for resources and their unceasing destruction of our natural environment, how about "communi-terrorism" to fight the forces of corporate depredation in our urban communities? Isn't life in our cities every bit as important to its inhabitants as life in our deserts or mountains? Just kidding about the terrorism part (I think).

MOTHER EARTH / SISTER SKY

If Abbey may be seen as an Old Testament kind of god, vengeful, full of fire and brimstone, then Terry Tempest Williams might, a generation later, be seen as his female counterpart. Mother, Earth Mother, heir to the same traditions as Abbey, to the tradition *of* Abbey, Terry is heir to older traditions as well—to a mysticism she came by through her family's Mormon religion and to an even more ancient tradition she's tapped into, held by the Navajo, that earth *is* mother. She also speaks of an "Erotics of Place" in her work, describes her love of the land in visceral terms. But she is more than mere lover to this land she cherishes, since she's made it her lifework to protect it with a ferocity equal to that of any bear protecting her cub. In this sense, in her role as guardian, the word "mother" seems appropriate, although Terry might not welcome such a label.

Terry Tempest Williams is so central to the new art form of creative nonfiction, so pivotal in its creation, that she may be seen as its center, at least in terms of natural-history writing.

And living here, Terry has been central to life at TKE for many years. I admire Terry as a writer more than I do almost any other. I view the world differently than she does; she is possessed of a spiritual dimension, a way of investing the ordinary, the everyday, with the odor of sanctity that in anyone else would make me uncomfortable, a way of "celebrating" land, water, sky, that coming from anyone else would seem self-congratulatory, as if the writer were pointing out the superiority of her own exquisite sensibility. All of which illustrates the enormous risks Terry takes when she writes as she does. Yet somehow, she avoids the gaping chasms of disbelief, the risk of hubris, seems honestly passionate and utterly compelling in her unswaying belief in wilderness. Each time I've read a new book of Terry's, I've wondered in amazement how she manages this. And I've come up with some explanations that make sense to me:

The first is her obvious and complete sincerity: Terry Tempest Williams is so impassioned, so infused (suffused) with love for the West that her rapture simply cannot be artifice.

The second is humor: For all her passion, sly wit glints like mica, reminding the reader that Terry knows fool's gold when she sees it, is willing to call it what it is.

The third is poetry: Terry is ever a poet, even if what she writes goes by the name of prose. There were moments in the "Hell" section of *Leap* that left me gaping at the page, saying aloud, "I knew she was good, but . . .", nuggets of dazzling lyricism that made my heart turn over, my breath shorten. She plays with language, with form and pattern, flies with it, fractures it, forces it to do her bidding, and if sometimes her views don't coincide with mine, so what, I say—anyone who can write like that can say whatever she damn well pleases, and maybe I'll even believe it, become a helpless convert.

The fourth is wisdom: Terry's wisdom comes from vulnerability, from the laying out of pain, of doubt, and from examining that pain, that doubt, using a writer's skill to analyze the causes and consequences of personal agony in a clear-eyed and honest way, and to then turn the experience into metaphor.

The fifth is the willingness to risk that is at the heart of any great writer's work: *temptress, terrifying, tempestuous, a template, a temple*—words that define Terry Tempest Williams in all her contradictory complexity. In *Leap* Terry risks more than most people do in a lifetime. She risks her family's love, her church's acceptance, her community's approval, takes risks with language, form, themes, and structure. That book is an act of blinding courage, personally, spiritually, literarily, and professionally. And if I'm too cynical to share with her all the joy that she finds in the *Garden of Earthly Delights*, am unable to empathize with her version of heaven, I certainly agree with her vision of the circles of hell and the possibilities inherent in restoration. Then, in *The Open Space of Democracy*, she risks everything that she has built professionally over her adult lifetime, leaving her prestigious New York publisher in order to say what she believes needs to be said about democracy, how it works, how it fails to work. Her new grass-roots activism is as grounded in land and community as is her written work. Indeed, as warrior, as seer, as visionary, Terry bears as much resemblance to Emerson and Thoreau as anyone in her and our lifetime, taking their vision and making it her own.

I first met Terry when, fresh from college, she came into the store to buy a book on birds. She introduced herself, and I felt a pang of familiarity as she told me she'd just earned a degree, had nearly finished a book but wasn't quite sure what to do next. If one didn't wish to teach, wasn't interested in a profession like law or medicine, what good were degrees? Or even books, if they didn't sell in large quantities. One had to eat, after all. I had an impulse (surprise, surprise) to give her some helpful advice. And since she had obviously had some experience in natural history *(The Secret Language of Snow* was almost complete, and her thesis had been the first draft of what would become *Pieces of White Shell)*, I suggested she go see my mom.

My mother, the classic example of the right person in the right place at the right time, had been an exception to the rule concerning the useless nature of degrees. In her forties, she had gone back to school for a masters in anthropology and had completed her degree just as the University of Utah's Museum of Natural History was opening its doors. Jesse Jennings, head of the anthropology department, was the museum's new director, and Mom had been his prize student. He hired her to set up a docent program and then to create and run the Junior Science Program, which taught the state's children about the earth, about the creatures which walk, crawl, and prowl its surface, through the linked sciences of anthropology, geology, biology.

Terry, knowledgeable in all three areas, came along at about the time Mother was thinking of retirement; Mom loved Terry, recommended that she (and one other young woman, Mary Gesicki) take her place. The two were at the museum for a good many years, and Terry published, while there, *Refuge* and *Coyote's Canyon*, along with *Pieces of White Shell* and *The Secret Language of Snow*.

Perhaps because of Mom, or perhaps out of respect for the store and its stock of good fiction, good poetry, good books on the wilderness, Terry has been a friend and constant customer at TKE and reads here whenever she publishes a new book. She's changed from the shy young woman who penned those early essays in *Pieces of White Shell*, the children's books *The Secret Language of Snow* and *Between Cattails* (both out of print, but they shouldn't be, they're lovely), into a woman of immense sophistication who is witty, articulate, compelling. But she is, if anything, more impassioned, more visionary than she ever was. It has been an education watching a first-class writer, not to mention thinker, emerge from the cocoon of that young woman besotted by wind, water, sky, and earth, by birds, turtles, and coyote, seeing her turn into someone who could revere all of that, still, and yet relate it to the larger concerns of literature, to man and womankind and *their* relationship to earth, to wilderness, to community, to the cosmos, to one another. She took the first step on this journey in *Refuge: An Unnatural History of Family and Place*, a book in which the observations of a naturalist were blurred, subsumed by the tears of a daughter watching a mother being eaten by cancer, even as her beloved bird refuge was drowning in the waters of the Great Salt Lake.

Refuge is a brilliant book, moving in a way that nonfiction is only infrequently. Its interweaving of natural history and personal memoir, its use of one as metaphor for the other, seemed wholly original, the first real example of a new form of literature. Other naturalists had written memoirs, of course, had applied the lessons of natural history to humanity, but no one had turned this usage into an art form the way Terry did in *Refuge*.

One of the things that is so terrifying about Terry Tempest Williams is the way that she gives of herself, lays herself bare—terrifying because it is easy to imagine her spending herself on others, so that nothing is left over for herself or for her work. She also lays bare the lives of those around her, or at least she did in *Refuge*, delving into the personal as she spoke of her own grieving, the grieving of her father and her brothers as her mother lay dying. And, because they had their own take on the subject of their feelings, when she came to our store, she brought them all along. Rather than reading from her book, Terry let them speak for themselves on the subject of their mother and wife, on Terry's accuracy or inaccuracy in depicting the process they all went through. It was obviously a painful experience for some but was, just as clearly, releasing, transforming, and was a lesson for all of us on the ways grief can be an ongoing process (nothing "closed" about it, the current adoration of the term "closure" notwithstanding). It was also one of the most moving hours in the history of The King's English.

Terry read from *Leap* off-site at a larger venue, a private school whose auditorium TKE borrowed for the occasion. It was the debut of that significant book and deserved, we thought, a wider audience than we could fit into the bookstore or the adjoining frame shop. The board of the Mountains and Plains Booksellers Association was in town for a meeting, and I was proud to have them in the audience, proud to be introducing what I believed to be Terry's most notable work to date—a book so brilliant, so wholly original, that I knew its most important reception would be here in her home state, where she took on so much that she disagreed with, risked so much. The board members, booksellers all, were in tears by the end of the reading. So was nearly everyone else in the audience.

She read there again when *The Open Space of Democracy* was first published, read during that breathless pre-election time in October 2004 when the fate of our entire democracy seemed to hang in the balance of that election's outcome. She spoke out passionately to the six hundred people packed into the auditorium, spoke about the need for action, yes, but the need to listen as well. The attention of the audience was rapt, people intent on her face, her voice, her words.

As a reader, Terry is a marvel. Her voice is low and personal, her wit always near the surface, spicing her emotion with humor, cooling its white-hot edges. Still, her passion is as obvious as is her absolute lack of guile—nothing Terry does is an act. When she signs books, she talks to every customer eye to eye, giving each one of them her full attention, dignifying the needs of those readers who wish to share their experience of cancer, of loss of faith, of loss of land, of loss of freedom. Terry pens lengthy inscriptions, more often than not, and as a consequence, her signings go on for hours. We know this heading into each event, and we plan for it, because Terry does nothing by half measures and seems to have the willingness, the capacity, to nurture anyone who needs nurturing, listen to anyone who has something to say. Mothering. Earth mothering. Conveying to each her conviction that the here and the now are our paradise, the land our Eden; that in wilderness is our salvation, and that we must protect it if we are to survive; that the earth was here in the beginning, that it is and ever shall be, world without . . .

THE BOOK OF REVELATION

If the earth was once "mother" to America's first peoples, it is fast becoming so again, here in the West where much of the "conquering" (read rich, white) population has (Mormons aside) rejected a celestial heaven and replaced it with a terrestrial one—replaced God with a natural spirituality akin to Thoreau's, and in so doing imbued our natural world with the attributes of religion.

A natural spirituality is hardly a new notion—if Native Americans held the earth as sacred, if Thoreau, Emerson, praised its spiritual glories, so in a different way did pantheists. It's not a bad notion, either, at least as notions that underpin religions go. But it is, nonetheless, a notion that has come to represent a religion—a religion that is fast acquiring a theology, a set of tenets, a (I shudder to think) dogma. And like most religions, once founded, proclamations are the order of the day, and dialogue is equated with sin. Which is why I view this new writing in the West as at once the best and the worst of writing: The worst because I fear the tyranny implicit in a proscribed way of viewing the land I live in, the land I love. For me, cynic that I am, all religion, all dogma is suspect.

And yet, and yet . . . The very rapture that mysticism such as Terry's inspires is the stuff of poetry, the stuff that makes words soar, leap off the page, as they do in *Leap*, in Dante-esque fashion, dazzling the reader's heart, yes, but mind as well, posing a thousand questions followed by as many answers, by affirmation that is as old as religion itself. How can this be wrong, this glorifying of the world we live in, singing of its vast, implausible beauty? How can it be wrong to treasure it, guard it?

And yet . . . it *can* be wrong if you're a poverty-stricken woman with a passel of kids and you live marginally on a patch of dry ground somewhere in Southern Utah—a patch the government has already saturated with nuclear fallout for decades, leached the water from with dams and with canal networks put in place to quench the insatiable thirst of Arizona and California—and if, now, that same government wants to "protect" this land, your land, by refusing to allow you to build anything on it because someone has seen a turtle crossing its perimeter.

I can see that the turtle, the desert tortoise, protected by the Endangered Species Act, matters, and I can see that the woman matters, too. So can Terry. Indeed, a part of the above example came from Terry, from *Red*. But she's one of the few who can, a trait that sets her apart. The thing I so hate about religion—or, for that matter, capitalism or any other "ism"—is that it removes the dialogue of fact-based logic from every problem. Every equation becomes a theorem "they" (they being the disciples, the imams, the rabbis, the priests, the theorists, the philosophers, the generals, the politicians . . .) claim to be true a priori. This is especially so for faith-based religion. Give me that old-time scholasticism every time; at least scholasticism allowed questions, attempted to answer them. It seems far more logical to try and explain faith based on reason than to attempt to turn reason on its ear, making one group's version of, vision of "reality" *into* a religion the way many of the new nature writers do. The new environmentalism-as-religion, at least in the wrong hands, doesn't even acknowledge questions, never mind carrying on a dialogue.

Don't get me wrong. I *am* an environmentalist. I believe the wilderness, open space need protecting, just as does community. I'm all for guarding, nurturing, leaving in peace the turtles and eagles and spotted owls that walk, crawl, and fly across our landscape. I get so mad, though, at people who drive around in their SUVs (urban tanks, Bill McKibbon calls them), poisoning our air and using up that same noxious air to lecture us about the environment, the wilderness. They don't seem to know what they're for, who they are, or *why*. They just know that they believe (or, more accurately, know what it is fashionable to believe).

At the risk of being boringly repetitive, what I believe in is choice. My favorite organization in the country is the ACLU, not because it's liberal (although I love it when it is) but because it is for choice. And because religion is, by its very nature, anti-choice, it scares me to death. People who are dead-sure they're right are capable of wishing death and destruction on the other side. Did you hear me espousing communi-terrorism? I'm my own best/worst example. I know I'm right about community, therefore, if community is threatened, let's bomb the bastards who threaten it.

No, let's not. And let's not spike trees or destroy equipment. Let's elect a few honest women and men and try to change things. Because without the rule of law (corrupt, disillusioning as it can be), all is anarchy. Without the rule of law we are no better than the animals that old-time nature writers glorified, but which are, for all their glory, still animals, not imbued with conscience as at least some of us (presumably) are.

To elect a few good people, however, in order to try to change things, to protect this land we live in, on, we need a movement. And who better to start such a movement than the writers who sing of wilderness, who believe change is necessary? Writers like Ed Abbey. Terry

Tempest Williams. Barry Lopez. And around we go—especially since, even if such a movement gathers force (as it has), the people subsequently elected don't all keep their promises. Politicians commonly fail to keep promises—money (possessed in large quantities by developers, by nuclear waste "management" companies) all too often speaks louder than principles, than promises. And if our government fails us (as it surely seems to do much of the time), what then?

There are no easy answers to this endless circle of quandaries, of course, just the duty to question, never forgetting the possibilities of dialogue, the need for balance.

EARTH NOTES

Barry Lopez won the National Book Award for *Arctic Dreams*. It is a monumental work about the land, its people, the *experience* of the land in the far north. His sensibilities, his vast knowledge, his questioning mind make his work fascinating; his writing lends it magic. His fiction, along with that nonfiction that, like Terry's, crosses fictional boundaries, is every bit as good—*Lessons from the Wolverine, Winter Count, Giving Birth to Thunder, River Notes, Desert Notes, Field Notes, Light Action in the Caribbean* are all, in their own ways, brilliant books.

TKE has hosted events for Barry twice, once before a large crowd at the university, the second time at the store. The first time he read *Crow and Weasel*, in its entirety. *Crow and Weasel* is, in a sense, a children's book—a wondrous fable and an adventure story which works as allegory. It is lovely to look at (the illustrations by Tom Pohrt are brilliant), blissful to read, divine to listen to. By picture-book standards, however, this magical tale about two friends (who are also two mythical creatures) journeying out into the world is a *long* children's book, a novella in fact. It took Barry Lopez well over two hours to read *Crow and Weasel* out loud and to answer questions about it.

He read from *Field Notes* several years later, and it was again a splendid reading. Again, it was a long reading—over two hours. By the time the questions were asked, his thoughtful, thorough answers given, the crowd was sated, ready to go home. They didn't stay to mingle, buy books—which, if not the entire point, we consider to be at least part of the purpose of such evenings, for author as well as bookseller.

I was talking with the buyer of one of the better bookstores in the West, and when I asked her, over one too many glasses of wine imbibed after a trade show dinner, which author gave the longest readings in the history of her store, she said without missing a beat, Barry Lopez. "He's good," she hastened to add. "Very good indeed."

He is very good. He is, in fact, one of the two or three best writers in the West who ground their work in wilderness, and his love of the earth, his knowledge of it, is a recurring and heartfelt theme in his books.

Another such writer is Rick Bass, who signed books for stock at our store, who read at the university where we sold his books, and whose fiction and nonfiction, *Platte River*, *Winter*, *The Ninemile Wolves*, *The Book of Yaak*, *In the Loyal Mountains*, *The Lost Grizzlies*, *The Sky, The Stars, The Wilderness*, share lyricism, passion, and an abiding love of the Montana landscape, a landscape which has produced a stunning array of writers over the past two decades, from Ivan Doig and William Kittredge to Clare Davis and Kevin Canty, from Rick Bass and Deidre McNamer to Mary Clareman Blew and the transcendant Melanie Rae Thon.

The freshest nonfiction voice out here in the West where the wind blows free belongs to Wyoming's Mark Spragg. His tale of growing up on a dude ranch just outside the confines of Yellowstone Park in Shoshone National Forest (*Where Rivers Change Direction*) is sure-footed and entertaining, terse, yet beautifully written. Hiding underground currents of pain in its piney pages, this tale is both witty and profound, the story of a mere boy doing a man's job caring for the dudes who were *his* children for two weeks at a time out in the wilderness where he knew more of life, survival, than any of them. Having lived with a father who was harsh taskmaster, Spragg learned from that stern but brilliant man not only the secrets of the natural world but also those harbored in the books that lined their living room; although many of the lessons were force-fed, that fact didn't diminish their value.

When we asked Mark Spragg our infamous holiday *Inkslinger* question—what he least wanted for Christmas, and what he'd trade it for—he said: "There's a South African playwright who'd been an alcoholic for years and he said he'd rather give up drink for a year than to have writer's block for one week in any given year." What Spragg himself wants in place of writer's block is, "any good sentence, any good paragraph, any good page." Judging by his memoir and his two wonderful novels, he's gotten his wish in spades.

THE GRAND STAIRCASE

There's a whole different sort of nature book, one which renders landscape, whether in vivid color or black and white, with photographs that record it, yes, but at a magical split-second in time—light glancing off a red wall of rock, drowning in a pool of water, illuminating the white-water froth of rapids, or the shadowed slit of a hidden canyon fissure. Ansel Adams and Eliot Porter are the legends in this field, Tom Till and John Telford modern-day giants. Indeed, Tom Till is a photographer with such an eye for beauty, for the shapes and colors that give the West its soul, that he may well become its chief chronicler, in a pictorial sense. He's given slide shows at TKE (I, thank God, was not working the projector), and on the screen his images take on a singular power, filling the room with splendor. Teresa Jordan, who wrote the text for his *Great Ghost Towns of the West*, is as fine a wordsmith as Till is a photographer. Best known for the lovely and honest *Riding the White Horse Home*, Jordan paints as well as she writes, using delicate, exquisite watercolors to evoke landscape, painting it in words with equally sure strokes in *Field Notes from the Grand Canyon*.

It was John Blaustein who was the first of such illuminators of the Western landscape to come to TKE. He visited TKE in our fledgling days and signed *The Hidden Canyon*, a lyrical light-suffused accompaniment to Ed Abbey's text which has recently been republished. Steve Trimble combines a like eye for beauty with both the knowledge of a naturalist and the writing of the best of this new breed of author/photographer. His *Blessed by Light* is light-struck, gorgeous, while *The People* is an exhaustive, insightful look—in photographs, in their own words, and in his text—at the Native Americans who inhabit our Southwest. Steve has signed at TKE a number of times and will again, I'm sure. His unauthorized biography of a local magnate, which is also an insightful look at development in the West, won the Utah Book Award for nonfiction in 2004.

There are a myriad of large and lavish books written as paeans to our part of the world by authors and photographers we've hosted at TKE. We've duly celebrated our most recently created wilderness area with two books, *Heart of the Desert Wild: Grand Staircase Escalante National Monument*, by Greer Chesher and photographer Liz Hymans, and *Wild and Beautiful: Grand Staircase Escalante National Monument* by Mark Taylor and photographer Anselm Spring. Photographer David Muench's *Utah* is a classic on the subject of this state, and Page Stegner (son of Wallace) rendered our grandest canyon gloriously in *Grand Canyon: The Great Abyss*. Few other corners of the globe lend themselves as readily to the probing attention of a wide-lens camera, a naturalist's pen, an artist's eye for what lies at the heart of landscape, as does our own. Few other landscapes lend such backbone to the literature of its inhabitants.

ANGLE OF REPOSE

Wallace Stegner, head of creative writing at Stanford until his death (Tobias Wolff now holds this position), was a master of fiction and nonfiction, of novels and stories, history and natural history alike. If Ed Abbey was the fiery Old Testament God of the new West, Stegner was at once seer and revelator, chronicler and ambassador. One of our nation's best writers, he was fair-minded, a realist, a humanist, a historian, a naturalist, an artist. Progenitor of Abbey and of Terry Tempest Williams, of Ellen Meloy, and Craig Childs on the one hand, precursor to Ivan Doig and Harriet Doerr, Kent Haruf and Barbara Kingsolver on the other, Stegner was the man who coined the phrase "a sense of place"—in a real sense the man who gave us our awareness of, our pride in, this place we call home. Wallace Stegner will ever stand at the head of the line of people who painted the West honestly, cared about it with passion tempered by pragmatism, wisdom.

I've loved Stegner's work since I read *Angle of Repose* in 1971 (it was then, and remains, one of my favorite novels of all time). He came to town a few years ago to deliver the Tanner Lecture, and after meeting him, I worked up the courage to write and ask him to come to TKE. I told him how I felt about his work, not expecting him to reply, certainly not guessing he'd agree to come. He was eighty-four then and had far too many demands on his time, even for a person half his age. His response was that he was "curious to see what has happened to 15th East [TKE's street] since 1931," and that, "I am putting the address down in my private address book. You will see me the first time I get to Salt Lake, but God knows when that will be. Meantime, many thanks for pushing and liking, or liking and pushing, my books." He never did come to TKE. He died later that year in an auto accident in New Mexico where he had gone to receive the Mountains and Plains Booksellers Association "Spirit of the West" award. With him died one of the great voices of our time.

HEAVEN'S GATE

If Stegner's voice resides still in the work of current Western writers, it resides too, in the books of such contemporary Western scholars as D. Michael Quinn, and Will Bagley and in that of a journalist whose perspective is global and whose writing is divine, Jon Krakauer. We first heard about Krakauer's book *Under the Banner of Heaven* while perusing the publicity grid (a prodigious document featuring all authors touring in a given season) for Bantam Doubleday Dell, in the spring of 2003. "Must refer to some high peak," we postulated, looking at the title. "Maybe in the Alps, or Katmandu. Someplace that brings out the obsessives and true believers he loves to write about." Little did we guess how right we were about the true believer part—not to mention the obsessive part. We sent a request for a Krakauer visit to our sales rep, Karen Hopkins, and when she next came to town reminded her of our plea. "Oh, no," she said, "he won't come to Salt Lake. He's already had death threats—and the book won't even be out for three months."

"Death threats?"

We were aghast. Confused, too. At least until she explained that the book was about *Mormons*, not *mountains*—not mainstream Mormons, either, but rather those of fundamentalist and polygamous persuasion. "The thesis of the book," Karen told us, "is the proclivity for violence of fundamentalism."

"Fits right in with death threats," we said.

"Especially since the core of the book deals with Ron and Dan Lafferty," she agreed.

"Oh," we said in open-mouthed unison. The infamous Ron and Dan Lafferty had killed their infant niece and their sister-in-law in cold blood—had done so, according to Dan's subsequent testimony, because God had told them to. "No wonder there have been threats. I'm sure the polygamists are in an uproar. But not mainstream Mormons, surely; they don't approve of polygamy any more than we do. And even if they aren't overjoyed at the prospect of an event concerning the Laffertys, that leaves half the city who will be avidly interested. We can put Krakauer in the big Catholic high school. It seats 1,100. And there's no place in the country more likely to garner that type of audience than Salt Lake City."

"I still don't think he'll agree to come. He's already said no. But I'll try."

No Room at the Inn

Thanks to Karen's efforts, Krakauer did say yes, and we were agog. *Into Thin Air* and *Into the Wild* were both runaway bestsellers, books that looked at the obsessive character of those who spend their lives conquering nature, who chase transcendental idealism to its logical end. Krakauer's name alone would assure a huge crowd, and his new subject matter was certain to generate interest bordering on mass hysteria in Utah. Polygamy is a dark secret here, subject of consuming curiosity for half the population while the other half does its best to ignore it.

We booked the Catholic high school and began planning our publicity campaign. Then prepublication copies of the book came out. Working in the very particular context of a single grisly murder, broadening his scope, first by moving back toward the roots of Utah polygamy buried deep in Mormon history, then out into its present-day enclaves, Krakauer made a compelling case for the connection between fundamentalism and violence that seemed absolutely universal in its implications. While he didn't spend much space making the argument that whatever holds true regarding the correlation of violence to fundamentalist belief in the single instance is true worldwide, still, by the end of the book the logic of this thesis seemed inescapable. If, under the tenets of most fundamentalist creeds, a man (and I use the word "man" advisedly since patriarchy seems inextricably linked to every sort of fundamentalism under heaven) is told by his God to perform a specific act, dialogue is superfluous, reason flies out the window, and any behavior becomes possible.

"Terrifying and timely," I said to Barbara and publicist Anne Holman when I had finished reading the book. "Just look at the Taliban, Al-Qaeda, Iran's mullahs, and Israel's orthodox— not to mention some born-again Christians."

"Let's stick to the subject at hand," said Barbara, ever the realist.

"But this is an *important* book. A book for our time. It's much broader in its implication and appeal than any ordinary tale of polygamy and murder."

"Not that tales of polygamy and murder are exactly ordinary," Barbara said. "You do know that The Church isn't going to like this, don't you?"

"You're right, they're not." It wasn't as much the subject of polygamy, or even Krakauer's noting of the fact that its roots come directly from the church's founding fathers (Joseph Smith and Brigham Young, among others) that would disturb the faithful—rather it was the rekindling of that topic in a manner that was bound to garner national publicity, make people who didn't know much about the LDS religion say, There they go again, those nuts in Utah. That and Krakauer's interest in the doctrine of blood atonement, another unsavory tenet from the church's early days—understandable in light of the horrific persecution early Mormons suffered, but for those fundamentalist groups who still cling to early doctrine, a clear basis for present-day doctrinal violence.

Although none of this ancient history was new to any of us, taken collectively, it was a pretty damning backdrop for Krakauer's thesis regarding fundamentalism and violence, tying it to Mormon roots as it did. Early Mormons were fundamentalists—and some *were* violent, however mainstream and peaceable members of the LDS church have become in the present. It was hard to see how anyone could argue that point; it was even harder to see how Mormons would be anything but upset at seeing their history tied in print to present-day violence, however tangentially—especially in what would obviously be a widely read book.

"We'd better call the high school and make sure they're clear about the subject of the book," I said. "They probably assume it's about mountains, since it's Krakauer. It wouldn't be fair not to warn them—especially if there's a firestorm of publicity."

"The school's Catholic, not Mormon; they won't mind."

"Let's call anyway."

They did mind, and so—when asked—did the Episcopal school. We were stunned. Part of the solidarity those of us on the "outside" of Mormonism experience stems from the fact that we are a community of our own, a fairly united community, whatever our differences. Indeed, one of the nicest things about being a non-Mormon in Utah is exactly that broad acceptance of anyone and everyone besides Mormons (at least religiously speaking), just as Mormons have a ready-made culture in which they are accepted.

Perhaps it was the current rift in the city over the selling of Main Street to the Mormons (a story for another time), the hostility it had engendered, the sensibility on both sides that calm must be restored, that fueled the reluctance of the private schools. Whatever the case, it left us in a pickle, to put it mildly. None of the public schools was an option, since the event was scheduled for the last half of July, and with school out for the summer, air-conditioning was off districtwide. Salt Lake records 100-plus-degree temperatures frequently in July and air-conditioning was essential.

The new library? It holds 320 people.

"Unacceptable," Krakauer's publicist told us. "You agreed to host 1,000."

We mulled possibilities all over town. Everything at the university was either unavailable, too small, acoustically impossible, or prohibitively expensive. The same was true of the other venues we looked at around the city. Symphony Hall would cost several thousand dollars to rent, and the community college, where we had hosted John Mortimer, was already booked. Desperate, I suggested Anne call the Catholic school back, beg them to reconsider. She did, and the answer was still no, the subject deemed too controversial. We were actually considering canceling the event when I remembered that an acquaintance, Geralyn Dreyfus, head of the Salt Lake Film Center, had called me about some project she had in mind. I hadn't called her back, and Geralyn was a force of nature, someone who knew literally everyone in town and unfailingly made things happen. Maybe she would have some ideas.

Geralyn had not only an idea but a theater. Although it would cost a few hundred dollars, it held 800 people. And she was starting a film/book series in which she wanted us involved—a series featuring authors such as William Styron and Michael Ondaatje. Did we want to be involved?

Euphoria is what I remember most about that day. And the event was back on track.

IN FOR A PENNY

There must have been something in the water or the wind that week, because no sooner had we called the publicist with the good news than we got calls from two other publicists in quick succession. The first, from Scribner, wanted to know if we would host an event for Sally Denton. Her book, *American Massacre*, had as its subject matter the infamous Mountain Meadows Massacre and was due out in late June.

"Oh, great, the church will love this," I told Barbara. "It's a good thing they aren't given to violence any longer."

The Mountain Meadows Massacre had occurred in the early days of the state's history, when the federal government was threatening the Mormons over polygamy, and persecution was at its height. In response, a group of Mormons disguised themselves as Indians and slaughtered a wagon train of people who were traveling across the state on their way to California. It had always been one of the dark secrets here, since the Mormons persistently ignored or denied it, covering up any evidence that came to light. Juanita Brooks had written a book on the topic in the '60s and Will Bagley had done a reading from his definitive and scholarly tome *Blood of the Prophet* at TKE only the year before; he had uncovered reams of new material definitively laying the blame for the atrocity at Mountain Meadows at the early church authority's door and causing quite a local commotion in the process. Judith Freeman's fine novel *Red Water* dealt with the same massacre, and feelings were high on both sides, the natural curiosity of nonbelievers exacerbated to a fever pitch by the denial and indignation of spokespersons for the church.

"Sure," we told Scribner, "we'd love to host Sally Denton."

"Good," the Scribner publicist said, "C-SPAN wants to film the event."

Next, Norton called, wanting to schedule a reading for a book entitled *Predators, Prey and Other Kinfolk: Growing Up in Polygamy*. We knew its author, Dorothy Solomon, whose now out-of-print *In My Father's House* had been a favorite of ours, and we said yes without hesitation. While the Mormon paper's review might be negative, still publicity was publicity, and *The Salt Lake Tribune* would inevitably review all three books, as would the local NPR stations. There was clearly an emergent theme in all of these works, that of Mormon fundamentalism—a theme it was past time to explore. Capitalizing on said theme, we sent out a postcard with a headline created by Sarah, one of our wonderful, literate grad students: *On Faith and Fundamentalism: Three New Books of Local and National Importance*. The card went on to list the books and authors, along with the dates and times of each reading.

IN THEIR FATHER'S HOUSE

Sally Denton was first on the postcard, and the patio was packed when she came to town. It was a hot 96 degrees, and the crowd grew sweaty and restive as the obviously local (un)talent hired by C-SPAN blundered about moving speakers, mikes, cords, amps, fiddling with knobs, and pushing buttons until well past 7:00 p.m. (the time when I was scheduled to introduce the author, something I had never done or even dreamed of doing on national TV). We passed out mineral water and monitored technical progress while I fought dry mouth and told myself to *breathe*. When they finally nodded, I did my bit, sighed with relief, and Sally read a stirring passage about the actual massacre of men, women, and children, making fresh assertions about the tragedy which virtually (if she's right) cleared the Indians of any involvement and all but named Brigham Young as an active co-conspirator in the atrocity.

There were Mormons and non-Mormons alike in the audience, and the ensuing discussion was lively (to put it mildly) as Denton's research was disputed by some, applauded by others, this one questioning source material, that one disagreeing with conclusions drawn from cited material, yet another agreeing passionately with what she said. There was a Goshute there who spoke up in support of her assertion that not only were Piutes not involved, but that they had fled the next day, knowing they would be blamed. Denton also asserted that the population in Cedar City, the flourishing town located near the site of the slaughter, dropped by half by the end of that year as people left the scene of what all knew to be a planned massacre.

It was a fascinating and chilling evening, and I couldn't help thinking what a TV show it was going to make, little dreaming that C-SPAN's sound problems had NOT been overcome: not only was the young man lurching from audience member to audience member attempting to pick up their questions on his antiquated boom mike (and not succeeding in this endeavor), but Ms. Denton's voice was not carrying into the TV mike (although the live audience could hear her plainly enough). C-SPAN was going to have to refilm the entire event—at a bookstore in Logan the following week.

Dorothy Solomon read on the same patio a few nights later—to many of the same people, although she also attracted a crowd of her own, most of whom either knew her personally or had read her previous book. Again, there were well over 100 people in attendance, again it was hot, but without C-SPAN's presence things went more smoothly. The audience, equally engaged, was less contentious, since Dorothy's story is personal rather than historical and deals not with mainstream Mormonism but with its fundamentalist fringes. Raised in a polygamous family, she had had trouble fitting into its confines even as a child, uncomfortable with the constant need to lie about her life and that of her family in order to avoid discovery, more and more driven to establish her own identity, more and more aware of the difficulty of doing so inside the closed society of which she was a part.

Her book is moving, wrenching in places, written with an incandescence which lends it startling power. When she told of her father's slaying under orders from Ervil LeBaron, a polygamist from a rival and violent family, of her own facing down of Rena Chenowyth, the actual murderer, both on national TV and in court (in order to prevent her from garnering profits from the killing), the crowd stilled, marveling at Dorothy's perseverance in the face of such anguish. No one could possibly have been angered by anything she said, and everyone, Mormon and non-Mormon alike, was in full sympathy with her. When a lone spectator did try to raise the issue of a connection between mainstream Mormonism (Dorothy is a practicing member of the Mormon church) and fundamentalist Mormonism, the crowd stared him down and Dorothy rebutted his thesis with a sharp sentence. This was *not* about mainstream Mormonism, it was about fundamentalism. A different kettle of fish.

BLOOD OF THE PROPHETS

So, for that matter, was *Under the Banner of Heaven*—about fundamentalism rather than mainstream Mormonism. Which is why, if history is to be believed, the need for security was self-evident (at least to those who live here). Local fundamentalists, from Ervil LeBaron to John Singer to the Lafferty brothers to Brian David Mitchell (otherwise know as Emmanuel and the man who kidnapped Elizabeth Smart), when threatened, are all-too-predictable.

New York felt even more strongly on the subject of security than we did, and at their prompting, I called the local detective I'd already used once or twice; his wife met with us, told us what security would cost and what it would and would not accomplish. "But before we take this on, why don't you go to the local precinct and see what the police are willing to do? If they feel there is a credible threat, they may assign patrolmen to you."

We took her advice and met with a desk sergeant, a quintessential bureaucrat who was at first unwilling to do anything; when finally convinced we might have a genuine security problem, he began speculating that a uniformed bicycle patrol might work.

"A *bike* patrol?" the publicist positively shrieked when informed of this novel notion. The last thing we want is to make it so obvious."

"Not to mention ineffectual," Barbara added after we hung up. "If there *were* trouble, what in the world good would uniformed patrolmen circling the theater on bicycles do?"

Anne decided to try another precinct—and was met by instant success, not to mention recognition. "Oh, we've already assigned two officers to Gloria Feldt when she comes (the director of Planned Parenthood was scheduled to visit TKE during this time period—yet another of our events about which the powers-that-be were not likely to be thrilled). We'll shake off a couple of vice [squad] to the theater."

Comforting, but by now we'd discovered that the theater had six different entrances. Would two officers be enough? We called the detective agency back, but they had had another case blow up and no longer had personnel available. At which point my daughter, a probation officer who works with teenagers, said, "Motheeer," in a voice very like those of her clients, "why didn't you ask *meee?*"

Ten minutes later I wondered why I hadn't, because she'd already lined up two adult probation officers who were eager to help. If we closed off the front entrances—easy, since the press would take up the first rows anyway—that left a professional at each of the other doors. But what if someone leapt out of the audience?

"Aren't you being a little paranoid?" Anne asked.

"Better safe than—" at which point inspiration struck. A young couple had moved into our house recently to help us get our disabled son out of bed in the mornings and to stay with him a couple of nights a week so that we could get a little more sleep. The young woman, Lisa, who had worked for us in the daytime for years, possessed the face of a Madonna and the martial arts skills of Bruce Lee. We could place her beside Krakauer, instruct her to open each book to be signed (thus positioning her between author and customers), and no one would guess that she was not an innocent bookseller. When asked, she agreed, and security was in place.

This was a new and lurid wrinkle on bookselling.

IN THE BELLY OF THE BEAST

Perhaps more surprising than the need for security was the hostile nature of the prepublication reviews, reviews positively vitriolic in their accusations that Krakauer was antagonistic toward mainstream Mormonism. In fact, Krakauer, in the book itself and in interviews, had taken great pains to distinguish Mormonism from its fundamentalist offshoots, saying that he'd been raised among Mormons in Oregon, that they'd been his playmates, his scout masters, his teachers, and that he'd liked and accepted them just as they had liked and accepted him. His book's subject was Mormon fundamentalism, he insisted, a very different subject from Mormonism per se.

Despite this insistence, despite the truth of it, obvious to anyone who had read the book, after Brandon Grigg's first story about Krakauer's soon-to-be-published book appeared in *The Salt Lake Tribune*, the authorities in the Mormon church launched a prepublication blitzkrieg of their own. They panned *Under the Banner of Heaven* unmercifully, claiming the book was anti-Mormon, anti-religion, and historically inaccurate as well. I had, by that time, read the book twice in galley form, had written a blurb for Book Sense and a long radio review, and I knew full well how wrongheaded such criticism was.

But not bad for business, Anne and I agreed, noting the stiffening to attention in the city as the awakening curiosity on both sides became almost palpable—especially after another blistering volley erupted from church authorities, this time occasioned by a *New York Times'* editorial on the book's topic. I imagined Doubleday publicity licking its corporate chops at the furor, as indeed it must have done; according to Krakauer, Doubleday promptly rushed another 350,000 copies into print—before the book was even out.

As if it hadn't done enough to boost sales, the church then penned an editorial of its own that was to run in the *Tribune* on the following Sunday, in tandem with one taking the counter position, for balance. This was the weekend before the event, and I knew that Brandon had another story scheduled for the *Tribune* as well. I called to see how major it was to be and was told it was a long piece—that he had reinterviewed Dan Lafferty, interviewed Krakauer. "It's slated for the front page," he said.

"Of the art section?"

"Of the paper."

"Wow," was my articulate response.

On Sunday, I opened the paper to an enormous headline concerning a death in a wilderness camp, a death that had occurred months before and was hardly the stuff of headline news. Disappointing, but there was nothing wrong with a headline in the arts section. I turned to section C. Nothing. Paged through to the book section. Still nothing. Began rifling through every section, frantic for some mention of Krakauer and finally found the face-off editorials—with no mention of the event or even the fact that Krakauer would be in town.

Our "alternative" newspaper, the major source of print news not monitored by the LDS church, had killed the story of the book's publication and the attendant controversy—all of which was breaking news here—while stories on Krakauer headlined the art sections of *The New York Times* and *The Los Angeles Times* on that same Sunday. A day before, Krakauer had been interviewed at length (along with a chilling interview with Dan Lafferty) by Ted Koppel on ABC.

Brandon's story did run in its entirety on Tuesday, two days before the event, albeit in a much lower profile position than originally planned. The next day, Krakauer was on the *Today Show*. Calls began to pour into TKE.

We scoped out the venue one last time the next day, and Thursday at 5:30 p.m., we descended on the theater once more, a SWAT team of booksellers, some stationed as ushers, some as security, some as salespeople. At 6:00 p.m., Jon Krakauer came in a side entrance, accompanied by his wife. She went off to get him a snack, and we spent the next hour in a tiny, hot office where, ably abetted by rare book dealer Ken Sanders, I opened cartons of books for Krakauer to sign. Outside, all was pandemonium as the theater filled and Anne and the other booksellers began turning people away. The press was there—cameramen and reporters from all four local TV channels along with reporters not only from Salt Lake's papers, but also from the wire services and local papers in Provo, Ogden, and Logan. Nothing like this had ever occurred at an author event in our memory, and I offered up a prayer to the book gods (the only ones I believe in). Thank you, I intoned silently, for encouraging the church authorities in the public expression of their outrage. May they continue to do so, world without end, Amen.

Krakauer expressed the same sentiments an hour later when someone in the audience asked how he felt about all the adverse publicity the church had created. "I'll tell you what my publishers thought," he said. "They said they couldn't in their wildest *dreams* have created or even hoped for this kind of publicity for the book. And the funny part is that the book is not anti-Mormon. It isn't *about* Mormons except in the historical sense. It's about extremism."

Why did reviewers, even *The New York Times*, take Krakauer to task for being unduly harsh in his treatment of mainstream Mormons? He wasn't. He treated Mormon *fundamentalists* harshly—deservedly so. But he was quite positive about present-day Mormonism, and there was not one thing he said about the roots of Mormonism that hadn't been said again and again by other historians and journalists—wasn't, in fact, historically accurate.

Reviewers aside, it was a fascinating evening. Two women leaning against the west wall of the theater listened intently while he read, and their hands shot up the second he announced that he would take questions. "Who were your sources?" they asked.

"I *never* reveal sources," he told them, and ignoring their still-waving hands (we had imposed a one-question-per-person limit), he called on someone else. We found out later that the two women were former sister-wives of Ron Lafferty.

Another multiple-questioner clearly possessed of an agenda was shouted down by the audience. Still another asked what Krakauer thought about Joseph Smith, the founder of Mormonism in the early 1800s. "Smith was an American genius," Krakauer responded. "That's what Harold Bloom said, and I agree with Bloom's assessment. Smith was a visionary and he had charisma. He would likely have accomplished as much in any age in which he was born."

"What do you think about women who live under polygamy?"

"That their position is unfair. When I began interviewing them, most would put on a good face, say they were happy with their sister-wives. But then, when I really got them talking, they would mention their jealousy, speak about how hard their lives could be."

This, like all his answers, was unhesitating; the swiftness of response, his climber's coolness under pressure clearly visible. Indeed, he never once equivocated or evaded that entire evening (maybe he should run for office—it would make a refreshing change), and by the end of the night, his absolute honesty was so apparent to us all that even the Mormons in the audience appeared almost reverent as they brought their books up to the stage to be signed (while Lisa stood guard at his side, opening each book for him, and the vice squad and probation officers unobtrusively scanned the crowd). Kurt Bench, a long-time LDS rare-book dealer who had been visibly angered by Sally Denton's reading and her response to questions, positively sang Krakauer's praises to me, while the author of the hour signed, and the press busily filmed and interviewed people waiting in the long line, books in hand.

At 10:00 p.m. the crowd had finally thinned. A student reporter from *The Daily Universe*, Brigham Young University's school newspaper, asked if he could do a quick interview while Krakauer signed more books for stock; Krakauer said sure, and the young reporter, fresh-faced, eager, but respectful, asked intelligent questions. Krakauer's responses were mild—until the subject of women came up. When asked to voice an opinion on women in the mainstream Mormon church, the author was once again blunt about the necessity for equality between the sexes, the absolute lack of it in Mormondom. "Women can't hold the priesthood," he pointed out. "Or any position of real authority within the church."

"Is that so terrible? They fill an important role in LDS society."

"If it's not an equal role, it can't help but create pain. Resentment. How could it not?"

The young man mulled this, and then his open features took on the look of revelation, as if he'd never really looked at women and his church from this angle before.

If there is a lesson in all this, it is one that Mormons, not booksellers, should take to heart. Would the LDS church only allow the bones of history to be exhumed, examined, reburied in public, that history would lose much of its power to shock, much of its consequent attraction. I mean this both figuratively and literally—a few years ago the bones at Mountain Meadows were hastily reburied two days after they were accidentally disinterred, thus preventing a thorough examination by forensic pathologists, an examination which might have shed much-needed light on the event.

Any number of atrocities have been committed in the name of religion over the years, from the Crusades to the Inquisition to the Salem witch trials. Once these atrocities are acknowledged publicly, they join the ongoing stream of history as it slides down the channel of centuries, a part of the past. It's the secrecy, the lies, and the covering up of documents and of facts that give events like the one at Mountain Meadows, half-forgotten doctrines such as blood atonement, the power to shock in the present. If Mormon authorities would let the victims of their own history join the long line of wronged—and recorded—victims of religion over time, a lingering narrative memory would be the only remaining echo. It is precisely those attempts to obfuscate, overwhelm, bully, and deny that give books like Krakauer's the attention they garner.

Not that *Under the Banner of Heaven* isn't a fine book. It is. A brilliant one. But its brilliance lies in the clarity of Krakauer's vision, the way his finely drawn particulars can be generalized so that, in the end, he is addressing a terrifying universal. He does, absolutely, deserve the bestseller status *Under the Banner of Heaven* attained, bestseller status that book would no doubt have achieved in its own right, although arguably not as quickly without the help of the authorities in the LDS church.

As I finish this section, my editor, a Mormon, gives voice to misgivings about some of what I've said. As we discuss her objections, instead of bristling I find myself wanting to understand how her views differ from mine and why. Who's being defensive, I wonder, her for having her religion questioned, or me for having my opinions questioned? We had the same sorts of discussions over the censorship chapter, and although we agreed to disagree on some issues, we both moved toward one another's positions on others, and by the time we arrived at the end of the book we were friends.

Face it, I tell my husband when he speaks of retirement, of moving to California where he can garden twelve months a year, this place is like no other. You'd miss it. I realize as I say this that I can echo Wallace Stegner's sentiments when he writes about Utah, "In spite of being a Gentile I discover that much of my youth is there, and a surprising lot of my heart." Besides, I point out to Kit, The King's English is in Salt Lake City. And what would I do without it?

Book Lists
Books on the West Published During TKE's First 25 Years

25 Western Fiction Titles Grounded in Place

1. *Ceremony*, Leslie Marmon Silko, 1977
2. *Legends of the Fall*, Jim Harrison, 1979
3. *Stones for Ibarra*, Harriet Doerr, 1984
4. *Lonesome Dove*, Larry McMurtry, 1985
5. *Fool's Crow*, Jim Welch, 1986
6. *Crossing to Safety*, Wallace Stegner, 1987
7. *Dancing at the Rascal Fair*, Ivan Doig, 1987
8. *Testimony of Mr. Bones*, Olive Ghiselin, 1989
9. *Animal Dreams*, Barbara Kingsolver, 1990
10. *All the Pretty Horses*, Cormac McCarthy, 1992
11. *The Meadow*, James Galvin, 1992
12. *Cowboys Are My Weakness*, Pam Houston, 1992
13. *Green Grass, Running Water*, Thomas King, 1993
14. *The Lone Ranger and Tonto Fistfight in Heaven*, Sherman Alexie, 1993
15. *Fata Morgana*, Lynn Stegner, 1995
16. *Blood Orchid*, Charles Bowden, 1995
17. *Elena of the Stars*, Chuck Rosenthal, 1995
18. *Plainsong*, Kent Haruf, 1999
19. *Place Last Seen*, Charlotte Freeman, 2000
20. *Sweethearts*, Melanie Rae Thon, 2001
21. *The Miracle Life of Edgar Mint*, Brady Udall, 2001
22. *The Last Report on the Miracles at Little No Horse*, Louise Erdrich, 2002
23. *Red Water*, Judith Freedman, 2002
24. *The Work of Wolves*, Kent Meyer, 2004
25. *An Unfinished Life*, Mark Spragg, 2004

25 Nonfiction Titles from the West

1. *This House of Sky*, Ivan Doig, 1978
2. *Basin and Range*, John McPhee, 1981
3. *The Desert Smells Like Rain*, Gary Paul Nabhan, 1982
4. *Solace of Open Spaces*, Gretel Ehrlich, 1985
5. *Cadillac Desert*, Marc Reisner, 1986
6. *Wild to the Heart*, Rick Bass, 1987
7. *Desert Solitaire*, Ed Abbey, 1988
8. *Sagebrush Ocean*, Steve Trimble, 1989
9. *Desert Notes, River Notes*, Barry Lopez, 1990
10. *Refuge: An Unnatural History of Family and Place*, Terry Tempest Williams, 1991
11. *Where the Bluebird Sings to the Lemonade Springs*, Wallace Stegner, 1992
12. *Hole in the Sky*, William Kittredge, 1992
13. *Eagle Bird*, Charles Wilkinson, 1992
14. *Riding the White Horse Home*, Teresa Jordan, 1993
15. *Temporary Homelands*, Alison Hawthorne Deming, 1994
16. *Down Canyon*, Ann Zwinger, 1995
17. *Place in Space*, Gary Snyder, 1995
18. *Homestead*, Annick Smith, 1995
19. *Where Rivers Change Direction*, Mark Spragg, 1999
20. *Canaries on the Rim*, Chip Ward, 2000
21. *The Blood Runs Like a River Through My Dreams*, Nasdijj, 2000
22. *Eye of the Blackbird*, Holly Skinner, 2001
23. *The Secret Knowledge of Water*, Craig Childs, 2001
24. *Running after Antelope*, Scott Carrier, 2001
25. *Anthropology of Turquoise*, Ellen Meloy, 2002

Chapter Nine

A FAR CRY FROM KENSINGTON

> [*"[As] the book business grows more removed from those who care about books beyond their function as commodity, the more a healthy reading society, and democracy, are endangered."*]

— Richard Howorth, Owner, Square Books, Oxford, Mississippi, (and Mayor of Oxford, MS), *Independent Bookselling and True Market Expansion*

✦

> [*"It's much better for us to have reps selling the list to 1,000 buyers across the country [who are] making independent decisions, than having five buyers deciding what is or isn't a worthwhile or viable book."*]

— A sales director of a top-ten publisher, speaking to *Publisher's Weekly* (sadly but understandably) on the condition of anonymity (ibid)

CATCH 22

Gerry Spence, the famous (some say infamous) defense attorney, was out on the patio at TKE fielding questions after a reading not long ago. In the process of thanking us for hosting his appearance, he delivered an impassioned, compelling defense of independent bookstores. "You're on a signing tour," Spence said, gesturing broadly, inviting the audience to tour with him. "You go from chain to chain and each one looks like the next one, a table here, (he pointed an accusatory finger at an imaginary table), one there . . ."

Spence paused in his best courtroom manner and looked out at the audience, hamming it up. "Did you know that my publisher has to *pay* for that table if we want my books on it?"

He paused again, examining us one by one. "Did you know my publisher has to pay the chain if they want my name on a sign hanging above *my* books on the table they had to pay the chain to use?"

This time he didn't wait, increased his rhythm. "Did you know that if my publisher *doesn't* pay the chain for that big ole banner with my name on it, they won't *hang* it? And did you know that there are only about six major publishers left in the country? That two of them are owned by Germans?

"Did you know that independent bookstores only sell about 25 percent of the books in this country and that the rest are sold by a couple of chains?"

Spence said all of this as if he couldn't quite believe it. He began to positively thunder as he went on. "And did you know that these independent bookstores are one of the last bastions guarding one of our most precious freedoms?

"You'd *better* support them," he finished, shaking his finger. "Or you'll be losing more than you know."

The only thing Gerry Spence got wrong in that lovely rant on our behalf was the market share possessed by independent bookstores—it's actually 16 percent and after declining for several years, is at long last stable, at least for the moment. The explanation promulgated by chains is that this is "progress," the "natural" forces of capitalism at work—that the proliferation of big-box and dot-com retailers is merely an example of "market expansion" and is as inevitable as the changing of the seasons. But the fact is, if independents don't survive, the multiplicity of choices we represent in terms of book titles available will narrow, not widen.

It's already happening. The number of high-quality midlist titles is diminishing as publishers respond to the chains' virulent pursuit of the chimeral bestseller list—the unending search for that one title that will firm up their bottom line for the year. As a result, less and less publisher energy is going into discovering and "growing" young authors, nursing them through successive books in an effort to bring them to natural maturity. Instead, it's do or die. A "young discovery" must prove out on the first book, or no one will even *look* at subsequent titles. Booksellers' ability to discover talent on the rise and to wait expectantly for second novels is withering, since the second novels often don't even appear if the first aren't bestsellers.

Capitalism at work? Progress? When two or three buyers from two or three chains and a dot-com retailer begin to decide what *all* the stores will offer and what *all* the publishers will print, is that capitalism at work? It's certainly not "progress." Not by anyone's standards. And it can hardly be called capitalism, either, since the chains don't make much money in the process. It's as if their own investors (along with our city governments, which so love to dole out subsidies to chains) *pay* national companies to move into communities and open new stores, to discount to the point that these stores lose money, and at the same time put local stores out of business. An odd breed of capitalism, a strange form for democracy to take.

It's like a giant Ponzi scheme—chains give the *appearance* of corporate good health and paint a rosy economic picture by claiming "expansion"; consequently, their stock goes up. But that so-called "expansion" consists of opening one new retail outlet after another (bankrolled by their stockholders and further subsidized by our local governments) while the older stores are, for the most part, barely breaking even—or losing money. The ultimate outcome, once this process has run its logical course, once stockholders finally start demanding profits, thereby limiting "expansion" is that the whole pyramid topples, as in the case of Toys "R" Us and Boston Market, among others. At this point, the chains take shelter in Chapter 11 and often begin to abandon the spaces they have occupied, leaving gaping black holes—alongside of those gaping black holes already left by local merchants that have been driven out of business. Worse, some developers entice the *same* chains they placed in a former development into their new ones, cannibalizing themselves (cannibalizing the community) in the process. Our cities and towns are left poorer in every way.

That our own local governments are actually helping to *shrink* rather than expand our tax base, even while such chain "expansion" is in *forward* motion (i.e., while new big-box stores are still opening, and before those black holes begin to appear), makes the whole thing doubly ludicrous. One might ask how enticing a chain to move *into* a community shrinks the tax base? The answer is that because chains send their profits *out of state*, hire most management-level employees from *out of state* (only the minimum-wage jobs go to locals), buy their goods *out of state*, contract for services from accountants, graphic design firms, PR companies, marketing firms, and attorneys *out of state*, the dollars spent in chain stores by local shoppers flow mostly *out of state*. Four studies, done in Austin, Texas; Santa Fe, New Mexico; the Andersonville area of Chicago, Illinois; and Midcoast, Maine, illustrate this, all finding that while local businesses send between 45 and 70 percent of the dollars spent in their stores back into the local economy, chains send back only 13 percent—less than one third the amount that is recirculated (spent) in the community by locals. In Salt Lake City we've convinced county government to conduct a like study; we would be surprised if the results are any different when said study is completed. Why, then, one must ask, do our local governments give chains benefits that make it so hard for local businesses to compete? "Myopic" is one word for such behavior.

However, even considering the unlevel playing field independent booksellers have been forced onto these past few years, the erosion of our market share has been surprisingly dramatic. The reason, I would submit, is that that chains and dot-coms have stumbled across an industry that is odd, yes, but only because its bottom line has never been solely about profit. And chains have taken those very systems meant to foster book publishing—peculiar but workable systems such as returns—and subverted them, using the book business in ways it was never meant to be used in the process.

Without doubt, the returns policy in the book industry is peculiar. Simply put, bookstores may return books to the publisher within one year after purchase—or six months or three months, or until out of print in some cases depending on the publisher—*if* the books are in saleable (read: perfect) condition. Why? Because otherwise booksellers would be far less likely to risk their money on unknown authors. And if there is one characteristic of the book business that is constant, it is change. Public taste changes; authorial styles go in and out of vogue as fast as does subject matter; fads disappear, reappear (how I wish I could forget Feng Shui, angels, and the ubiquitous G spot); authors often change focus in midcareer, some have one good book, twenty lousy ones, another good one; some only *write* one book (like Harper Lee), while others write something wonderful every third effort.

The downside to returns is this: in the good old (pre-chain) days, returns held at about 10 to 15 percent. Which made the entire system workable. We independent bookstores bought books we liked the looks of, books we honestly thought we could sell and felt good about recommending to readers. When we got the books from the publishers, we read most of them, and we hand-sold them (we still do). Consequently, the majority of the books we bought ended up in the happy hands of readers, where they belonged. Publishers remaindered (read: put on fire sale) the returns they did get back, earned enough on the 85 to 90 percent they sold us to cover the cost of the books that didn't sell, and made fortunes on the best-sellers. There was plenty of money in this process to allow publishing houses to publish the midlist titles that are the backbone of bookselling (not to mention the backbone of reading); books by authors whose work sells well, gets good reviews, but is unlikely to hit bestseller lists; books by new writers whose first efforts might not sell in great quantity, but who will mature over time into solid, saleable authors; brilliant books that sell in small quantity but that get rave reviews and may well make up "the canon" tomorrow, be those books that will live on in classes at universities and on the shelves of book collectors and passionate readers.

Publishers could also afford to warehouse what has ever been the true bread and butter of the book industry: backstock. I'm speaking of older commercial novels that still sell well, like *Gone With the Wind*, *Hawaii*, *The Prince of Tides*; classic mysteries and thrillers from *Gaudy Night* and *Woman in White* to *Our Man in Havana*, and brilliant new ones like *Motherless Brooklyn*, *The Curious Incident of the Dog in the Night-Time*, *The Constant Gardener*; classic novels from *Pride and Prejudice*, *War and Peace*, and *Jane Eyre* to *Absalom, Absalom*; *Gravity's Rainbow*; *Angle of Repose*; *Tin Drum*; *Catch 22*; *The House of the Spirits*; *Love in the Time of Cholera*; *Ragtime*; *Transit of Venus*, *Midnight's Children*; *A Fine Balance*; *The Blind Assassin*—the books that link us to our past, help us to understand our present, make our future imaginable.

So what is different now? For one thing, chains use the returns policy to buy books on margin—i.e., to bet on the come, pick up titles that have the look of "bestsellers," to "stack 'em deep and discount 'em steep," selling such enormous quantities (for little or no profit) that bestsellers are created simply by the hype. Capitalism at work, some might say, although again, this practice has so far accomplished little except to *lose* bushels of money for big-box and dot-com retailers alike (not to mention publishers, once the returns come back), and thus can hardly be described as capitalism with a capital C. In fact, here's the problem with the new corporate system: The books that chains pick to stack and rack don't always (or even usually) turn into bestsellers; sometimes (often) they bomb, utterly. When this happens, the chains send all those big, big stacks of unsold books back to the publishers—which practice is one significant reason returns leapt from 15 percent to somewhere between 35 and 40 percent (statistics vary depending on the source) after the so-called superstores began mushrooming around the country. In fact Richard Howorth (past president of ABA, mayor of Oxford, Mississippi, and owner of Square Books) quotes an Open Book Publishing study which found that "The return rate for national chains is approximately fifty percent higher than the returns of the average independent store." The consequence of these staggering returns? The price of books skyrocketed along with the returns rate as publishers struggled to recoup their losses the only way they could (besides, of course, reducing the number of titles published, which is an even more terrifying new reality than skyrocketing prices).

Ask yourself this question: Has the onslaught of "superstores" and dot-com retailers really saved anyone money? Has it saved *you* money, gentle reader? I doubt it. On the contrary, if you're a frequent buyer of books, you've probably spent a fortune in terms of higher book prices this past decade—not to mention money wasted on bad books purchased because some publisher gave some chain extra money to put said books on a "power isle," hang a banner above them.

Co-op is another peculiar practice of the book business, one that booksellers engaged in with savvy and discretion for many years. It has now been subverted and is again resulting in (among other things) the skyrocketing price of books. Co-op was the allowance that bookstores could apply for as a sort of PR/advertising budget for a given title. We used it to advertise a book in the newspaper when an author was coming to town or to feature a specific book that we liked in a newsletter. Chains, on the other hand, use co-op dollars for such unsavory practices as "power isle placement" (something no publisher has ever offered TKE, this involves giving bookstores money to put specific titles up front in spaces where customers will see them as soon as they walk in the door); "Distinguished Young Author Series" (how weird is it to know that publishers *pay* to have their authors become "distinguished," rather than paying those who *are* distinguished?), or in-store banners—those colorful hanging strips of cardboard or plastic bearing authors' names and book titles, which publishers pay chains to display. In other words, publishers are paying (being coerced to pay, in my opinion) huge sums of money to chains to do what most self-respecting stores do on their own—display and promote books. Worse, because chains have so much buying power, they convince publishers to give them ever more of these spurious allowances, allowances that have not always been made available to independents.

Co-op practices and returns policies are just two examples illustrative of the changes occurring in the book business. Our industry is changing so profoundly, so rapidly, that it's hard to see *how* it will all end up. For most independent booksellers, however, the *books*, each and every one of them, remain more important than the bottom line; life counts for more than money. That may be a shocking philosophy in our country, in our century, but it is a vital one if we are to maintain our collective sanity.

To understand how the whole industry worked once upon a time, not so long ago, and why it no longer does work this way, it is useful to take a look at a few of its nuts and bolts. In order to do that, it is probably best to begin with an overall picture.

First, to state the obvious, the book is written, then accepted by an agent who in turn sells it to a publisher. What goes on in the publishing house has been addressed in other places—suffice it to say the book is edited, jacketed, blurbed, and catalogued, then sold to retailers and wholesales. Some of what occurs inside wholesalers, discount houses, and chains once they receive the books, has already been described. Which leaves us with the part of the book industry I know about firsthand, the flow of books from the publishing house, via the sales rep, to independent bookstores and from there into the hands of the reader.

Perhaps the most interesting leg of the journey from editor to bookstore—because it's so little-known—is the pivotal role sales reps play in the book business. As a job title, the phrase "sales rep" is singularly unexciting. It conjures an image of someone who drives too fast, drinks too much, and worries about such subjects as sales ratios, return rates, and co-op pools; someone who carries around a cell phone into which she speaks far too loudly, using less than perfect grammar, while traveling endlessly on planes, trains, and buses; a corporate yes-woman who smiles and smiles and says whatever her boss or customer wishes to hear.

The book rep as a species does *not* fit this stereotype. On the contrary, reps tend to be overeducated for their job descriptions (Harvard, Yale, Columbia, and Princeton are the alma maters of a few of the reps I know well enough to be familiar with such details of their lives, and many have master's degrees, one or two, Ph.D.s), rebellious (otherwise, given their degrees, they'd be lawyers, doctors, or, in the book business, editors), and antibureaucratic by nature. They're a restless breed, easily bored, happy to be on the move, disruptive if forced into a mold or a rigid framework of rules. They're honest (in this business it pays to be), and they love books.

For a taste of that sensibility, here is how Harcourt rep John Hopkins recently described a day's work to his regional manager: "'Pavese personifies a death who attends us like an old familiar, a remorse or vice we cling to, an enemy beloved.' (*The Demon and the Angel*, Hirsch). These were my exact thoughts as I navigated my salesmobile to the first calls of the season, thinking obsessively about the sales challenges which lay ahead, objections to be met, goals to be achieved, agonizingly small and joyously large order quantities to be written legibly on multipart NCR forms, and yes, the envelope to be addressed to the order-processing department in Orlando, Florida, preparatory to the long, hazardous drive to the branch post office, followed by the triumphant act of actually placing the envelope in the proper slot. I was reminded of George C. Scott in the part of General George S. Patton viewing the aftermath of centuries of warfare, 'I love it so.' As the song has it, I had been looking for *duende* in all the wrong places. I was to find it lurking in the very activity of book sales, its Millerian denouement drawing ever near. (An extra order of Biggie Fries always helps me get through the day) . . . " (If you enjoyed this riff, you should hear his "bad poets" CD.)

Why are reps and the work they do so important to readers? Because every editor believes in every one of his or her books—or pretends to, which amounts to the same thing. Book reps are the oh-so-necessary filters that sort hype from reality, bring bookstores the grain, leaving the chaff behind for the discount houses, grocery stores (and chains, in my opinion). Book reps know full well that every book can't be miraculously good, that many aren't even sort of good. They also know what the area of expertise is for each bookstore with which they deal, and they become expert at matching the best books on their lists with the needs of each of their (many) stores.

Without reps, independent bookstores wouldn't exist. Publisher's catalogues tout every book as the best in its category, just as editors do. Reps read, distill, interpret, winnow, so that each bookstore ends up with only several hundred of the 175,000 titles published each year. They do this by attending sales conferences three or four times a year, where they listen to countless editors spouting off about each of the books on their "list" (those titles that a publisher brings out in a single season). Since most editors pitch each book as if it were the Bible, and since any given book is subject to return, it doesn't behoove book reps to believe everything they hear—if they did they'd sell every book on their list as if it *were* the Bible, convince us, the booksellers, to buy them all. But because we get full credit for returns, half of the books would be sent back to the publisher, and the reps would be docked half of their paychecks.

All of which is to say that book reps take what they hear from their editors with a grain (or a bucket-full) of salt, read the books on their lists, think about the bookstores in their territories (every publisher carves the country up geographically and gives each of its reps a chunk), and then match the books to the stores, just as, later, booksellers read and then match books up to readers. So, for instance, will the Harvard/Yale/MIT rep, Patricia Nelson, sell a book on the Urban Architecture of Japan to TKE? No, she won't even try. She'll sell enough copies at Hennessey & Ingalls in Santa Monica and Builders Booksource in Berkeley to satisfy her publisher. But what she *will* sell to TKE is *Painters and the American West*, a lively, lovely art book which uses the glorious Anschutz Collection from Denver as a vehicle to discuss Western art's ties to American and world art—because that is a book she knows we, in turn, will sell to our customers.

That's the role of the rep—to get into the hands of booksellers those books that are the specialty of each of the hundreds (there used to be thousands) of odd, idiosyncratic stores that specialize in this, that, and the other, to know their territory *and* their books well enough to do this with the maximum sell-through (even in the book business we use a few such terms) and the minimum of returns.

If reps need to know their editors, then book buyers need to know their reps. Remember the story of my buying binge during my trial partnership with my second would-be partner, Kristine? Granted, competing to see who could buy the most, spend the most in the shortest time, was over-the-top behavior, but the personality of your average book buyer is addictive at the best of times, and buying books is such an adrenaline high for most of us that we can easily be whipped into a feeding frenzy at the mere prospect of the next book by, say, Michael Ondaatje, Isabel

Allende, or Salman Rushdie. In the grips of this frenzy we don't always stop to ask how good (or bad) a particular book by one of the above actually is, or how saleable; we're like druggies in a crack house, and once devoted to an author, would buy all of their work in quantity if we could. Oddly it is the rep, the *sales*person, who frequently applies the brakes, telling us this is a lesser Allende (hard to imagine), a brilliant but dark Ondaatje, an unreadable Rushdie (actually none of Rushdie's books are unreadable, but some, like *Satanic Verses*, are more difficult than others).

The only other brake I know of, aside from our own knowledge and that of reps, is budget. That, however, is a concept most buyers reject out of hand, claiming they need the freedom to buy unhampered, that there is no way to predict what will appear on the next list, from the next house, no way to make an "open to buy" policy work in the book business. I, too, claimed this need for freedom for twenty-three years before finally realizing that if we didn't buy a new book until we sold or returned an old one, we could avert bankruptcy (better to come to this knowledge late in life than not at all).

CHAOS THEORY

Once the book gets to the bookseller the fun begins—and also the agony. A peculiarity of the book business that is perhaps appropriate for people who love, live with, the written word is the plethora of paper that is its chief characteristic—and I'm not talking here about the pages of paper in the books we sell. Each store deals with several hundred publishers. Each publisher publishes tens, sometimes hundreds of books each season. Every season each title is described in a catalogue, listed on order forms, on sell sheets, in publicity material. Each book must appear in *Books in Print* (computerized now, but the same idea applies), on wholesaler and publishers' inventories, and on our inventory system. Each listing must include title, author, ISBN (every book has its own standard book number), price, category (hardback or paperback, fiction or non, adult or children, etc. etc. etc.). Worse, each publisher has a different set of order forms, different types of invoices, different statements.

Nothing is standard. Numbers on statements sometimes appear in horizontal rows, sometimes in vertical columns; discounts are not uniform; some publishers charge freight and some don't; returns policies differ, and so do co-op allowances. All of this varies from publisher to publisher and from year to year inside a *given* publisher; if the reader is lost in all this, so, let me tell you, is the unschooled bookseller. It takes years, literally, to learn the ins and outs of the book industry—and I'm just talking the business part, never mind the glorious infinity of the books themselves.

The obvious answer to all of this industry-wide scatiness is, of course, the computer. And as you might have guessed, TKE was dragged kicking and screaming (or, more accurately, moaning and whining) into the computer age well after everyone else. When Barbara bought into TKE in 1987, we were still doing inventory control out of shoe boxes (well, not quite, but file boxes shaped and sized like shoe boxes). We'd sell books by writing down titles, authors, and publisher information on a tablet we kept at the desk, while customers cooled their heels—although they'd usually end up buying another book or two while they waited, so the system did have some advantages. We'd then ring up the books on the cash register, and at night, whoever worked would mark off each book sold on its inventory card and pull for reorder those cards that showed low stock quantities. Orders were made each week by sorting all the pulled cards by publisher or wholesaler, adding in the special orders, and calling each vendor to place an order.

It was actually an effective system—in some ways better than the computer, since Judy, who for years did all our backstock ordering, had the sales history of each book right before her eyes when she was deciding how many of a given book to reorder, how fast we needed to get each one. Now, we must click to three separate screens to glean that same information. But customers did have to wait while we wrote down titles, we had to do an annual inventory manually, title by title (groan), and admittedly there is an abundance of information computers can generate by sorting the data in different ways—sales by section, by date, inventory turns by section, by date—that our card system couldn't provide.

So Barbara and I went shopping (one of our favorite activities). We looked at computer systems at The Waking Owl, at Dolly's Bookstore in Park City, at BYU in Provo, and could see flaws, advantages in each system. We finally settled on one used by BYU, knowing that Linda Brummett was happy with it, and that we could get it serviced locally, so that we would *never* be some anonymous voice at the end of an 800 number begging for help from strangers.

Two months later, the computer company was swallowed up (so what else is new?) by a larger company in Philadelphia.

The trouble began before that, however. The system we purchased, which had been such a good fit for the huge BYU store, was inordinately complex for a small store like ours. Because it worked on PIC system instead of DOS, it was incomprehensible to anyone but the company technicians and required daily computer *programming* to keep it operational (hardly my field, or Barbara's). The system crashed time and time again that first month, and since our inventory was now on said computer, our business was in constant chaos. We were on the phone several hours a day at first, two or three times a week by the second month. Worse (from Barbara's point of view), the system needed a "restore" (whatever that means) once a month, the "restore" took five hours, and since TKE was open seven days a week, the only way to get it done was to start it going at 4:00 a.m. Barbara, for one, was not happy with the system.

We've made our peace with technology by now, have a new system that remains operational most of the time and gives us information—and speed—not available before. But technology is by no means a panacea. Convincing staff to access the information in their own brains is growing increasingly difficult as booksellers become more and more dependent on the computer. "You know perfectly well that John Steinbeck wrote *The Grapes of Wrath*," I tell one highly educated employee. "So, please, walk over to the shelf, pick up the book, and hand it to the customer who asked for it. Don't type the title into the computer as if you'd never heard of it. That's chain behavior. Chain employees may not know who wrote *The Grapes of Wrath* but you *do*. You've got a brain and a great background in books; that's why we hired you."

The booksellers at TKE do have great brains, as do most employees of independent bookstores. They also share a passion for books, a trait that makes booksellers, whether at TKE or in any independent bookstore, a great community to be a part of. And with or without computers, I like to think we use those brains, that knowledge and passion to good ends.

EVERYTHING YOU NEED

We're part of a larger community as well, however—that of the city in which we live. In a business sense we participate in that community through our charitable giving, yes, but through events as well, dragging our bookselling dog and pony show out into the public arena on a regular basis. At TKE we've always done events—author events such as you've read about in these pages, sure, but all kinds of other book-related activities as well. We do them in the store, in schools, at public venues. We have clubs and activities for children and for adults, sell books at fund-raising events (in a single week, recently, we sold Molly Ivins' books for the ACLU when they brought her to town, Richard Patterson's books for Utahns for Choice, and the Dalai Lama's books for the Mediation Conference).

Such activities are good for business, needless to say, and sometimes they make money in the process. We do so many of them that it should be old hat, nothing to get exercised about. But in fact, every time I do something that involves a public speech of any kind, however brief, whether it's a book presentation or an introduction, moments of personal terror are involved. Recently, I did a Mother/Daughter Book Club presentation that should have been a breeze, since I do such things frequently, usually capably. But this time I was dreadful. At the last minute they told me my presentation time was to be cut in half, so I tried to hurry—and ended up saying nothing at all, or at least nothing of interest, about each of the twenty-some books.

That was bad enough. But never has terror become a self-fulfilling prophecy more completely than it did when I was asked to introduce the authors who had won the awards at the Mountains and Plains Booksellers Association Awards Banquet. Piece of cake, one might suppose, since as an MPBA board member I'd been head of the selection committee, had read each book two or three times, loved them all.

I've spent days laboring over the introductions, especially the one for *The Blood Runs Like a River Through My Dreams*. The book had tremendous impact on me, both because it was wonderfully written, underhewn with blistering anger and passion, and because its author had had an adopted son who had died from his seizures. At night when we hold our son, when his seizures are particularly violent, we wonder whether he'll wake up or not. This book has made me face that fear more squarely than I had before and given me, somehow, new tools for doing so. I owe the author a debt, one I can pay by honoring him with my words. Instead, I fail to pronounce his name correctly. I try mightily. I meet him before the dinner, and at that time think I know how to say *Nas*disch—which, by the way is spelled NASDIJJ—can you see the problem? As usual, I've gotten it wrong. "It's Nas*degee*," he says with a soft "g" that makes the second syllable glide to completion. "It's Athabascan," he adds, "not an easy language. But don't worry. You'll do fine."

Ha. I took five years of high-school French and placed dead last on the list of those who made it into second-year French in college. Musically I'm tone deaf, and although I do fine with lyrics, I couldn't repeat a musical line if my life depended on it. My brain just doesn't seem to connect to my ears—who knows, maybe that's why I like to read so much.

During dinner I say the author's name over and over again to Bobby Sommer from Changing Hands Bookstore in Tempe, Arizona. Nas*deeeege*, I say, shaking Bobby's hand. Nas*deeeege*, he reminds me, lifting his glass in a toast. He says it again, while bowing his head in mock prayer. Nas*deeeege*, I repeat, bowing my own head, praying I can hold on to those syllables. I should be able to. There are only two of them . . .

I introduce the art book first, and do fine—it's a good introduction in fact. I've hit on a theme the author considers to be central to the book, and have delivered it in a firm (for me) voice. I can do this, I think. Nas*deeeege*, I tell myself.

But I get in trouble on introduction number two. It's a kids' picture book, and when I say that this story about a purple pig going west to find adventure speaks to children rather than adults, I think I'm paying it a compliment, *am* paying it a compliment by my lights (I'm not wild about children's books that use Faulknerian language to get review attention, but that kids find incomprehensible). The author, however, in accepting the award, assures the audience that adults, too, will like her book. Hearing her words I realize I've insulted her, albeit unintentionally, and for a long moment after she takes her seat, I'm immobilized. The silence drags out until I force myself out of my chair, paper in hand, and since I have no choice but to carry on, I walk to the podium, begin the first line of introduction #3. And when the time comes, I say —with a nasal a, a flat e—N*a*sgee.

I could have just glossed over my mispronunciation at that point. No one would have even noticed. But I didn't. I stopped and apologized. Knowing I'd put emphasis on the wrong syllable, I tried again, said, "Nass*geeeesche*."

Wrong again, I thought and said, "The lisp doesn't help, does it?" trying for a laugh, but just embarrassing myself further; I apologized once more into a deafening silence.

I went on with my introduction, then, but each time I came to his name I mispronounced it. I said Nas*disch* I said Nas*dije*, I even said Na*dd*ish, at one point. But not once did I manage Nas*deeeege*.

I still squirm when I think about it, even though Nasdijj was very kind that night, talked to me about my son, the bookstore, E-mailed me later on. Performance anxiety is a bad thing for a bookseller to have, since we're expected to sail with full confidence out in front of an audience, a radio mike, even a TV camera, to do so with alarming frequency, winging it about this author, that book. And usually we can. Sometimes we're even good. And sometimes we aren't.

FAMILY MATTERS

There are countless associations in this business for which one is asked to do workshops, sit on panels, introduce authors, sit on boards. There's the ABA, BEA, MPBA, and IBA (Intermountain Booksellers Association, now defunct, but active for the first 20 years we were in business). Locally there's VP (Salt Lake Vest Pocket Business Coalition, a group of locally owned independent businesses), The Chamber of Commerce, ACLU (self-protection in any community), NAWBO (National Association of Women Businesses Owners), along with The Great Salt Lake Book Festival, Writers at Work, Booked: Books Behind Bars (a literacy program for jails), The Humanities Council, The Literacy Coalition, The Arts Council. In addition, we do presentations for women's political, social, and gardening clubs; for book clubs; for meetings of the Stanford Club, PEO (an organization for women which has something to do with education, but don't ask what its initials stand for—it's members are sworn to secrecy, and even my mom won't spill the beans), the Town Club, the Alta Club, Boys & Girls Clubs, the list goes on.

Independent bookstores are a community resource, in other words. And community outreach is good PR, good for business. It is also something we do because we are part of a community. Sometimes it's hard to do, especially if you have performance anxiety, or are short on sleep or time, but we do it anyway. All of us do. And I've found that if you do give to your community, are an active part of your community, then they're a part of you, too. A comforting part when the chips are down. And the chips were down for us, not long ago.

A couple of years after I bought the building that houses TKE, I went to city hall to apply for a parking variance. I jumped through incredible hoops (city government being what it is) before obtaining the variance, which allowed a restaurant to be built behind us. For eighteen years this restaurant (now Fresco's) existed in one form or another, operated with a minimum of fuss, and provided our neighborhood and the city at large with a great deal of pleasure in the process—their food's fabulous. Then a medical student moved into our area from out of state to do his internship. He decided, after he'd been here a month or two, that he didn't like being close to a business that was open at night, didn't like the noise, or the fact that people sometimes parked in front of his house.

He complained to the city, and when they investigated and officially found that the restaurant was legal and did not violate any noise or parking ordinances (we do, after all, live in a city, so no one owns the streets, and the nights aren't ever entirely still, even in Utah), said neighbor descended into the bowels of city hall and researched old zoning variances—including the one obtained by yours truly in 1977. After some study, he hired an attorney and appealed the legality of the variance. Before we knew it, a hearing had been called before the city's Board of Adjustment, and the fate of both our businesses (since they co-exist in one building using one variance) was mortally threatened.

"How can they *do* this," I fume to my husband.

"Anyone can sue anyone about anything," he tells me, and when I rail at him that they shouldn't be able to, that it's not right, he says, "Only when you're the one being sued."

Since my husband has also told me only a fool is represented by her spouse, I hire a lawyer. Then I call customers, especially those who live in our neighborhood, and I write a defense of our position. After that, I wait in absolute terror. What if no one bothers to show up in our defense? What if the opposing attorney twists facts, makes two businesses that are in legal compliance, are long-standing members of their neighborhood and community, look as if they are merely nuisances? What if they make us change our hours, scale back our operations? They could drive us out of business, close us down.

The room is packed. Standing room only. For once I don't have performance anxiety and deliver my speech with absolute conviction, outraged that one man's complaints can throw into doubt the right of two long-time business owners to exist. What's the matter with city government, I want to know. Don't businesses have *any* rights? Each person that stands up echoes that question. Aside from the intern, his wife, and one other neighbor, everyone there wants to testify in our favor. Some are frequenters of the restaurant. Most shop at the bookstore. And everyone wants, *demands*, to know how the rights of someone who has just moved to town, moved into a situation that had existed for years before he arrived, dares to throw such turmoil into the midst of our community. Everyone there says something about the role that the store and the restaurant have played in the fabric of their lives. TKE had done book fairs in the schools of almost every one of their children, helped libraries buy books, given books and gift certificates again and again to the charities they support, read to their kids at story hour (we've had a weekend story hour at TKE for years), recommended books to see them through divorce, death, child-bearing, child-rearing, mid-life crises, or to simply make their vacations memorable for more than the scenery. The outpouring of support and affection is overwhelming, and suddenly the kaleidoscope of life shifts into a lovely pattern for us, makes sense, in a new way, of what we all do.

Aside from being moved, I am also impressed. People who buy books are so *smart*. One after another they give articulate, impassioned, sometimes witty testimony on our behalf. And one long-time customer, Steve Prescott, a doctor by trade, sums the whole thing up much more effectively than any of the lawyers, making the point that this isn't about justice, about law upholding justice, which is what our judicial system is supposed to do, but rather about one individual who dislikes a business attempting to use law as a weapon against that business, trying to manipulate an old regulation in order to pursue a vendetta—that to allow him to do so would subvert justice and harm the entire community in the process, since the businesses are valuable and long-standing members of that community.

Thank you to Steve Prescott. Thanks to everyone who came that day. For making sense of this community we're all part of and for underlining our connection to it and to one another. For getting to the heart of the matter.

The phrase "sense of place," so commonly used to describe literature grounded in nature, could as aptly be used to describe community, since (as I have said before) one landscape is as important to our lives as is the other. And if we need community as much as we do nature, it seems logical by extension that the proliferation of chains and dot-com retailers and the consequent loss of local business is as harmful to the world we all live in as is the depredation of our environment—that the movement toward global economics, with its inevitable erasure of the locally owned, of communal connection, is destructive in more ways than we can presently imagine.

BRAVE NEW WORLD

In addition to serving as community resources, being integral members of their communities, booksellers have a community of their own. Each region has an organization invested in saving the collective hides of its members, and the ABA (American Booksellers Association) is trying to do so on a national scale. It's an organization committed to not just advocacy, however, but to education as well, offering all manner of publications, panels, and seminars to further the success of independent booksellers in this changing world we face. Almost every independent bookseller in the country, including myself, belongs to ABA. In the past few years the ABA has filed lawsuits against publishers and national chains to level the playing field between independents and chain bookstores. It has also started Book Sense and BookSense.com.

Book Sense, "Bookstores for Independent Minds," was begun by the raucous group of Northern California booksellers who have been at the forefront of activist resistance to "corporate" (read: large national chains) bookselling since the first so-called superstore opened. ABA took the Book Sense idea and ran with it, forming a national network of over 1,200 member-booksellers, many of whom contribute to a national bestseller list, a national list of new recommendations from forthcoming titles (books that have not yet been released, or are just hitting the shelves in bookstores) called Book Sense Picks, and a gift-card network in which gift cards purchased at any Book Sense store are redeemable at any other Book Sense store nationwide, as well as online through BookSense.com.

Why is all of this important? The Book Sense bestseller list provides a perfect answer. Most bestseller lists are compiled from sales of reporting stores *and* from sales of wholesalers—and yes, this means counting the same book twice. Not only that, but since wholesalers do not sell to readers but to other stores, and since the majority of the books they sell go to chains, the resultant "bestseller lists" report *not* figures that describe the book purchases of a cross-section of *readers* across the country, but rather a list of what chains *want* readers to buy (i.e., what chains chose to rack and stack up—and then, as often than not, return, unsold, to the publisher). Sometimes, the hype generated by the appearance of those books (which, remember, have not yet been sold to readers and are not officially on sale at all) on the bestseller list may become a self-fulfilling prophesy, and voila, the book *becomes* a bestseller before it has officially been published—a fact which irrefutably proves that it was not readers who put it there.

Feel duped? You should.

Book Sense is an anodyne to this duping process—a list of books that *are* bestsellers because people in independent stores all across the country actually *bought* the books and took them home to read. The result is a quality list, too, since readers by and large have excellent taste. One need only compare recent lists from both Book Sense and *The New York Times* to see what I mean.

Book Sense also created the unique "Book Sense Picks"—a testament to just how much booksellers love to read and recommend new titles. The galleys we receive, fight over, and divvy up we *really do read*—not just at TKE but at independent stores everywhere. Collectively, we have great taste in books, and we put quality before the bottom line, choosing books we like, rather than trying to guess which ones will be "commercial." The nuggets we find are reported not just individually to each store's customers via newsletters, but to Book Sense so that they can craft the latest "Picks" list—which is created every month by culling out brand-new books (many by new authors or from small presses ignored by others) that independent booksellers liked well enough to review.

BookSense.com is a website where readers see the Book Sense Picks and Bestseller lists, and, more importantly, find local independent bookstores that are Book Sense members. Users simply input a zip code and are shown a list of participating stores nearby. The site also allows bibliophiles to find the websites of Book Sense stores (to shop online) and stores that accept the popular Book Sense gift cards. The BookSense.com project is an effort by independents to come up with a system that uses the Internet effectively and inexpensively in order to service customers in cyberspace.

CROSSING TO SAFETY

I'm sitting in a meeting in Phoenix, Arizona, a meeting called by the ABA and Book Expo America (BEA)—the company that puts on the book industry's national trade show. (In the 1990s the ABA sold the trade show in order to focus more directly on programs to benefit booksellers.) The purpose of the day's meeting is to help decide which authors will appear for the trade show breakfasts (one thousand people, mostly booksellers, attend each one). Every breakfast is to have three speakers, and the list of possibilities as submitted by publishers is 44 pages long. As we scan down a page, Emoke b'racz from Malaprops in North Carolina says in an accent originating somewhere west of the Ukraine and south of Washington D.C., "Isabel Allende is a *for sure*, as far as I'm concerned." Gayle Shanks from Changing Hands in Phoenix nods, and so do I. Across the table, Richard Howorth from Square Books in Oxford, Mississippi agrees, but Miriam Sonz from Powell's in Portland raises an eyebrow. A nonfiction buyer with a penchant for the political, she clearly feels that fiction is already hogging the limelight. We bandy names about: Queen Noor, Peter Matthiessen, Dan Rather, Joyce Carol Oates, Quincy Jones. Everyone nods agreement at Peter Matthiessen; he'll fill the slot at the second breakfast that Allende will fill at the first. But what about the glitz?

What *about* the glitz, I wonder. How can you get glitzier than Isabel Allende or Peter Matthiessen? BEA officials don't see it that way, though, and they wonder aloud about the possibility of Rodney Dangerfield. We groan.

Dan Rather?

Silence.

Wynton Marsalis?

This brings nods again, especially when a Saturday night concert is suggested in addition to the breakfast. We've got our "big three," now, but who do we put with them? As we negotiate our way through celebrity names, complaining at the paucity of literary choices, cracking jokes about some, it becomes increasingly apparent to me, attending this meeting for the first time, just how broad the base of knowledge in the room, how passionate the feelings of each person at the table. These are the people who buy books for some of the best independent bookstores in the country, and I can see their abiding love for books quiver in the air as one or another throws out an opinion for or against this or that author. They're not just talking to say something, they *know* whereof they speak. They've read previous books by all the authors represented (with the exception of a movie star or two), thought about them, reviewed them, sold or chosen not to sell them, and they feel passionately about each and every one.

Carl Lennertz (formerly of Book Sense) exemplifies the same mix of passion and prejudice, knowledge and enthusiasm. I am standing with him on the floor of Changing Hands Bookstore that evening, and we're deep in conversation about the new Ondaatje—until, as we near the mystery section, Carl pulls out the latest Michael Connelly, asking me whether I've read it. I haven't, I tell him, but I will, and I grab *A Drink Before the War*, the debut mystery novel by Dennis Lehane. He hasn't read that one, and I begin enthusing about *Mystic River* (Lehane's most recent book at that time). Carl then asks if I've read Alan Furst's books, which I have. On we go like two drunks, reeling around the store pulling books off the shelves willy nilly, enthusing about this one, panning that one. Our eyes start to glitter, our pulses to pound . . . No, we're not falling in love, we're just booksellers doing what we love most. We exchange E-mails the next week. "Nice to meet a fellow book nut," we both agree.

At another such meeting two years later, I bump into Mark Nichols, also from Book Sense. We enthuse about Richard Powers' new novel, *The Time of Our Singing*, which we both love, and agree that it, along with *Atonement*, by Ian McEwan, Rohinton Mistry's *Family Matters,* and William Trevor's *The Story of Lucy Gault* are the best of that year's crop of novels. Less boisterous than Carl, Mark speaks of the books he loves with quiet passion; his knowledge of books is staggering. He has a long history of bookselling in his past and has spent the majority of a lifetime working with, devoted to, books. The same is true of the rest of the Book Sense staff.

And that's why we're going to succeed against all odds, against the best efforts of corporate America. Because as booksellers, we're a community engaged in the business of books—a business that is both an art and a calling.

LATE NIGHT DOUBTS WHILE WATCHING MY SON

Back arched, Nick cants his head left, as if listening. His eyes moon sideways, but only part way, and when I say, "Breathe," there's a pause as though he wants to look back at me. "Breathe," I say again, and then his eyes do shift toward me—only slightly, yet I can tell he's trying to focus, and "Breathe," I tell him again. He doesn't, but his eyes still strain in my direction, his hand, though stiff, doesn't flail, and we hang like that, on the tip of the seizure, fighting the descent, trying to find purchase in reality.

This earth feels a little like that to me as I add yet another paragraph. September 11th has long since come and gone and the world is in seizure, buckled by the misfiring currents of war, of fundamentalist mania and of patriotism-gone-mad, forced to assume a shape that beggars sanity, denies all compassion. Yet I tell myself that if we all hang on, breathe, focus our collective consciousness on what's good about humanity, on the individual roles we each play in our common history, maybe we'll survive this nightmare we seem bent on creating for ourselves. And I can't help but feel that in some essential way the business of books, books themselves, are a part of an attempt to focus: another a way of breathing.

Book Lists

10 Books From Inside the Book Business

1. *Cody's Books: The Life and Times of a Berkeley Bookstore*, Pat Cody and Fred Cody, 1992
2. *This Business of Books: A Complete Overview of the Industry from Concept Through Sales*, Claudia Suzanne, 1995
3. *Old Books, Rare Friends: Two Literary Sleuths and Their Shared Passion*, Leona Rostenberg and Madeline Stern, 1997
4. *Used and Rare, Travel in the Book World*, Lawrence and Nancy Goldstone, 1997
5. *Bookstore: The Life and Times of Jeannette Watson and Books & Co.*, Lynne Tillman, 1999
6. *The Business of Books: How the International Conglomerates Took Over Publishing and Changed the Way We Read*, Andre Schiffrin, 1999
7. *The Forest for the Trees: An Editor's Advice to Writers*, Betsy Lerner, 2000
8. *The Book Business: Publishing Past, Present, and Future*, Jason Epstein, 2001
9. *Making the List: A Cultural History of the Bestseller List 1900-1999*, Michael Korda, 2001
10. *Stet: An Editor's Life*, Diane Athill, 2001

25 Books From Inside Community and Business

1. *Soul of a New Machine*, Tracey Kidder, 1981
2. *Growing a Business*, Paul Hawken, 1987
3. *Servant Leadership*, Paul Stevens, 1990
4. *The Republic of Tea*, Bill Rosenszeig, 1992
5. *Getting to Yes*, John Bradshaw, 1992
6. *No Thanks, I'm Just Looking*, Harry Friedman, 1992
7. *The Great Game of Business*, Jack Stack, 1994
8. *Leadership and the New Science*, Margaret Wheatley, 1994
9. *When the Canary Stops Singing* (women in biz) Pat Barrenthe, 1994
10. *Up Against the Wal-Marts: How Your Business Can Prosper in the Shadow of Retail Giants*, Don Taylor and Jeanne Archer, 1994

11. *City Comforts: How to Build an Urban Village*, David Sucher, 1994
12. *Soul of a Business*, Charles Garfield (ed.), 1997
13. *The City After the Automobile*, Moshe Safdie, 1997
14. *Changing Places: Rebuilding Community in an Age of Sprawl,* Richard Moe and Carter Wilkie, 1997
15. *Who Moved My Cheese: An Amazing Way to Deal Wwith Change in Your Work and in Your Life*, Spencer Johnson and Ken Blanchard, 1998
16. *Going Local*, Michael Shuman, 1998
17. *Natural Capitalism*, Paul Hawken, 1999
18. *The New New Thing*, Michael Lewis, 1999
19. *Why We Buy*, Paco Underhill, 1999
20. *Soul of a Citizen*, Raul Rogat Loeb 1999
21. *Slam-Dunking Wal-Mart*, Al Norman, 1999
22. *Better Not Bigger*, Eben Fodor, 1999
23. *The Hometown Advantage: How to Defend Your Main Street Against Chains Stores . . . and Why It Matters*, Stacey Mitchell, 2000
24. *Suburban Nation: The Rise of Sprawl and the Decline of the American Dream*, Andreas Duany, Elizabeth Plater-Zyberk, and Jeff Speck, 2000
25. *Ethics for the New Millennium*, Dalai Lama, 2001

Chapter Ten

HARRY POTTER AND
THE NEW MILLENNIUM

[
"From there to here, from here to there,
funny things are everywhere."

— DR. SEUSS, *One Fish Two Fish Red Fish Blue Fish*
]

[
"That is all very well, Little Alice," said her grandfather,
"but there is a third thing you must do.
You must do something to make the world more beautiful."

— BARBARA COONEY, *Miss Rumphius*
]

Who knows what's right and what's wrong? Maybe the whole book industry, or at least the independent part, is engaged in fantasy, in conjuring up an ideal world of books and of community that is so out of touch with reality it can't possibly exist—or last, if it does still exist. I hope that's not the case, but even if complete and utter catastrophe is lurking around some corporate corner, for now the book world is still vital, still vibrant, and while it is true that independents have lost market share, we remain the ones who read, who make the new and important discoveries in fiction and nonfiction, children's books and poetry—the ones who bother to look at the second novels of authors whose first books didn't become best-sellers and first novels by unknown authors. It is thanks to our mining of the still-rich mother lode of books that are published each year (and thanks to Book Sense for making our voices heard, sending word of our discoveries abroad in the world) that the industry continues to function successfully—at least if success is defined as getting good books into the hands of good readers. Title lists, while generally shrinking, continue to provide grist for our mills, and, for every large publisher that is swallowed by another, a new small press springs up, ready to fill whatever vacuum is left. The book world as TKE has known it these past three decades (almost) still exists. And one of the *best* parts of that world *is* the stuff of fantasy: children's books. The children's room at TKE is one part magic and two parts invention, mixed with the sorcerous skill of a madcap crew of children's booksellers, mostly mothers, who are themselves two parts magic and one part knowledge, and as creative as any of the authors whose books they sell. Lana, Marilyn, Janet, Becky, Margaret, Vivian, and Emily have made the children's room such a success over the years that all Barbara and I can do is stand back and marvel.

DRAGON *SONGS* AND DRAGON *SINGERS*

The first children's author to come to TKE for a signing was Arnold Lobel, a quiet, gentle man to whom fame over his recent Caldecott Award (for *Fables*) seemed more a matter for bewilderment than an accolade. He arrived at TKE in a rental car, was clad in one of the wide-lapeled suits that were de rigueur in the late seventies, and he lavished such kindly attention on the children who had come to see him that they fairly glowed with it. He was the perfect match for gentle Marilyn, who ran the children's room back then. She was utterly starstruck.

Marilyn had quite another reaction to our next guest. This famous author (who shall remain nameless in these pages) was unhappy with our every arrangement—insisted the table was wobbly (although it seemed solid and square with the floor to us), the pen inadequate, the room too warm. She refused to sign books or to visit with children until we secured her a new and "stable" signing table and a better pen (although if she had wished to sign with a fountain pen and considered only black ink suitable, we still maintain she should have brought her own). A hundred kids cooled their heels waiting in a warm line (she was right about the temperature) while she toe-tapped and stared at the ceiling, and we rushed up to the restaurant to borrow another table.

When Ms. Nameless finally decreed that our arrangements had passed muster, she directed one of us to patrol the line of small persons waiting so patiently for her attention and collect names on yellow "stickies". Another bookseller was to stand between our author's own royal personage and the children hoping to meet her, take each book from the eager hands of its owner, hold the book open to the signature page, the sticky at the ready. Nameless would then grab the book, sign it while looking at the sticky (heaven forbid that she'd engage in conversation with a child or even exchange a glance), then pass said book to our third staff member, who would blow her signature dry, close the book, and hand it back to the child. Thus, Nameless could preside over an entire hour-long signing and never touch the hand (or heart) of a single child. The children were merely bewildered, but we were neophytes then and we were stunned.

Tomi de Paola had a similar operating style as far as the mechanics of signing books, at least. He arrived at TKE in state in a white stretch limo complete with entourage. This highly trained troupe went immediately to work setting up roughly the same system for signing books that Ms. Nameless had employed—but to very different effect. Tomi was a genial man (as we could see from his outfit, which was multicolored down to the laces in his shoes) who *talked* to the children, engaged with each of them. The fact that he finessed the autographing piece of the visit with a slick system merely meant that he could spend more time twinkling at each of the hundred-plus kids who wanted to connect with him. He joked around with them, made them laugh, and they loved him. He was supposed to return to TKE a year later, but, alas, his publisher has a set-in-stone policy requiring two stores to participate in each city's visit, and the publicist couldn't find another store willing to host a signing on a Sunday in Salt Lake. Not even for Tomi de Paolo, author of *Strega Nona* and *The Legend of Bluebonnet*.

Eric Carle was equally organized, equally genial, and we were equally thrilled to have him at TKE; arranging his visit was just a matter of our publicist talking to his publicist. Jack Prelutsky, on the other hand, may in fact be the author we worked hardest to woo. He was scheduled to visit Deseret Book and a local children's bookstore in Salt Lake (not, thank the Lord, on Sunday) and Janet Lund, our children's room wunderkind, had tried for weeks to convince his publisher that he should come to TKE as well. All the publicist would agree to was a ten-minute visit to "sign stock" (to autograph the copies of his latest book that we had on hand, no customers allowed). The book in question was *The Dragons Are Singing Tonight*, a splendid collection of his poems, the subject of which was dragons, be they large, small, fat, or spindly, each one splendidly illustrated by Peter Sis. I had asked Janet if she'd go all-out in the kids' room, make it a dragon's paradise (I don't ask much of my employees, do I?), and she outdid herself, decking the room with dragon mobiles, dragon posters, stuffed toy dragons, mechanical dragons, dragon cutouts—she even had dragons eggs, made by her daughter Anna (then three years old), who had come to help (and to meet Jack Prelutsky). Dragons hung from the ceilings, danced on the walls, draped over the displays, and best of all, Janet brought along the dragon costume she'd made Anna for Halloween, complete with a green felt dragon head and a long green tail.

Prelutsky was enchanted with fey, large-eyed Anna. Anna, however, far from enchanted with him, was terrified—to her present-day chagrin since she refused to have her picture taken with Master Jack, thus losing the opportunity to appear with him on the dust jacket of his next book. He seemed equally bewitched by Anna's mother, Janet, with whom he flirted in an all-in-good-fun manner. He also flirted with Julie, and with Becky, from whom he ordered a hand-embroidered Dragon T-shirt (she made it up, sent it to him, and he wore it for the rest of his tour).

Peter Sis was Prelutsky's perfect foil, watching quietly, drawing gorgeous pictures on the books he signed, chiming in occasionally, if only to egg Jack on. We all had a wild and wacky afternoon, lost touch with time, and, as a result, the deadly duo was well over an hour late to their official signing at our rival's store. We should have felt guilt but we didn't. We felt instead a heady triumph, since Jack Prelutsky promised before he left that he'd come back to TKE. He did, when *Pizza the Size of the Sun* was new, and his visit was as successful as we'd hoped, although a far less joyous one. Jack Prelutsky was ill—too ill to be on tour, really, but stubborn enough to keep his promises. We were grateful to him and we did feel guilty that time. He should have been home in bed, not schlepping from bookstore to bookstore.

GUESS HOW MUCH WE LOVE YOU

Elizabeth Winthrop, whose *Dumpy La Rue* was named one of the ten best children's books of 2001 by *The New York Times*, first came to Salt Lake City on a signing tour when *Battle for the Castle* was new (she almost always includes Salt Lake City on her tours as she has a cousin here to whom she is close). The sequel to the classic *Castle in the Attic* (one of our favorite middle-reader fantasies of all time), this chapter book was eagerly anticipated by grade-schoolers, teachers, and parents alike. To top it off, she had two terrific picture books newly out that year—*I'm the Boss* and *Asleep in a Heap*. Elizabeth, who writes everything from books for toddlers to books for adults with equal aplomb, has a canniness concerning the toddler sensibility, a knack for combining a child's-eye view of the monstrous unfairness of life with charm and humor, which makes her picture and chapter books completely enchanting. As a consequence, she has an enormous and ardent following. And to top all of *that* off, we had just opened our new children's room, had poured the concrete on the adjoining parking lot that very day, so aside from signing books, she carved her autograph into the still-soft cement curb. It's visible there yet, as is the signature of David Macauley, who visited TKE on the same glorious day.

The Way Things Work was brand-new and had taken the country by storm the way few nonfiction children's books ever have. It was on everyone's list, adult and children alike, of the most coveted gifts of the year. His previous books, among them *Castle, Pyramid,* and *Unbuilding*, were classics of architectural wonder long stocked in TKE's children's room. Even better, Macauley (who has since won the Caldecott) was about as nice a man as one could dream up as a children's author: funny, kind, a wonder with kids. Elizabeth was equally divine, and we can't think in retrospect of anyone we'd rather have had sign our cement than the pair of them.

Actually, we wouldn't have minded a signature in cement by Sam McBratney as well. Sam came to TKE when *Guess How Much I Love You* was in its millionth (unbelievable, unless you've read the book) printing. He's Irish, with the obligatory red hair and accent, and talked to each and every child as if said child was his dearest personal friend. When his wife walked into the store, she looked around, clapped her hands and "Oh," she said, "a wee *cozy* place. Everything in America is so big. We'll come back here, we will, I'm tellin' you."

Demi's would be another autograph to feature in concrete. When she came to TKE, instead of talking about her lovely book *The Empty Pot*, she spoke with the children about the ways they might make their own pots full, asking each of them what they most wished for, wished to be, adding to their imaginary kettles the magic of their dreams. She also told a story Anna remembers to this day—of buying an umbrella (which she was assured was absolutely unique) at an Asian festival, only to see the exact replica bobbing toward her a few minutes later, held by the man who was to become her future husband. The children gathered around Demi like worshippers at a shrine, and I doubt any of them have forgotten that day.

Nor are they likely to forget Jan Brett (author of, among other things, *The Mitten*, *Wild Christmas Reindeer*, and *Annie and the Wild Animals*), who is about as nice a person as we have met, ever. As pretty as a storybook princess or everyone's memory of their first-grade teacher, Jan is married to a scrappy musician who plays the violin in the Boston Symphony Orchestra. Joe manages Jan Brett's appearances with finesse, measuring the length of the line of children in order to estimate how long it will take his wife to autograph her way through it, determining whether she will have time to draw pictures, personalize her autographs, or merely sign her name. Jan, meanwhile, in her element with children and adults alike, holds us all in thrall even as Joe keeps an eye on his watch and his wife's schedule. The two of them are the team from heaven, selling books by the buckets while they us charm utterly.

THE GOOD, THE BAD, AND THE GOOFY

A children's author who strikes a very different note to equally good effect is Jon Scieszka, author of *The True Story of the Three Little Pigs* (written by the wolf, who swears, evidence notwithstanding, that he was framed). When Scieszka read on the patio, children were laughing until they cried (so were their parents). His outlandish imagination and his ability to skew a situation slightly, thus making it wildly funny, have wooed a whole new generation of readers. His series of transitional readers collectively called "Knights of the Kitchen Table" are especially appealing to those hard-to-get-at boys who would rather play ball than look at books. Along with his madcap picture books, this series sells like hotcakes—and he's every bit as funny in person as he is in print.

So is Lemony Snickett (his real name is David Handler and I love his mysteries too), whose books tap into that same group of children who are (barely) ready to read chapter books. By the time they have whizzed through each book in *The Series of Unfortunate Events*, they are raring to go and can't wait for the next one. And like Scieszka, Snickett keeps them all snickering, in person as well as in print. One memorable moment from Lemony Snickett's signing came when he was teasing a small child; the child laughed right along with him—until suddenly she stopped, looked up at him, and said, "Okay, that was fun, but I've had enough for now." Suiting her actions to her words, she swished a hand through the air in dismissal and walked away on sturdy child's legs. Nonplussed for a second, he then grinned a huge grin, laughing at himself, not at her.

LOCAL HEROES

There are many other stories, other children's authors who have come to TKE—such wondrous chroniclers of the natural world as Byrd Baylor and Jean Craighead George; gentle geniuses like Allen Say, Avi, David Kirk, Tom Barron, Ted Rand, Jeff Brumbeau; and nationally known local wonders like Carolyn and Mark Buehner (whose picture books are equal parts cleverness and charm, from *Taxi Dog* to *With a Spoon Not a Shovel* to *Snowmen at Night*); Gloria Skurzynski and Alane Ferguson (a mother-daughter team whose mysteries, published by Sierra Club and each set in a national park, are bestsellers in our store every year, and whose individually authored books sell equally well); Barbara Williams (whose *Titanic Crossing* was a national bestseller and who is considered the doyen of chapter book writers locally); and lovely talented Ivy Ruckman, darling of all of us.

But my personal favorite of all the talented children's writers in this state is Ann Edwards Cannon, whose name you keep hearing in these pages—perhaps because she's one of my favorite people on this earth. And I maintain that the quality of her writing could be predicted by the quality of her parenting. The mother of five bumptious boys, she has always said that the divine secret of parenting is benign neglect. Ann practices what she preaches, maintaining a calm demeanor when the school calls to tell her that this boy has broken an ankle, that one has a shoulder out of joint or a black eye or a bloody nose. But she's long on empathy when it's really needed, recognizing the pain lurking behind a scowl, seeming to know instinctively when a tantrum has been sparked by anguish rather than a snit. She acts accordingly, meting out sympathy instead of anger when the situation so merits. She echoes this sensibility in her books, *Cal Cameron by Day, Spiderman by Night; Sam's Gift; Shadow Brothers; Amazing Gracie; Great Granny Rose and the Family Christmas Tree; I Know What You Do When I Go to School; On the Go with Pirate Pete and Pirate Joe;* and *Charlotte's Rose* (which won the Pen/Faulkner Award for its age category, as well as the Utah Book Award). Her writing probes, for all her humor, for the sore spot that motivates a child's or teenager's truculence, rage, tears. I've never met a person more fully acquainted with her own and others' vulnerability, or one able to explore as artfully the boundary between pain and humor, the way humor can flush the sting from a wound. Ann also recognizes that "magical" part of children's thinking, understands their easy assumption that they are the axis on which the world turns, the sorcery implicit in the wonder with which they view that world. Ann herself views the world with a combination of humor, empathy, and imagination. Who wouldn't like to be her child?

HARRY POTTER IN CHAINS

We sold more of Harry Potter V than Harry Potter IV, sold eight hundred copies in 24 hours, hosted a midnight pajama party complete with owls and snakes, sorcerers and witches. But the publication of Potter IV, *Harry Potter and the Goblet of Fire*, was one of those moments when readers, books, and booksellers came together to make magic in unforgettable ways.

The entire nation was celebrating on July 8, 2000, whole families sharing the thrill of a new Harry Potter, bonding over a book. And despite the best efforts of chains, superstores, dot-coms, and discount retailers, that Harry Potter Day was an independent booksellers' event. We had found Harry Potter, we had endeared him to our readers, and in the end, he was ours in the minds of the public. We were, at the time, as down-and-out as Rowling-the-welfare-mother was before she sold her first book, as down-and-out as Harry was when he lost his parents. We *were* (and are) the Harry Potters of the book world in some sense and like Harry, we were ever-resourceful, willing to try any- and everything in our fight for survival.

Initially, we ordered two hundred copies of *Harry Potter and the Goblet of Fire*, knowing it would sell hugely, but also knowing that the warehouses, dot-coms, price clubs, and other such outlets would go into a marketing frenzy of publicized discounting in order to cannibalize each other, burying the bottom line for everyone in the process. How badly would that hurt our own sales? We knew most of our customers would be loyal, but how loyal? We'd go light, pre-sell the book, we decided, take orders, plan events to which the book would be the ticket and see what happened. We opted, after much soul searching, not to open at midnight, since it seemed unconscionably late for kids (not to mention a bunch of over-the-half-century-mark booksellers), so we planned several breakfasts, complete with games, contests, treasure hunts, stories, costumes, and magicians. We also advertised drive-up curbside service for "Potter Pickups," starting at 7:00 a.m. The reservations filled up in the first week and our "hold" list grew past one hundred. It was time to order more.

We placed a big order with our distributor. The books would arrive by the 6th of July our distributor assured us. We called on July 1 and were told the same thing. We called on July 3 to make sure the books were shipping and were told they would go out that afternoon. On July 6, no books had come, and when we called we were told a few shipments had been delayed but had gone out that morning. We called on July 7, but couldn't get through. All day we dialed and heard busy signals. "Don't worry," Janet (our kids room dynamo) told us, "I've checked three times and they've sworn that everything is in order."

But I kept calling—until finally, at 3:30, I got a (bored) operator on the phone and furnished her with name, account number, and the date and number of the purchase order for the missing books.

"I'm sorry," a Lily Tomlin voice, slightly Southern in inflection, says after a pause during which she is presumably searching her computer screen, "but I don't have your affidavit on file."

"What affidavit?" I try to keep the panic out of my voice.

"The one you were told to fax us when you ordered the books."

"No one said anything about an affidavit. I know, because I was standing there when the order was placed. Anyway, I signed an affidavit with the publisher weeks ago, promising I wouldn't put the books on sale until July 8."

"But you didn't sign one with *us*." She savors the "us", doesn't even try to keep the triumph out of her voice. Gotchya, she's obviously thinking. And, just as obviously, she's enjoying the thought. "We can't *ship* without that affidavit."

"What—are you telling me we're not going to have the books tomorrow?" My voice has risen two octaves.

"That is correct, ma'am."

"But we called and checked three times. Three times you told us all was well and that we would get our books on time."

"I can't help that, *ma'am.*"

"I've promised books to two hundred customers. Two hundred *children*. You can't do this to us. You can't do this to them."

"I can't help that, *ma'am.*"

She says the "ma'am" with such relish I think I'll scream. Instead I ask to speak with her supervisor.

"Certainly, *ma'am.*"

I hear a series of clicks, followed by a moment's silence and then a dial tone.

One hour (of dialing and redialing) later: "Let me talk to your supervisor."

"What is this regarding?" (Different voice, same insufferable tone, same Southern accent, this one thicker.)

"An order. One you didn't ship."

"What's your account number?"

I give it.

"Your P.O. Number?"

I give it.

"That's a Harry Potter shipment and I can tell you from the sca'reeeen that you have no affidavit on file, ma'aaam."

"Let me talk to your supervisor. And please stay on the line until you're sure I've got her. I don't want to be disconnected again."

"Yes, ma'aaaaam."

After a number of ominous electronic clicks, I am connected with the supervisor, and an identical litany occurs. I assure her for the fifth time that we were *never* told that we needed to sign another affidavit, and she says for the fifth time, "But it was our *policy* to tell every account who placed an order that they needed to fill out and return an on-sale-date affidavit to us.

"Well someone on your end messed up then, because you *didn't* tell us about the affidavit. I know. I heard the order placed. The question is, what do we do now? We need those books."

"Without that affidavit . . ."

"Look, it's Friday. Tomorrow's D-day. The affidavit's irrelevant because with or without it, it's legal to put the books on sale tomorrow. Ship them now. Fed Ex them. This is your fault and that's the least you can do at this point."

"It's too late for Fed Ex. They've already been to our warehouse. I could get them out UPS . . ."

"But UPS doesn't deliver on Saturday. You know that as well as I do."

"If you'd called earlier . . ."

"I *did* call earlier. I couldn't get through. And when I finally did, one of your operators disconnected me. We're going to have hundreds of children descending on the store tomorrow, and what are we going to tell them? You've *got* to get me those books, damn it!"

"There's no reason to be vulgar."

"Yes there is. It was your responsibility to get those books to us and it's your contractual obligation to do so."

"If you'd like to file a compliant . . ."

"Why can't you just ship the books today? Call Fed-Ex, *please*. It's your responsibility."

"I've told you, ma'am, Fed Ex is gone. I could get them out UPS, but . . ."

"But UPS doesn't deliver on Saturday. We've been down this road; it's a Catch-22, isn't it?"

"Beg pardon?"

"Oh, nothing."

6:00 p.m. and I'm in tears. So is Janet. So is her daughter Anna, who is desperate for *Harry Potter and the Goblet of Fire*, and who's been told all two hundred copies have been promised to customers—that she'll have to wait until Monday. Julie says, "There are always the chains. They start selling at midnight and the books might be discounted . . ."

"The chains? The *chains*? But can we . . ." I reconsider. Why not . . . After all, as the cliché goes, all is fair in love and war. And between the independents and the chains, it is definitely war. "Maybe there'll be time to . . . " Salvation in sight, we begin to plan. Emily (who's 17 and doesn't mind staying up late) will make a few midnight forays, armed with her mother's credit card . . .

6:00 a.m. and Emily arrives at the store. Julie, Janet, and Margaret are hanging Harry Potter royal banners, hiding golden balls for the Quidditch treasure hunt, setting up the Honey Duke Candy Store and tables for breakfast at Hogwarts. The pile of holds is being carried to the curb, and the press is beginning to arrive when Emily pulls up. She hauls a box from her car. It doesn't look very big. "That's it?" I hiss.

"The good news is the books were discounted 40 percent. The bad news is they had a limit of 10. I went to three stores . . . "

Why didn't you call me, I want to yell. But she's young, she's stayed up until 1:00 a.m. traipsing from store to store and we have 30 more copies than we had before. "What time do they open this morning?"

"Media Play opens at 9:00."

"Okay, let's put the assigned names on the first 10 of these, put the rest out, and at 9:00, we'll get some more and pull the other 20 holds. Julie, do you know when the price clubs open?"

"9:30, I think"

7:00 a.m: Five employees are running the Hogwarts breakfast event, seating the trio of musicians dressed up as Harry, Hermione, and Ron; two are handling the curbside service, another the treasure hunt, two are scurrying from chain to chain gathering copies, while the last two (I'm one of them) work the desk parceling out the holds to people in the line that has formed and backed out onto the sidewalk. It moves forward slowly because so many of the people waiting are there for holds; we have to sort through two hundred names, a tedious business even though we've alphabetized. Everyone is smiling, joking, buzzing with excitement, kids and adults alike. Harry has eclipsed the Easter Bunny, one customer laughs. And Santa, another agrees. We laugh with them and look anxiously out the window. No books in sight.

9:09: Not counting the books that are on hold for people, we're down to two copies. The line is even longer than before and we move ever more slowly, fumbling with coins and bags, stalling for time. I hear a car squeal to a stop out front, glance out the window and see Emily racing for the side door, box in hand. I give the next customer in line, a small boy with anxious eyes, such a huge smile that he backs away a step.

9:17: Emily had managed to round up another 47 copies but even the chains are running low now. Five not-on-hold books left and the line is longer than before, still full of children with eager eyes and adults with foolish grins. Parent after parent jokes that Mom and Dad are in a constant fight over who *gets* to read aloud at night, rather than who *has* to, and when their kids say, "Thanks, but I'd rather read the book to myself," their parents say "No way, we'll read it to you!" Reading aloud, it seems, has replaced television as the number-one family activity.

I look at the eager, trusting faces of the children in line. Costco opens at 9:30. "Can I wrap those for you?" I ask a woman who is picking up three copies we had already held under her name. I know I'm only postponing the inevitable but it can't hurt to try. "Yes, that would be grand," she says, and I beam at her. With only one of us at the desk, the line will slow down even further.

9:47: A rash of customers has been picking up holds, so we still haven't run out. I'm handing the last available copy to an adolescent with acne and a pierced tongue, when Nancie pops her head around the corner. She's a bit wan, but she holds a thumb up and mouths, "70."

"Seven OHHH?" I mouth back, and she nods. I grin and so does she.

11:57: Seventeen copies left, plus a remaining 33 on hold. Customers in line are less familiar, no longer our regulars. Barnes & Noble stores have run out, they tell us. So has Media Play. No news on Borders. Susan Pixton, an attorney who moonlights at the bookstore to feed her book-habit, is listening to my tale of our hour-by-hour flirtation with disaster. "Do you have enough to last?" she asks.

"Probably not, but they gave Nancie a hard time at Costco, humiliated her. They wouldn't even give her a box to carry the books out in. She refuses to go back and I can't blame her."

"I've got a Costco card—I'll go. It would take more than someone at a price club telling me I'm buying too much to bother me. I'll be back."

1:15: Two copies left when in walks Susan with 57 more.

Result? An $8,500 day (only visits by Isabel Allende, Margaret Atwood, Jan Brett, or Jon Krakauer ever reap such riches), a couple hundred happy children, several hundred happy parents, and among the staff, a welter of conflicting emotions: joy, camaraderie, fatigue—and triumph. We never actually ran out of Harry Potter, and now, when the chains have run low or are out, we have a few left on hand and another two hundred due in from the distributor on Monday morning—the order they refused to ship us the day before.

We feel shame, as well, however; we have had commerce, *committed* commerce, with the enemy. It was an act of survival we tell ourselves, a successful piece of guerrilla warfare. But we still feel guilt. It was fun, though, we have to admit, even if a reminder that it is a not-very-brave-new world that we live in, full of chains, e-commerce, and corporate insanity.

The fact is, it wasn't the victory over the chains that we reveled in, it was the act of handing those plump green volumes, 700-plus pages each, to all of those eager children and their equally eager parents. We wouldn't have traded that experience for anything, would have done almost anything to prolong it, to avoid the disappointment we would have seen on the faces of the children if we had had to say, "Sorry, we're out of *Harry Potter and the Goblet of Fire.*"

We are, after all, booksellers first and foremost. And what's a bookseller supposed to do besides sell books?

BOOK LISTS
Children's Books Published During TKE's First 25 Years

35 Favorite Children's Picture Books

1. *The Grouchy Ladybug*, Eric Carle, 1977
2. *Bill and Pete*, Tomi de Paola, 1978
3. *Fables*, Arnold Lobel, 1980
4. *Miss Rumphius*, Barbara Cooney, 1982
5. *The Napping House*, Audrey and Don Wood, 1984
6. *Wilfrid Gordon McDonald Partridge*, Mem Fox, 1985
7. *If You Give a Mouse a Cookie*, Laura Numeroff, 1985
8. *George Shrinks*, William Joyce, 1985
9. *Polar Express*, Chris van Allsburg, 1985 (1985 was a good year)
10. *Weaving of a Dream*, Marilee Heyer, 1986
11. *Animalia*, Graeme Base, 1987
12. *Nativity*, Julie Vivas, 1988
13. *We're Going on a Bear Hunt*, Michael Rosen, illustrated by Helen Oxenbury, 1989
14. *The Mitten*, Jan Brett, 1989
15. *Rosie and the Rustlers*, Roy Gerrard, 1989
16. *The True Story of the Three Little Pigs*, Jon Scieszka, 1989
17. *Chicka Chicka Boom Boom*, Bill Martin, 1989 (another good year)
18. *More, More, More, Said the Baby*, Vera Williams, 1990
19. *The Empty Pot*, Demi, 1990 (and another)
20. *The High Rise Glorious Skittle Skat Roarious Sky Pie Angel Food Cake*, Nancy Willard, 1990
21. *Martha Speaks*, Susan Meddaugh, 1992
22. *On the Day You Were Born*, Debra Frasier, 1992
23. *Grandfather's Journey*, Allen Say, 1993
24. *Stellaluna*, Janell Canon, 1993
25. *Guess How Much I Love You?*, Sam McBratney, 1995
26. *Lilly's Purple Plastic Purse*, Kevin Henkes, 1996
27. *Fanny's Dream*, Caralyn Buehner, 1996

28. *Hush, Little Baby*, Sylvia Long, 1997
29. *Pete's a Pizza*, William Steig, 1998
30. *I Know What You Do When I Go to School*, Ann Cannon, 1999
31. *Olivia*, Ian Falconer, 2000
32. *Dumpy La Rue*, Elizabeth Winthrop, 2001
33. *Dear Mrs. LaRue*, Mark Teague, 2002
34. *Tree of Life*, Peter Sis, 2003
35. *Wild About Books,* Judy Sierra, 2004

5 Favorite Books of Children's Poetry
1. *A Light in the Attic*, Shel Silverstein, 1981
2. *New Kid on the Block*, Jack Prelutsky, 1984
3. *Joyful Noise*, Paul Fleischman, 1988
4. *Insectlopedia*, Doug Florian, 1998
5. *Amber was Brave, Essie Was Small*, Vera Williams, 2001

35 Favorite Middle Reader Books
1. *A Bridge to Teribithia*, Katherine Paterson, 1977
2. *The Westing Game*, Ellen Raskin, 1978
3. *The Indian in the Cupboard*, Lynne Reid Banks, 1980
4. *Dear Mr. Henshaw*, Beverly Cleary, 1983
5. *Mandy*, Julie Edwards, 1984
6. *One-Eyed Cat*, Paula Fox, 1984
7. *Ordinary Princess*, M. M. Kaye, 1984
8. *Sarah Plain and Tall*, Patricia MacLachlan, 1985
9. *The Castle in the Attic*, Elizabeth Winthrop, 1986
10. *Redwall*, Brian Jacques, 1986
11. *Hatchet*, Gary Paulsen, 1987
12. *Matilda*, Roald Dahl, 1988
13. *The Devil's Arithmetic*, Jane Yolen, 1988
14. *Number the Stars*, Lois Lowry, 1989

15. *Maniac McGee*, Jerry Spinelli, 1990
16. *True Confessions of Charlotte Doyle*, Avi, 1990
17. *Shiloh*, Phyllis Reynolds Naylor, 1991
18. *The Watsons Go to Birmingham—1963*, Christopher Paul Curtis, 1995
19. *Gooseberry Park*, Cynthia Rylant, 1995
20. *Holes*, Lois Sacher, 1995
21. *The View from Saturday*, E. L. Konigsburg, 1996
22. *The Daydreamer*, Ian McEwan, 1996
23. *Ella Enchanted*, Gail Carson Levine, 1997
24. *Harry Potter and the Sorcerer's Stone*, J. K. Rowling, 1997
25. *Shakespeare Stealer*, Gary Blackwood, 1997
26. *Shadow Spinner*, Susan Fletcher, 1998
27. *The Wreckers*, Iain Lawrence, 1999
28. *A Series of Unfortunate Events, The Bad Beginning: Book the First*, Lemony Snickett, 1999
29. *Esperanza Rising*, Pam Munoz Ryan, 2000
30. *Because of Winn-Dixie*, Kate DiCamillo, 2001
31. *Love That Dog*, Sharon Creech, 2001
32. *Charlotte's Rose*, Ann Edwards Cannon, 2003
33. *Goose Girl*, Shannon Hale, 2003
34. *Artemis Fowl*, Eoin Colfer, 2003
35. *Ida B.,* Katherine Hannigan, 2004

25 Favorite Young Adult Books

1. *Beauty*, Robin McKinley, 1978
2. *Jacob Have I Loved*, Katherine Paterson, 1980
3. *Tiger Eyes*, Judy Blume, 1981
4. *Dicey's Song*, Cynthia Voight, 1983
5. *Moves That Make the Man*, Bruce Brooks, 1985
6. *Memory*, Margaret Mahey, 1987
7. *Eva*, Peter Dickinson, 1989
8. *Weetzie Bat*, Francesca Lia Block, 1989

9. *Shabanu, Daughter of the Wind*, Suzanne Fisher Staples, 1990
10. *Amazing Gracie*, Ann Edwards Cannon, 1991
11. *Down River*, Will Hobbs, 1992
12. *The Giver*, Lois Lowry, 1993
13. *Make Lemonade*, Virginia Euwar Wolff, 1993
14. *Flour Babies*, Anne Fine, 1994
15. *Under the Blood Red Sun*, Graham Salisbury, 1994
16. *Catherine Called Birdie*, Karen Cushman, 1994
17. *Golden Compass*, Philip Pullman, 1995
18. *Unlikely Romance of Kate Bjorkman*, Louise Plummer, 1995
19. *Lost Years of Merlin*, T. A. Barron, 1996
20. *Whirligig*, Paul Fleischman, 1998
21. *Monster*, Walter Dean Myers, 1998
22. *Speak*, Laurie Halse Anderson, 1999
23. *Whale Talk*, Chris Crutcher, 2001
24. *Sisterhood of the Traveling Pants*, Ann Brasheares, 2001
25. *Eragon*, Christopher Paolini, 2002

WHAT'S PAST IS
PROLOGUE

W hether a single soul is lost in some personal perdition, or an entire people is imprisoned, story—in the form of memory, of hope, or of simple escape—can provide salvation. Stories are pivotal to human existence. So are the people who pass them on. Readers, along with writers, are the glue that holds human history together. Anonymous, ravenous—readers devour books. And they exercise judgment, read intelligently, almost by definition, if they do so with any frequency.

Readers are hard to please, and even harder to manipulate. Or at least the best of them are—and there are millions of the best around the world today. It was our faith in readers that gave us the courage to start TKE, to keep going early on when we began to surmise how little we actually knew about the "business" of books. And it was our ongoing faith in the constancy of readers' *need* for good books that kept us going when the book business seemed to be falling apart, dumbing down, malling itself into mediocrity as the "superstores" descended on us all like a plague of corporate locusts.

"Do what you do best," we kept telling ourselves. "Pick good books, pass them on. That's all that counts in the end." And although that might sound absurdly naive, it was true then and it still is. That's what makes the book business such a glorious occupation—the best one I know or can imagine.

BOOK LIST
25 Books on Reading Books

1. *Letters to Alice on First Reading Jane Austen*, Fay Weldon, 1985
2. *Reading and Writing*, Robertson Davies, 1993
3. *Where We Stand: Women Poets on Literary Tradition*, Sharon Bryan (ed.), 1993
4. *You've Got to Read This: Contemporary American Writers Introduce Stories that Held Them in Awe*, Ron Hansen and Jim Shepherd (ed.), 1994
5. *A Gentle Madness: Bibliophiles, Bibliomanes and the Eternal Passion for Books*, Nicholas Basbanes, 1995
6. *Reading in Bed: Personal Essays on the Glories of Reading*, Steven Gilbar, ed. (it would be even better if he'd included more women), 1995
7. *Ruined by Reading*, Lynn Sharon Schwartz, 1996
8. *The History of Reading*, Alberto Manguel, 1996
9. *New York Public Library's Books of the Century*, edited by Elizabeth Diefendorf, 1996
10. *Great Books: My Adventures with Homer, Rousseau, Woolf, and other Indestructible Writers of the Western World*, David Denby, 1996
11. *How Proust Can Change Your Life: Not a Novel*, Alain de Botton, 1997
12. *Old Books, Rare Friends*, Leona Rostenberg and Madeleine Stern, 1997
13. *Book Notes: America's Finest Authors on Reading, Writing, and the Power of Ideas*, Brian Lamb, 1997
14. *The New Lifetime Reading Plan*, Clifton Fadiman and John S. Major, 1997
15. *Ex Libris*, Ann Fadiman, 1998
16. *Why Read the Classics?*, Italo Calvino, 1999 (new translation)
17. *For the Love of Books*, Ronald B. Shwartz, 1999
18. *A Passion for Books*, Harold Rabinowitz and Rob Kaplan, 1999
19. *Lost Classics*, Michael Ondaatje et al, 2001
20. *How to Read and Why*, Harold Bloom, 2001
21. *The Book That Changed My Life*, Diane Olsen, (ed.) 2001
22. *Letters of a Young Novelist*, Mario Vargas Llosa, 2002

23. *Reading Lolita in Tehran*, Azur Nafisi, 2003
24. *Book Lust: Recommended Reading for Every Mood, Moment, and Reason*, Nancy Pearl, 2003
25. *Shelf Life: Romance, Mystery, Drama, and Other Page-Turning Adventures from a Year in a Bookstore*, Suzanne Strempek Shea, 2004

[APPENDIX]

RECOMMENDED READING LISTS
FROM INDEPENDENT BOOKSTORES
ACROSS THE COUNTRY

Some of these lists were compiled by bookstore owners, some by store managers or buyers, some by a combination of the above, and many aren't fully representative of a particular store's breadth and depth, but taken together they aptly illustrate the collective knowledge, the astonishing diversity, and the vitality of America's independent bookstores. The fact that they each interpreted the instructions differently illustrates another trait we all share—independence!

ANDERSON'S BOOKSHOP
Naperville, Illinois — Founded 1875

Children's
Elephant! Elephant: A Book of Opposites, Francisco Pittau
The World that Loved Books, Stephen Parlato
The Boy Who Looked Like Lincoln, Mike Reiss
Falling for Rapunzel, Leah Wilcox
Wake the Dead, Monica A. Harris
Wild About Books, Judy Sierra, illustrated by Marc Brown
The Train of States, Peter Sis
Baby Brains, Simon James
Jungle Gym Jitters, Chuck Richards
The Neighborhood Mother Goose, Nina Crews
Skippyjon Jones, Judy Schachner
Kitten's First Full Moon, Kevin Henkes
Knuffle Bunny: A Cautionary Tale, Mo Willems
Ida B., Katherine Hannigan
A Mango-Shaped Space, Wendy Mass
So B. It, Sarah Weeks

The Tale of Despereaux, Kate DiCamillo
Airborn, Kenneth Oppel
I, Jack, Patricia Finney
Eragon, Christopher Paolini
Wolf Brother: Chronicles of Ancient Darkness, Michelle Paver
Saving Francesca, Melina Marchetta
Luna, Julie Anne Peters
Double Helix, Nancy Werlin
Phineas Gage, John Fleischman
A Woman for President, Kathleen Krull, illustrated by Jane Dyer

Adult
The Miracles of Santo Fico, D. L. Smith
Last Days of Summer, Steve Kluger
These Is My Words, Nancy E. Turner
Point of Impact, Stephen Hunter
Snow in August, Pete Hamill
Population: 485, Michael Perry

The Persian Pickle Club, Sandra Dallas
The Devil in the White City, Erik Larson
Shadow Divers, Robert Kurson
Corelli's Mandolin, Louis De Bernières
Middlesex, Jeffrey Eugenides
The Many Lives & Secret Sorrows of Josephine B.,
  Sandra Gulland
The Secret Life of Bees, Sue Monk Kidd
The Color of Water, James McBride
Plainsong, Kent Haruf
The Lovely Bones, Alice Sebold
Empire Falls, Richard Russo
Ender's Game, Orson Scott Card
Angela's Ashes, Frank McCourt
Of Beetles and Angels, Mawi Asgedom
Mitten Strings for God, Katrina Kenison
Sacred Hoops, Phil Jackson
Life of Pi, Yann Martel
The Sparrow, Mary Doria Russell
Outlander, Diana Gabaldon
Birds without Wings, Louis De Bernières
Case Histories, Kate Atkinson

ARIEL'S BOOKSELLERS
New Paltz, New York — Founded 1971

Most Popular Books in the 1970s
Stranger in a Strange Land, Robert A. Heinlein
Slaughterhouse-Five, Kurt Vonnegut
The Masks of God Vol. 1-5, Joseph Campbell
The Hero With a Thousand Faces, Joseph Campbell
The Magus, John Fowles
One Flew Over the Cuckoo's Nest, Ken Kesey
The Whole Earth Catalog, Stewart Brand
Man and His Symbols, Carl G. Jung
One Hundred Years of Solitude, Gabriel García Márquez
Our Bodies, Ourselves, Boston Women's Health
  Collective
Be Here Now, Ram Dass
The World of M.C. Escher, J. L. Locker
The Teachings of Don Juan, Carlos Castaneda

If You Meet the Buddha on the Road, Kill Him,
  Sheldon B. Kopp
Watership Down, Richard Adams
The Foxfire Book, Eliot Wigginton
Fear of Flying, Erica Jong
Cutting Through Spiritual Materialism,
  Chögyam Trungpa
Gravity's Rainbow, Thomas Pynchon
Carrie, Stephen King
All the President's Men, Carl Bernstein &
  Bob Woodward
The Lives of a Cell, Lewis Thomas
Pilgrim at Tinker Creek, Annie Dillard
The Woman Warrior, Maxine Hong Kingston
Zen and the Art of Motorcycle Maintenance,
  Robert M. Pirsig
Ragtime, E. L. Doctorow
Even Cowgirls Get the Blues, Tom Robbins
Interview With the Vampire, Anne Rice
Coming into the Country, John McPhee
World of Wonders, Robertson Davies
Diet for a Small Planet, Frances Moore Lappé
Roots, Alex Haley
Fear and Loathing: On the Campaign Trail '72,
  Hunter S. Thompson
Moosewood Cookbook, Mollie Katzen
Gnomes, Will Huygen
The Complete Book of Running, James F. Fixx
The Shining, Stephen King
*The Origin of Consciousness in the Breakdown of the
  Bicameral Mind*, Julian Jaynes
The Thorn Birds, Colleen McCullough
The Road Less Traveled, M. Scott Peck
The World According to Garp, John Irving
Final Payments, Mary Gordon
Going After Cacciato, Tim O'Brien
The Dancing Wu Li Masters, Gary Zukav
The Uses of Enchantment, Bruno Bettelheim
Gödel Escher Bach, Douglas R. Hofstadter
The Hitchhiker's Guide to the Galaxy, Douglas Adams
The Snow Leopard, Peter Matthiessen
Sophie's Choice, William Styron
The Old Patagonian Express, Paul Theroux

Most Popular Books in the 1980s
A Confederacy of Dunces, John Kennedy Toole
The Clan of the Cave Bear, Jean M. Auel
The Right Stuff, Tom Wolfe
Stretching, Bob and Jean Anderson
A People's History of the United States, Howard Zinn
Midnight's Children, Salman Rushdie
The Soul of a New Machine, Tracy Kidder
Of Wolves and Men, Barry Lopez
The Tao of Pooh, Benjamin Hoff
The Color Purple, Alice Walker
The Mists of Avalon, Marion Zimmer Bradley
Ironweed, William Kennedy
The Name of the Rose, Umberto Eco
The Bonfire of the Vanities, Tom Wolfe
". . . And Ladies of the Club," Helen Hooven Santmyer
Iacocca: An Autobiography, Lee Iacocca
"Surely You're Joking, Mr. Feynman," Richard P. Feynman
White Noise, Don DeLillo
The Man Who Mistook His Wife for a Hat, Oliver Sacks
The Tao of Physics, Fritjof Capra
Lonesome Dove, Larry McMurtry
Maus: A Survivor's Tale Vol. 1, Art Spiegelman
The Handmaid's Tale, Margaret Atwood
Presumed Innocent, Scott Turow
The Songlines, Bruce Chatwin
Misery, Stephen King
World's End, T. C. Boyle
The Bean Trees, Barbara Kingsolver
The Joy Luck Club, Amy Tan

Most Popular Books in the 1990s
Possession, A. S. Byatt
Iron John, Robert Bly
A Year in Provence, Peter Mayle
The Prince of Tides, Pat Conroy
The Firm, John Grisham
All The Pretty Horses, Cormac McCarthy
The English Patient, Michael Ondaatje
Women Who Run With the Wolves, Clarissa Pinkola Estes
She's Come Undone, Wally Lamb
A Return to Love, Marianne Williamson
Bastard Out of Carolina, Dorothy Allison

The Shipping News, E. Annie Proulx
Nobody's Fool, Richard Russo
Chicken Soup for the Soul, Jack Canfield
A History of God, Karen Armstrong
The Bird Artist, Howard Norman
Corelli's Mandolin, Louis De Bernières
A Civil Action, Jonathan Harr
Angela's Ashes, Frank McCourt
Primary Colors, Anonymous
Infinite Jest, David Foster Wallace
Longitude, Dava Sobel
Cold Mountain, Charles Frazier
Tuesdays with Morrie, Mitch Albom
A Walk in the Woods, Bill Bryson
The Four Agreements, Don Miguel Ruiz
The God of Small Things, Arundhati Roy
Into Thin Air, Jon Krakauer
The Perfect Storm, Sebastian Junger
The Hours, Michael Cunningham
Colors of the Mountain, Da Chen
Girl in Hyacinth Blue, Susan Vreeland

BOOKS & BOOKS
Coral Gables and Miami Beach, Florida —
Founded 1982

Favorite Books to Hand Sell Over the Past 22 Years
Running in the Family, Michael Ondaatje
Continental Drift, Russell Banks
Waiting for the Barbarians, J. M. Coetzee
Miami, Joan Didion
Black Sun, Geoffrey Wolff
Cathedral, Raymond Carver
July's People, Nadine Gordimer
Memoirs, Pablo Neruda
This Boy's Life, Tobias Wolff
The Color Purple, Alice Walker
Aunt Julia and the Scriptwriter, Mario Vargas Llosa
The Sportswriter, Richard Ford
The House of the Spirits, Isabel Allende
Sylvia Beach and the Lost Generation, Noel Riley Fitch
Bright Lights, Big City, Jay McInerney

One Writer's Beginnings, Eudora Welty
The Corpse Had a Familiar Face, Edna Buchanan
Miami Blues, Charles Willeford
The Last Good Kiss, James Crumley
LaBrava, Elmore Leonard
Up for Grabs: A Trip through Time and Space in the Sunshine State, John Rothchild
Tourist Season, Carl Hiaasen
Going to Miami, David Rieff
Enduring Love, Ian McEwan
Interview with the Vampire, Anne Rice
Three Trapped Tigers, G. Cabrera Infante
Book Deal, Les Standiford
Florida Poems, Campbell McGrath
Tropical Deco, Laura Cerwinske
The Secret Names of Women, Lynne Barrett
Los Gusanos, John Sayles
The Blind Assassin, Margaret Atwood
The Book of Illusions, Paul Auster
Bel Canto, Ann Patchett
Emperor of the Air, Ethan Canin
Angela's Ashes, Frank McCourt
New York in the 50s, Dan Wakefield
Under Cover of Daylight, James W. Hall
The Known World, Edward P. Jones
The Clearing, Tim Gautreaux
The Volcano Lover, Susan Sontag
Breath, Eyes, Memory, Edwidge Danticat
Anywhere But Here, Mona Simpson
Dreaming in Cuban, Cristina Garcia
Light Years, James Salter
The Color of Water, James McBride
The Joy Luck Club, Amy Tan
Louisiana Power & Light, John Dufresne

BOOKSHOP SANTA CRUZ

Santa Cruz, California — Founded 1966

The Adventures of Huckleberry Finn, Mark Twain
Angle of Repose, Wallace Stegner
The Aran Islands, John Millington Synge
Beautiful Losers, Leonard Cohen

Billy Budd, Herman Melville
Curious George, H. A. Rey (children's book)
Declaration of Independence (2nd Paragraph), Thomas Jefferson
Epitaph for a Peach, David Mas Masumoto
Howl and Other Poems, Allen Ginsberg
The Lice, W. S. Merwin (poems)
Light in August, William Faulkner
Love and Death in the American Novel, Leslie A. Fiedler
My Dark Places, James Ellroy
The Old Man and the Sea, Ernest Hemingway
On the Road, Jack Kerouac
One Hundred Years of Solitude, Gabriel García Márquez
The Quiet American, Graham Greene
Refuge: An Unnatural History of Family and Place, Terry Tempest Williams
The Scarlet Letter, Nathaniel Hawthorne
Song of Myself, Walt Whitman (poems)
Sound and the Fury, William Faulkner
Snow Country, Yasunari Kawabata
Twenty Love Poems and a Song of Despair, Pablo Neruda (poems)
Two Years Before the Mast, Richard Henry Dana, Jr.
The Winding Stair, W. B. Yeats (poems)
Why Are We in Vietnam?, Norman Mailer

BOOKWORKS

Albuquerque, New Mexico — Founded 1984

Favorite Authors

Rudolfo Anaya
Jimmy Santiago Baca
Steve Brewer
Howard Bryan
Denise Chávez
Craig Childs
Rick Collignon
Jennifer Owings Dewey
James D. Doss
Max Evans
Nasario García
Kirk Gittings

Joy Harjo
Steven F. Havill
Joe Hayes
Kate Horsley
Tony Hillerman
Betsy James
Marcia Keegan
Barbara Kingsolver
Barry Lopez
Cheech Marin
Michael McGarrity
N. Scott Momaday
Tony Mares
Lee Marmon
Demetria Martinez
Carolyn Meyer
David Muench
John Nichols
Simon J. Ortiz
Louis Owens
Jake Page
Suzanne Page
Slim Randles
V. B. Price
Kit Sargeant
Connie Shelton
Susan Slater
Leslie Marmon Silko
Marc Simmons
Patricia Clark Smith
Mark Spragg
Stewart L. Udall
Alisa Valdes-Rodriguez
Judith Van Gieson
Pablita Verlarde
Terry Tempest Williams

BOULDER BOOKSTORE
Boulder, Colorado — Founded 1973

Recommended Fiction by Author
Desert Solitaire: A Season in the Wilderness,
    Edward Abbey
Flatland: A Romance of Many Dimensions,
    Edwin A. Abbott
The Long Dark Tea-Time of the Soul, Douglas Adams
The Ultimate Hitchhiker's Guide to the Galaxy,
    Douglas Adams
Getting Even, Woody Allen
The Iron Tracks, Aharon Appelfeld
Bless Me, Ultima, Rudolfo A. Anaya
Alias Grace, Margaret Eleanor Atwood
Good Bones and Simple Murders,
    Margaret Eleanor Atwood
Moon Palace, Paul Auster
Giovanni's Room, James A. Baldwin
Come to Me: Stories, Amy Bloom
Midwives, Chris A. Bohjalian
Water Music, T. Coraghessan Boyle
The Illustrated Man, Ray Bradbury
Something Wicked This Way Comes, Ray Bradbury
Startide Rising, David Brin
Lost Souls, Poppy Z. Brite
*Burning in Water, Drowning in Flame: Selected Poems
    1955-1973*, Charles Bukowski
The Master and Margarita, Mikhail Bulgakov
Cadillac Jukebox, James Lee Burke
At the Jim Bridger: Stories, Ron Carlson
The Genesis Code, John Case
Death Comes for the Archbishop, Willa Cather
The Mysteries of Pittsburgh, Michael Chabon
The House on Mango Street, Sandra Cisneros
Loose Woman: Poems, Sandra Cisneros

The Eagle Catcher, Margaret Coel

The Alchemist, 10th Anniversary Edition, Paulo Coelho,
    Alan R. Clarke (translator)

The Prince of Tides, Pat Conroy

The Archivist: A Novel, Martha Cooley

Microserfs, Douglas Coupland

Shampoo Planet, Douglas Coupland, Judith Regan

Sphere, Michael Crichton

The Best of Roald Dahl, Roald Dahl

Shark Dialogues, Kiana Davenport

Fifth Business, Robertson Davies, Gai Godwin

Corelli's Mandolin, Louis De Bernieres

The Charm School, Nelson DeMille

The Last Summer of Reason, Tahar Djaout

The Waterworks, E. L. Doctorow

Blake's Therapy, Ariel Dorfman

A Yellow Raft in Blue Water, Michael Dorris

The World's Wife, Carol Ann Duffy

*Alexandria Quartet: Justine, Balthazar, Mountolive, and
    Clea, Boxed Set, 4 Volumes*, Lawrence Durrell

The Invisible Circus, Jennifer Egan

Erasure: A Novel, Percival L. Everett

The Monk Downstairs, Tim Farrington

Birdsong, Sebastian Faulks

Yolanda's Genius, Carol Fenner

Faerie Tale, Raymond E. Feist

Unicorn's Blood, Patricia Finney

The Dangerous Lives of Altar Boys, Chris Fuhrman

Billy, Albert French

Roadkill, Kinky Friedman

The Meadow, James Galvin

The Aguero Sisters, Cristina Garcia

For the Sake of Elena, Elizabeth George

Harvest, Tess Gerritsen

Virtual Light, William Gibson

*The Simpsons: A Complete Guide to Our Favorite
    Family*, Matt Groening

The White Bone, Barbara Gowdy

The Museum of Clear Ideas: New Poems, Donald Hall

Snow in August, Pete Hamill

Chocolat, Joanne Harris

The Garden of Eden, Ernest Hemingway

Dune, Frank Herbert

Smilla's Sense of Snow, Peter Hoeg

About a Boy, Nick Hornby

High Fidelity, Nick Hornby

*Chasing Rumi: A Fable about Finding the Heart's True
    Desire*, Roger Housden

The Bone People, Keri Hulme

Their Eyes Were Watching God, Zora Neale Hurston

M Butterfly, David Henry Hwang

A Prayer for Owen Meany, John Irving

A Son of the Circus, John Irving

The Remains of the Day, Kazuo Ishiguro

Middle Passage, Charles R. Johnson

The Complete Stories, Franz Kafka

The Prodigal Spy, Joseph Kanon

Desolation Angels, Jack Kerouac

Sometimes a Great Notion, Ken Kesey

Carrie, Stephen King

The Year of Living Dangerously, Christopher J. Koch

Immortality, Milan Kundera

Slowness: a Novel, Milan Kundera

*Angels in America: A Gay Fantasia on National Themes,
    Part One: Millennium Approaches; Part Two:
    Perestroika*, Tony Kushner

Your Oasis on Flame Lake, Lorna Landvik

Lady Chatterley's Lover, D. H. Lawrence

The Dispossessed, Ursula K. Le Guin

Memoirs Found in a Bathtub, Stanislaw Lem,
    Christine Rose, Adele Kandel

The Fortress of Solitude, Jonathan Lethem

Einstein's Dreams, Alan P. Lightman

Cloud Mountain, Aimee Liu

Moon Tiger, Penelope Lively

Motel of the Mysteries, David Macaulay

My Little Blue Dress, Bruno Maddox

*Wicked: The Life and Times of the Wicked Witch of the
    West*, Gregory Maguire

Shadow Ranch: a Novel, Jo-Ann Mapson

Zenzele: A Letter for My Daughter, J. Nozipo Maraire

Defiance, Carole Maso

At Play in the Fields of the Lord, Peter Matthiessen

The Moon and Sixpence, W. Somerset Maugham

Blood Meridian: Or the Evening Redness in the West,
    Cormac McCarthy

Downhome: An Anthology of Southern Women Writers,
  Susie Mee
Fugitive Pieces, Anne Michaels
Focus, Arthur Miller
The Romantics: A Novel, Pankaj Mishra
Black Robe: A Novel, Brian Moore
In the Cut, Susanna Moore
The Man Without Qualities: A Sort of Introduction and
  Pseudoreality Prevail, Robert Musil
Moonlight on the Avenue of Faith, Gina Barkhordar Nahai
Mama Day, Gloria Naylor
Vurt, Jeff Noon
Bounty Trilogy, Charles Nordhoff, James Norman Hall
The English Patient, Michael Ondaatjc
Survivor, Chuck Palahniuk
Small Vices, Robert B. Parker
Italian Neighbors, Tim Parks
An Instance of the Fingerpost, Iain Pears
The Club Dumas, Arturo Pérez-Reverte
The Book of Disquiet, Fernando Pessoa
American Visa: Short Stories, Wang Ping
Grass Dancer, Susan Power
Gates of Fire: An Epic Novel of the Battle of Thermopylae,
  Steven Pressfield
Roxanna Slade, Reynolds Price
Heart Songs and Other Stories, E. Annie Proulx
Mason & Dixon, Thomas Pynchon
Ishmael, Daniel Quinn
The Fountainhead, Ayn Rand
The Trees, Conrad Richter
Half Asleep in Frog Pajamas, Tom Robbins
Jitterbug Perfume, Tom Robbins
Homeport, Nora Roberts
Housekeeping, Marilynne Robinson
In a Dry Season, Peter Robinson
Ride the Wind, Lucia St. Clair Robson
American Pastoral, Philip Roth
Ecstasy Club: A Novel, Douglas Rushkoff
Nobody's Fool, Richard Russo
Sarum: The Novel of England, Edward Rutherfurd
Sorrow Floats, Tim Sandlin
Kissing in Manhattan, David Schickler
The Reader, Bernhard Schlink

The Lovely Bones, Alice Sebold
Cock and Bull, Will Self
The Killer Angels, Michael Shaara
Sam Shepard: Seven Plays, Sam Shepard
Getting a Life: Stories, Helen Simpson
A Blessing on the Moon, Joseph Skibell
The Gary Snyder Reader: Prose, Poetry, and Translations,
  1952-1998, Gary Snyder
Mountains and Rivers Without End, Gary Snyder
The Man Who Fell in Love with the Moon: A Novel,
  Tom Spanbauer
Maus: A Survivor's Tale 2 Vol. Boxed Set, Art Spiegelman
Collected Stories of Wallace Stegner
Perfume: The Story of a Murderer, Patrick Suskind
Last Orders, Graham Swift
Follow Your Heart, Susanna Tamaro
The Secret History, Donna Tartt
Imagining Argentina, Lawrence Thornton
Adrian Mole: The Lost Years, Sue Townsend
The Holy Man, Susan Trott
Ladder of Years, Anne Tyler
Morality Play, Barry Unsworth
The Body Eclectic: An Anthology of Poems,
  Patrice Vecchione, Editor
Welcome to the Monkey House, Kurt Vonnegut
Brief Interviews with Hideous Men, David Foster Wallace
Fools Crow, James Welch
Little Altars Everywhere, Rebecca Wells
Trainspotting, Irvine Welsh
Harm's Way, Stephen White
Bellwether, Connie Willis
Written on the Body, Jeanette Winterson
The Waves, Virginia Woolf
When Nietzsche Wept: a Novel of Obsession,
  Irvin D. Yalom
We, Yevgeny Ivanovich Zamyatin
Germinal, Emile Zola

BYU BOOKSTORE
Provo, Utah — Founded 1906

Still Being Recommended, Still Selling Well
The Discoverers, Daniel J. Boorstin
To Kill a Mockingbird, Harper Lee
Walking Across Egypt, Clyde Edgerton
A Town Like Alice, Nevil Shute
This House of Sky, Ivan Doig
John Adams, David McCullough
Bird by Bird, Anne Lamott
Tuesdays with Morrie, Mitch Albom
My Grandfather's Blessings, Rachel Naomi Remen
Kitchen Table Wisdom, Rachel Naomi Remen
One Hundred Years of Solitude, Gabriel García Márquez
A Circle of Quiet, Madeleine L'Engle
Wilfrid Gordon McDonald Partridge, Mem Fox,
   illustrated by Julie Vivas
Collected Poems, Leslie Norris
Amusing Ourselves to Death, Neil Postman
Angle of Repose, Wallace Stegner
Refuge: An Unnatural History of Family and Place,
   Terry Tempest Williams
Punished by Rewards, Alfie Kohn
Night, Elie Wiesel
Recollected Essays, Wendell Berry
From Dawn to Decadence, Jacques Barzun
Pride and Prejudice, Jane Austen
Ex Libris, Anne Fadiman
The Poisonwood Bible, Barbara Kingsolver
The Princess Bride, William Goldman
Ender's Game, Orson Scott Card
Things Fall Apart, Chinua Achebe
Adventures of Huckleberry Finn, Mark Twain
The Grapes of Wrath, John Steinbeck
Bellwether, Connie Willis
Cry, the Beloved Country, Alan Paton
Mere Christianity, C. S. Lewis
My Great-Aunt Arizona, Gloria Houston, illustrated by
   Susan C. Lamb
And There Was Light, Jacques Lusseyran
My Name Is Asher Lev, Chaim Potok
Undaunted Courage, Stephen E. Ambrose

The Chronicles of Narnia, C. S. Lewis
Fugitive Pieces, Anne Michaels
Straight Man, Richard Russo
Chronicles of Prydain, Lloyd Alexander
Tacky the Penguin, Helen Lester
Homesick: My Own Story, Jean Fritz, illustrated by
   Margot Tomes

CAPITOLA BOOK CAFÉ
Capitola, California — Founded in 1980
* An asterisk indicates that the author has read in the store.

Favorite Fiction to Sell in the Last 25 Years
All the Pretty Horses, Cormac McCarthy
Atonement, Ian McEwan*
The Blind Assassin, Margaret Atwood
The Bone People, Keri Hulme
The Curious Incident of the Dog in the Night-Time,
   Mark Haddon
Dirt Music, Tim Winton*
Flaubert's Parrot, Julian Barnes
Gould's Book of Fish, Richard Flanagan*
Housekeeping, Marilynne Robinson
If on a Winter's Night a Traveler, Italo Calvino
July's People, Nadine Gordimer
Life Is Elsewhere, Milan Kundera
Long for this World, Michael Byers
Mating, Norman Rush
Motherless Brooklyn, Jonathan Lethem
The Mysteries of Pittsburgh, Michael Chabon
The Name of the Rose, Umberto Eco
No Great Mischief, Alistair MacLeod
Open Secrets, Alice Munro
Peace Like a River, Leif Enger*
Snow Crash, Neal Stephenson*
The Stone Diaries, Carol Shields*
The Things They Carried, Tim O' Brien*
Where I'm Calling From, Raymond Carver
Where Rivers Change Direction, Mark Spragg*

Favorite Nonfiction to Sell in the Last 25 Years
Another Place at the Table, Kathy Harrison*
A Civil Action, Jonathan Harr
Confederates in the Attic, Tony Horwitz*
Counting Coup, Larry Colton*
Don't Let's Go to the Dogs Tonight, Alexandra Fuller*
Endurance, Alfred Lansing
Foreign Correspondence, Geraldine Brooks*
The Haunted Land, Tina Rosenberg
Jihad vs McWorld, Benjamin R. Barber
King Leopold's Ghost, Adam Hochschild*
Maverick's: The Story of Big-Wave Surfing, Matt Warshaw*
Nickel and Dimed, Barbara Ehrenreich*
Parting the Waters, Taylor Branch
Personal History, Katharine Graham
The Power Broker, Robert A. Caro
A Problem from Hell, Samantha Power
The Professor and the Madman, Simon Winchester*
Refuge: An Unnatural History of Family and Place,
    Terry Tempest Williams*
Rowing to Latitude, Jill Fredston*
The Spirit Catches You and You Fall Down,
    Anne Fadiman
Swimming to Antarctica, Lynn Cox*
There Are No Children Here, Alex Kotlowitz
*We Wish to Inform You That Tomorrow We Will Be Killed
    With Our Families*, Philip Gourevitch*
What's the Matter with Kansas? Thomas Frank
Young Men and Fire, Norman Maclean
The Zanzibar Chest, Aidan Hartley

**Below the Radar: Great Books and Authors
That Deserved More Attention from Critics and
Book Buyers**
Country of My Skull, Antjie Krog
Death Without Weeping, Nancy Scheper-Hughes
The Debt to Pleasure, John Lanchester*
The Devil's Highway, Luis Alberto Urrea*
Emma's War, Deborah Scroggins
The Hiding Place, Trezza Azzopardi
Kalimantaan, C. S. Godshalk*
Letters from Yellowstone, Diane Smith
Looking for History: Dispatches from Latin America,

Alma Guillermoprieto*
A Hundred Little Hitlers, Elinor Langer*
Red Water, Judith Freeman*
The Sheep Queen, Thomas Savage
Marianne Wiggins
Susan Straight*

**Best of the West: Western Authors We Love Who
Have Read at Our Store**
Sherman Alexie
Mark Arax
Kim Barnes
Judy Blunt
Ivan Doig
Judith Freeman
Pam Houston
Teresa Jordan
William Kittridge
Craig Lesley
Barry Lopez
Gregory Martin
John Maclean
Muffy Mead-Ferro
Russell Rowland
Annick Smith
Rebecca Solnit
Mark Spragg
Thomas Steinbeck
Brook Williams
Terry Tempest Williams

CHANGING HANDS
Tempe, Arizona — Founded 1974

Fiction
The Milagro Beanfield War, John Nichols
The Dispossessed, Ursula K. Le Guin
Zen and the Art of Motorcycle Maintenance,
    Robert M. Pirsig
Humboldt's Gift, Saul Bellow
Happy All the Time, Laurie Colwin
Song of Solomon, Toni Morrison

The World According to Garp, John Irving
The Book of Laughter and Forgetting, Milan Kundera
Sophie's Choice, William Styron
A Confederacy of Dunces, John Kennedy Toole
What We Talk About When We Talk About Love,
    Raymond Carver
The House of the Spirits, Isabel Allende
The Mists of Avalon, Marion Zimmer Bradley
Ironweed, William Kennedy
Love Medicine, Louise Erdrich
Empire of the Sun, J. G. Ballard
Love in the Time of Cholera, Gabriel García Márquez
Ender's Game, Orson Scott Card
The Sportswriter, Richard Ford
Thomas and Beulah, Rita Dove
The Bonfire of the Vanities, Tom Wolfe
The Bean Trees, Barbara Kingsolver
The Emperor of the Air, Ethan Canin
The Remains of the Day, Kazuo Ishiguro
The Joy Luck Club, Amy Tan
The Things They Carried, Tim O'Brien
A Thousand Acres, Jane Smiley
Imagining Argentina, Lawrence Thornton
The Prince of Tides, Pat Conroy
All the Pretty Horses, Cormac McCarthy
The English Patient, Michael Ondaatje
Consider This, Señora, Harriet Doerr
Corelli's Mandolin, Louis De Bernières
The Risk Pool, Richard Russo
Snow Falling on Cedars, David Guterson
A Fine Balance, Rohinton Mistry
Ladder of Years, Anne Tyler
The Hotel Eden, Ron Carlson
Fugitive Pieces, Anne Michaels
Mama Day, Gloria Naylor
Birds of America, Lorrie Moore
House of Sand and Fog, Andre Dubus III
Jayber Crow, Wendell Berry
Interpreter of Maladies, Jhumpa Lahiri
Balzac and the Little Chinese Seamstress, Dai Sijie
Bel Canto, Ann Patchett
Morality for Beautiful Girls, Alexander McCall Smith
The Curious Incident of the Dog in the Night-Time,

Mark Haddon
Old School, Tobias Wolff

Nonfiction
The Lives of a Cell, Lewis Thomas
Working, Studs Terkel
The Woman Warrior, Maxine Hong Kingston
Coming into the Country, John McPhee
The Origin of Consciousness and the Breakdown of the
    Bicameral Mind, Julian Jaynes
The Uses of Enchantment, Bruno Bettelheim
The Snow Leopard, Peter Matthiessen
The Road Less Traveled, M. Scott Peck
The Dancing Wu Li Masters, Gary Zukav
Gödel, Escher, Bach, Douglas R. Hofstadter
A People's History of the United States, Howard Zinn
The Soul of a New Machine, Tracy Kidder
Of Wolves and Men, Barry Lopez
The Country Between Us, Carolyn Forché
Axe Handles, Gary Snyder
Paula, Isabel Allende
The Tao of Physics, Fritjof Capra
The Man Who Mistook His Wife for a Hat, Oliver Sacks
Gathering the Desert, Gary Paul Nabhan
A Brief History of Time, Stephen Hawking
Home Cooking, Laurie Colwin
A New Path to the Waterfall, Raymond Carver
This Boy's Life: A Memoir, Tobias Wolff
Iron John, Robert Bly
Refuge: An Unnatural History of Family and Place,
    Terry Tempest Williams
Genius: The Life and Science of Richard Feynman,
    James Gleick
The Book of Life: An Illustrated History of the Evolution
    of Life on Earth, Stephen Jay Gould
Naturalist, Edward O. Wilson
A Civil Action, Jonathan Harr
Longitude, Dava Sobel
The Spirit Catches You and You Fall Down,
    Anne Fadiman
The Professor and the Madman, Simon Winchester
The Orchid Thief, Susan Orlean
Where Rivers Change Direction, Mark Spragg

The Tipping Point, Malcolm Gladwell
The Blood Runs Like a River Through My Dreams,
 Nasdijj
Fast Food Nation, Eric Schlosser
Seabiscuit: An American Legend, Laura Hillenbrand
John Adams, David McCullough
Breaking Clean, Judy Blunt
Reading Lolita in Tehran, Azar Nafisi

CHAPTER ONE BOOK STORE
Hamilton, Montana — Founded 1974

Favorites (in no particular order whatsoever)
West with the Night, Beryl Markham
Indian Creek Chronicles, Pete Fromm
*James Barber's Immodest But Honest Good Eating
 Cookbook*, James Barber
Sometimes a Great Notion, Ken Kesey
The Brothers K, David James Duncan
The Way It Is, William Stafford (poetry)
Tough Trip through Paradise, Andrew Garcia
The Mouse and His Child, Russell Hoban
Riddley Walker, Russell Hoban
Possession, A. S. Byatt
A Primate's Memoir, Robert M. Sapolsky
Road-Side Dog, Czeslaw Milosz
Abbey's Road, Edward Abbey
The Watch, Rick Bass
Henderson the Rain King, Saul Bellow
Animal Dreams, Barbara Kingsolver
Jayber Crow, Wendell Berry
Endurance, Alfred Lansing
The Ascent of Rum Doodle, W. E. Bowman
Essays of E. B. White
Cross-Country Cat, Mary Calhoun
In Trouble Again, Redmond O'Hanlon
Mona Lisa Overdrive, William Gibson
Uncle Shelby's ABZ Book, Shel Silverstein
The Known World, Edward P. Jones

CODY'S
Berkeley and San Francisco, California — Founded
1956

Andy Ross's List of Recommended Summer Reading
The Poisonwood Bible, Barbara Kingsolver
Animal Dreams, Barbara Kingsolver
*We Wish to Inform You That Tomorrow We Will Be
 Killed with Our Families*, Philip Gourevitch
A Widow for One Year, John Irving
Gates of Fire, Steven Pressfield
Roman Blood, Steven Saylor
Lying on the Couch, Irvin D. Yalom
Straight Man, Richard Russo
Sick Puppy, Carl Hiaasen
The Flanders Panel, Arturo Pérez-Reverte
Berkeley! A Literary Tribute, ed. Danielle La France
Jasmine, Bharati Mukherjee
Season of the Monsoon, Paul Mann
Small World, David Lodge
The White Hotel, D. M. Thomas
Why Not Me?, Al Franken
Memoirs of a Geisha, Arthur Golden
Another Life, Michael Korda
Saints and Villains, Denise Giardina
City of Light, Lauren Belfer
The Killer Angels, Michael Shaara
Native Tongue, Carl Hiaasen
A Philosophical Investigation, Philip Kerr
Class, Paul Fussell
Snow Falling on Cedars, David Guterson
The Ends of the Earth, Robert D. Kaplan
I Should Have Stayed Home, ed. Roger Rapoport
The Codicil, Tom Topor
The Deal, Peter Lefcourt
White Man's Grave, Richard Dooling
The Robber Bride, Margaret Atwood
Stones for Ibarra, Harriet Doerr
The Pillars of Hercules, Paul Theroux
The Eight, Katherine Neville
Los Alamos, Joseph Kanon
Locked in the Cabinet, Robert B. Reich
Great Books, David Denby

Damascus Gate, Robert Stone
Doctor Generic Will See You Now, Oscar London, M.D., W.B.D.
Booked to Die, John Dunning
Brain Storm, Richard Dooling
Face Time, Erik Tarloff

CRAWFORD DOYLE BOOKSELLERS
New York City, New York — Formerly Burlington Books, founded 1938

Favorite Books to Hand Sell in the 80s and early 90s
A Wreath for the Enemy, Pamela Frankau
So Long, See You Tomorrow, William Maxwell
Hotel Du Lac, Anita Brookner
Not That Sort of a Girl, Mary Wesley
Winter's Tale, Mark Helprin
Ironweed, William Kennedy
Spartina, John Casey
The All of It, Jeannette Haien
Crossing to Safety, Wallace Stegner
The Counterlife, Philip Roth
Foreign Affairs, Alison Lurie
The Songlines, Bruce Chatwin
The Parnas, Silvano Arieti
A Dance to the Music of Time, Anthony Powell
Housekeeping, Marilynne Robinson
The Reader, Bernhard Schlink (handsold pre-Oprah)
Clara Callan, Richard B. Wright (a contemporary Canadian not the late great American writer)
Miss Garnet's Angel, Salley Vickers
When I Lived in Modern Times, Linda Grant
Ali and Nino, Kurban Said
A Month in the Country, J. L. Carr
Silk, Alessandro Baricco
The Emigrants, W. G. Sebald
The Curious Incident of the Dog in the Night-Time, Mark Haddon
The Crazy Hunter, Kay Boyle
The Transit of Venus, Shirley Hazzard
Achilles, Elizabeth Cook
The Last Life, Claire Messud
I, the Divine, Rabih Alameddine

The Question of Bruno, Aleksandar Hemon
Stoner, John Williams
Cold Mountain, Charles Frazier
Her Privates We, Frederic Manning
The Heather Blazing, Colm Tóibín
Memoirs of a Geisha, Arthur Golden

ELLIOTT BAY BOOK COMPANY
Seattle, Washington — Founded 1973

A Buyer's List of Favorite Books
The Business of Fancydancing, Sherman Alexie
Keeping a Rendezvous, John Berger
   (also his novels: *G.*, *To the Wedding*, *Pig Earth*)
News of the Universe, Robert Bly
The Way of the Animal Powers, Joseph Campbell
Where I'm Calling From, Raymond Carver
This House of Sky, Ivan Doig
Memory of Fire Trilogy, Eduardo Galeano
In the Heart of the Heart of the Country, William H. Gass
Braided Creek, Jim Harrison and Ted Kooser
Haboo, Vi Hilbert (A book of tales from the local Salish people by an esteemed tribal elder)
We've Had a Hundred Years of Psychotherapy and the World's Getting Worse, James Hillman and Michael Ventura
The Gift: Imagination and the Erotic Life of Property, Lewis Hyde
The Remains of the Day, Kazuo Ishiguro
Always Coming Home, Ursula K. Le Guin
Evening Train, Denise Levertov
Arctic Dreams, Barry Lopez
Beloved, Toni Morrison
Cities of Salt, Abdelrahman Munif
Reading Lolita in Tehran, Azar Nafisi
The Book of Questions, Pablo Neruda
The English Patient, Michael Ondaatje
An Atlas of the Difficult World, Adrienne Rich
Even Cowgirls Get the Blues, Tom Robbins
The God of Small Things, Arundhati Roy
The Essential Rumi, Coleman Barks, Translator
The Joy Luck Club, Amy Tan

Storm Watch, Barbara Earl Thomas
Sometimes the Soul, Gioia Timpanelli
If You Want to Write, Brenda Ueland
Refuge: An Unnatural History of Family and Place,
   Terry Tempest Williams

A Slightly Longer List of Favorite Authors
Diana Abu-Jaber
Nuha Al-Radi
Agha Shahid Ali
Julia Alvarez
Isabel Allende
Margaret Atwood
Paul Auster
James Baldwin
Russell Banks
Andrea Barrett
Rick Bass
Wendell Berry
T. C. Boyle
Bill Bradley
Rebecca Brown
Roberto Calasso
Peter Carey
Hayden Carruth
Anne Carson
Michael Chabon
Nien Cheng
Noam Chomsky
Sandra Cisneros
Jill Ker Conway
Edwidge Danticat
Louis De Bernières
Charles D'Ambrosio
Madeline DeFrees
Don DeLillo
Joan Didion
Annie Dillard
Michael Dorris
Roddy Doyle
Slavenka Drakulić
David James Duncan
Timothy Egan

Dave Eggers
Leif Enger
Louise Erdrich
Clarissa Pinkola Estés
Nuruddin Farah
Carolyn Forché
Richard Ford
Charles Frazier
Judith Freeman
Tess Gallagher
Cristina García
Gabriel García Márquez
Allen Ginsberg
Francisco Goldman
David Guterson
Jessica Hagedorn
Sam Hamill
Joy Harjo
Seamus Heaney
Jim Heynen
Bill Holm
Pam Houston
Pico Iyer
Jane Jacobs
Ted Joans
Charles Johnson
Edward P. Jones
Mary Karr
Yelena Khanga
Barbara Kingsolver
William Kittredge
Carolyn Kizer
Etheridge Knight
Jon Krakauer
Gish Jen
Ha Jin
Jacob Lawrence
Chang-rae Lee
Li-Young Lee
Jeffrey Lent
Vyvyane Loh
David Malouf
Micheline Aharonian Marcom

Peter Matthiessen
Nathan McCall
Cormac McCarthy
Ann-Marie MacDonald
Colleen J. McElroy
Ian McEwan
Terry McMillan
W. S. Merwin
Anne Michaels
Rohinton Mistry
David Mitchell
Lorrie Moore
Walter Mosley
Bharati Mukherjee
Alice Munro
Haruki Murakami
Gary Paul Nabhan
Jill Nelson
Kathleen Norris
Ben Okri
Amos Oz
Orhan Pamuk
Brenda Peterson
Caryl Phillips
E. Annie Proulx
Robert Michael Pyle
Jonathan Raban
Nancy Rawles
Red Pine
Rainer Maria Rilke
Pattiann Rogers
J. K. Rowling
Norman Rush
Salman Rushdie
Edward W. Said
Roger Sale
Marjane Satrapi
W. G. Sebald
David Sedaris
Vikram Seth
Shan Sa
Leslie Marmon Silko
Mona Simpson

Annick Smith
Zadie Smith
Gary Snyder
Rebecca Solnit
Malidoma Patrice Somé
Susan Sontag
Ahdaf Souief
Art Spiegelman
William Stafford
Neal Stephenson
Art Thiel
Robert Farris Thompson
Abraham Verghese
William T. Vollmann
Alice Walker
David Foster Wallace
James Welch
Rebecca Wells
John Edgar Wideman
Tobias Wolff
Yu Hua
Howard Zinn

FOUNTAIN BOOKSTORE
Richmond, Virginia — Founded 1988

1984, George Orwell
A Natural History of the Senses, Diane Ackerman
Candide, Voltaire
Strange Wine, Harlan Ellison (actually, anything by Harlan Ellison)
Hamlet, Shakespeare
Blue Belle, Andrew Vachss
A Farewell to Arms, Ernest Hemingway
The Sparrow, Mary Doria Russell
Susie Bright's Sexwise
The Half-Mammals of Dixie, George Singleton
The poetry of Byron
Ten Little Indians, Sherman Alexie
The Stars My Destination, Alfred Bester
The Futurological Congress, Stanislaw Lem
Winnie the Pooh, A. A. Milne
The Places That Scare You, Pema Chödrön
The Last Temptation of Christ, Nikos Kazantzakis
Animalia, Graeme Base
A Prayer for the Dying, Stewart O'Nan
Affinity, Sarah Waters
Stories of Your Life and Others, Ted Chiang
Fox in Socks, Dr. Seuss
Kitchen Confidential, Anthony Bourdain
Cod, Mark Kurlansky
Dirty Work, Larry Brown

THE GALAXY BOOKSHOP
Hardwick, Vermont — Founded 1988

Crossing to Safety, Wallace Stegner
The Canada Geese Quilt, Natalie Kinsey-Warnock
Stranger in the Kingdom, Howard Frank Mosher
Postcards, Annie Proulx
All the Pretty Horses, Cormac McCarthy
Smilla's Sense of Snow, Peter Hoeg
Sophie's World, Jostein Gaarder
Longitude, Dava Sobel
Fugitive Pieces, Anne Michaels

Corelli's Mandolin, Louis De Bernières
The Jump-Off Creek, Molly Gloss
In the Fall, Jeffrey Lent
We Die Alone, David Howarth
River Thieves, Michael Crummey
The Known World, Edward P. Jones
Eventide, Kent Haruf

HARVARD BOOKSTORE
Cambridge, Massachusetts — Founded 1932

All-Time Staff Favorites
A People's History of the United States, Howard Zinn
The Wind-Up Bird Chronicle, Haruki Murakami
The New York Trilogy, Paul Auster
The Crying of Lot 49, Thomas Pynchon
The Lord of the Rings, J. R. R. Tolkien
Jane Eyre, Charlotte Brontë
Lolita, Vladimir Nabokov
1984, George Orwell
One Hundred Years of Solitude, Gabriel García Márquez
The Catcher in the Rye, J. D. Salinger
Crime and Punishment, Fyodor Dostoevsky
On the Road, Jack Kerouac
Alice's Adventures in Wonderland, Lewis Carroll
The Brothers Karamazov, Fyodor Dostoevsky
The Age of Innocence, Edith Wharton
Don Quixote, Miguel De Cervantes
Perfume, Patrick Süskind
Ulysses, James Joyce
Anna Karenina, Leo Tolstoy
The Complete Stories of Flannery O'Connor
Cry, the Beloved Country, Alan Paton
Dracula, Bram Stoker
The Eagles Die, George Richard Marek
Emotionally Weird, Kate Atkinson
The Handmaid's Tale, Margaret Atwood
Infinite Jest, David Foster Wallace
Kitchen, Banana Yoshimoto
London Fields, Martin Amis
Moise and the World of Reason, Tennessee Williams
Movie Wars, Jonathan Rosenbaum

Paradise Lost, John Milton
Persuasion, Jane Austen
The Tortilla Curtain, T. C. Boyle
Visions of Excess, Georges Bataille
Where the Wild Things Are, Maurice Sendak
A Wild Sheep Chase, Haruki Murakami
Beloved, Toni Morrison
The Counterfeiters, André Gide
The Bell Jar, Sylvia Plath
The Blind Owl, Sadegh Hedayat
The Complete Works of Edgar Allan Poe
The Count of Monte Cristo, Alexandre Dumas
Dealing with Dragons, Patricia C. Wrede
The Earthsea Trilogy, Ursula K. Le Guin
Ecology of Fear, Mike Davis
Franny and Zooey, J. D. Salinger
History of the Peloponnesian War, Thucydides
How the Garcia Girls Lost Their Accents, Julia Alvarez
Kabuki: Circle of Blood, David Mack
Of Human Bondage, W. Somerset Maugham
The Satanic Verses, Salman Rushdie
The Sheltering Sky, Paul Bowles
Tristram Shandy, Laurence Sterne
The Well of Loneliness, Radclyffe Hall
The Wicked Pavilion, Dawn Powell
Collected Stories of V. S. Pritchett
War and Peace, Leo Tolstoy
Babel-17, Samuel R. Delany
Dora, Sigmund Freud
Empire Falls, Richard Russo
For Whom the Bell Tolls, Ernest Hemingway
Girl in Landscape, Jonathan Lethem
Goodbye to All That, Robert Graves
Ham on Rye, Charles Bukowski
Like Life, Lorrie Moore
Mao II, Don DeLillo
Random Family, Adrian Nicole LeBlanc
Revolutionary Road, Richard Yates
The Stranger, Albert Camus
Humboldt's Gift, Saul Bellow
White Noise, Don DeLillo
Atlas Shrugged, Ayn Rand
Bastard Out of Carolina, Dorothy Allison

The Days Run Away Like Wild Horses Over the Hills, Charles Bukowski
Delta of Venus, Anaïs Nin
Fast Food Nation, Eric Schlosser
Ficciones, Jorge Luis Borges
Go Ask Alice, Anonymous
The Hitchhiker's Guide to the Galaxy, Douglas Adams
The Iliad, Homer
On Photography, Susan Sontag
The Republic, Plato
Shockproof Sydney Skate, Marijane Meaker
The Society of the Spectacle, Guy Debord
Strangers in Paradise, Terry Moore
The Sun Also Rises, Ernest Hemingway
A Wrinkle in Time, Madeleine L'Engle
Dubliners, James Joyce
Breakfast of Champions, Kurt Vonnegut
No Logo, Naomi Klein
The Aeneid, Virgil
Ariel, Sylvia Plath
Charlotte's Web, E. B. White
Curious George Learns the Alphabet, H. A. Rey
Enormous Changes at the Last Minute, Grace Paley
The Heart Is a Lonely Hunter, Carson McCullers
Henry VIII, Shakespeare
I, Claudius, Robert Graves
The Lost Continent, Bill Bryson
The Master and Margarita, Mikhail Bulgakov
On the Origin of Species, Charles Darwin
Pursuit, Erica Funkhouser
Rosencrantz and Guildenstern are Dead, Tom Stoppard
Rule of the Bone, Russell Banks
Youth in Revolt, C. D. Payne
The Ogre, Michel Tournier
Things Fall Apart, Chinua Achebe
Angels in America, Tony Kushner
Days and Memory, Charlotte Delbo
Selected Poems of Delmore, Schwartz
Democracy in America, Alexis De Tocqueville
Fahrenheit 451, Ray Bradbury
Go Dog Go, P. D. Eastman
Johnny the Homicidal Maniac, Jhonen Vasquez
The Last Samurai, Helen DeWitt

Living My Life, Emma Goldman
Maus: A Survivor's Tale, Art Spiegelman
The Metamorphosis, Franz Kafka
Othello, Shakespeare
Siddhartha, Herman Hesse
Simulations, Jean Baudrillard
Slouching Towards Bethlehem, Joan Didion
Time-Life Pictorial Atlas (thanks, Churchill)
Written on the Body, Jeanette Winterson
The Deptford Trilogy, Robertson Davies
The Unbearable Lightness of Being, Milan Kundera
Bird by Bird, Anne Lamott
Blindness, José Saramago
The Bluest Eye, Toni Morrison
The Botany of Desire, Michael Pollan
The Brothers Karamazov, Fyodor Dostoevsky
Easy Riders, Raging Bulls, Peter Biskind
Cannery Row, John Steinbeck
Middlemarch, George Eliot
The Feminine Mystique, Betty Friedan
Gateway, Frederik Pohl
The Great Gatsby, F. Scott Fitzgerald
Oedipus, Sophocles
Short Stories of Saki
The Sound and the Fury, William Faulkner
Twelfth Night, Shakespeare
The Waste Land, T. S. Eliot
Geography of the Heart, Fenton Johnson
A Thousand Clowns, Herb Gardner
Brave New World, Aldous Huxley
Calvin and Hobbes, Bill Watterson
Catch-22, Joseph Heller
A Confederacy of Dunces, John Kennedy Toole
Dangerous Liaisons, Choderlos De Laclos
Native Son, Richard Wright
The Story of Ferdinand, Munro Leaf
In Search of Respect, Philippe Bourgois
Laughable Loves, Milan Kundera
Lute Player, Norah Lofts
Moll Flanders, Daniel Defoe
Mrs. Dalloway, Virginia Woolf
Nicomachean Ethics, Aristotle
Poems of Gerard Manley Hopkins

Tender Is the Night, F. Scott Fitzgerald
The Thirty Years' War, Geoffrey Parker
Understanding Media, Marshall McLuhan
The Great Unraveling, Paul Krugman
Low Life, Luc Sante
The Member of the Wedding, Carson McCullers
Mere Christianity, C. S. Lewis
Père Goriot, Honoré De Balzac
The Phantom Tollbooth, Norton Juster
A Portrait of the Artist as a Young Man, James Joyce
The Principia, Isaac Newton
To Kill a Mockingbird, Harper Lee
The Woman in the Dunes, Kobo Abe
The Raj Quartet, Paul Scott
All Quiet on the Western Front, Erich Maria Remarque
The Birth of Tragedy, Friedrich Nietzsche
The Collected Stories of Eudora Welty
The Origins of Totalitarianism, Hannah Arendt
The Longest Journey, E. M. Forster
Fear and Loathing in Las Vegas, Hunter S. Thompson
I Lost It At the Movies, Pauline Kael
Lady Chatterley's Lover, D. H. Lawrence
Life on Mars, David Getz
A New Path to the Waterfall, Raymond Carver
The Brothers K, David James Duncan
The Picture of Dorian Gray, Oscar Wilde
R. S. Thomas Collected Poems
A Room of One's Own, Virginia Woolf
The Last Temptation of Christ, Nikos Kazantzakis

KEPLER'S BOOKS
Menlo Park, California — Founded in 1955

Our Staff's Favorite Books Over the Years
1800s
Pride and Prejudice, Jane Austen

1930s
Murder on the Orient Express, Agatha Christie
Death on the Nile, Agatha Christie
And Then There Were None, Agatha Christie

1950s

The Member of the Wedding, Carson McCullers
Lolita, Vladimir Nabokov
Charlotte's Web, E. B. White
The Cat in the Hat, Dr. Seuss

1960s

The Empire City, Paul Goodman
A Confederate General from Big Sur, Richard Brautigan
Catch-22, Joseph Heller
One Flew over the Cuckoo's Nest, Ken Kesey
Hiroshima Mon Amour, Marguerite Duras
A Personal Matter, Kenzaburó Óe
The Cantos, Ezra Pound
Who's Afraid of Virginia Woolf? Edward Albee
Mastering the Art of French Cooking, Julia Child,
     Louisette Bertholle, and Simone Beck
Dune, Frank Herbert
Where the Wild Things Are, Maurice Sendak
Alexander and the Wind-Up Mouse, Leo Lionni
The Tin Drum, Günter Grass
In a Shallow Grave, James Purdy
Swimmy, Leo Lionni
Sylvester and the Magic Pebble, William Steig

1970s

The Bluest Eye, Toni Morrison
The Temple in Man, R. A. Schwaller de Lubicz
The Man Died, Wole Soyinka
Fear and Loathing in Las Vegas, Hunter S. Thompson
The Last Whole Earth Catalog, Stewart Brand, editor
Cities of the Red Night, William S. Burroughs
Tarantula, Bob Dylan
Selected Poems, Ted Hughes
Kesey's Jail Journals, Ken Kesey
In Patagonia, Bruce Chatwin
The Lorax, Dr. Seuss
The Westing Game, Ellen Raskin
The Princess Bride, William Goldman
From the Mixed-Up Files of Mrs. Basil E. Frankweiler,
     E. L. Konigsburg
Bridge to Terabithia, Katherine Paterson
Stuart Little, E. B. White

The Cricket in Times Square, George Selden
Are You There God? It's Me, Margaret, Judy Blume
Ira Sleeps Over, Bernard Waber
Where the Sidewalk Ends, Shel Silverstein

1980s

The Name of the Rose, Umberto Eco
Dream of Glass, Jean Mark Gawron
I, Leonardo, Ralph Steadman
The Chalice and the Blade, Riane Eisler
A Thief of Time, Tony Hillerman
Frankenstein, Mary Shelley,
     Barry Moser (illustrator)
America, Jean Baudrillard
Waterland, Graham Swift
Blood Meridian, Cormac McCarthy
The Bonfire of the Vanities, Tom Wolfe
The Things They Carried, Tim O'Brien
Music of the Swamp, Lewis Nordan
Joe, Larry Brown
"My Father's Dragon," Ruth Stiles Gannett
Outrageous Acts and Everyday Rebellions, Gloria Steinem
A Light in the Attic, Shel Silverstein
The Eight, Katherine Neville

1990s

Hamlet's Mill, Giorgio De Santillana &
     Hertha Von Dechend
Mountains and Rivers Without End, Gary Snyder
The Famished Road, Ben Okri
Virtual Archaeology, Maurizio Forte
The French Laundry Cookbook, Thomas Keller
The General in His Labyrinth, Gabriel García Márquez
In the Palm of Darkness, Mayra Montero
The Sirius Mystery, Robert Temple
Almanac of the Dead, Leslie Marmon Silko
Where White Men Fear to Tread, Russell Means
And the Ass Saw the Angel, Nick Cave
The Consumer, M. Gira
Classic Crews, Harry Crews
Cry Me a River, T. R. Pearson
The Same River Twice, Chris Offutt
Stranger Music, Leonard Cohen

You Can't Win, Jack Black
Blindness, Jose Saramago
Killer on the Road, James Ellroy
The Things They Carried, Tim O'Brien
Interpreter of Maladies, Jhumpa Lahiri
Sophie's World, Jostein Gaarder
The Flanders Panel, Arturo Pérez-Reverte
Stellaluna, Janell Cannon
Kiss the Girls, James Patterson
Misadventures in the 213, Dennis Hensley

2000s (so far)
The Death of Vishnu, Manil Suri
Dante's Inferno, Sandow Birk
Leonardo da Vinci: Leonardo (Taschen edition)
In the Hand of Dante, Nick Tosches
Angels and Demons, Dan Brown
The Collected Works of Chögyam Trungpa
The Secret Life of the Lonely Doll, Jean Nathan
Poetry of Pablo Neruda, 2003
Selected Non-Fictions of Jorge Luis Borges
Unequal Protection, Thom Hartmann
The Iron Triangle, Dan Briody
Old School: A Novel, Tobias Wolff
You Are Not a Stranger Here, Adam Haslett
Embers, Sandor Marai
The Eyre Affair, Jasper Fforde
Reality, Peter Kingsley
The Little Friend, Donna Tarte
My Sister's Keeper, Jodi Picoult
The Sex Lives of Cannibals, J. Maarten Troost
The Millennium Problems, Keith Devlin
The Key to the Golden Firebird, Maureen Johnson
Lethal Seduction, Jackie Collins
Why Girls Are Weird, Pamela Ribon
Secret Celebrity, Carol Wolper
Beginner's Luck, Laura Pedersen
Rocko and Spanky Go to a Party, Kara and Jenna Lareau

LENOX HILL BOOKSTORE
New York City, New York — Founded 1997
(Owned by Jeannette Watson, founder of Books &
Co., New York City, New York, founded in 1977)

Lives of the Monster Dogs, Kirsten Bakis
The Wilder Shores of Love, Lesley Blanch
Invisible Cities, Italo Calvino
The Book of Mercy, Kathleen Cambor
A Month in the Country, J. L. Carr
On the Black Hill, Bruce Chatwin
The Deptford Trilogy, Robertson Davies
The Book of Ebenezer Le Page, G. B. Edwards
Deep River, Shusaku Endo
The Dead of the House, Hannah Green
A Journey with Elsa Cloud, Leila Hadley
The All of It, Jeannette Haien
Mariette in Ecstasy, Ron Hansen
Dalva, Jim Harrison
Hidden Journey, Andrew Harvey
Winter's Tale, Mark Helprin
The Mambo Kings Play Songs of Love, Oscar Hijuelos
Ancient Futures: Learning From Ladakh,
    Helena Norberg-Hodge
A Book of Bees and How to Keep Them, Sue Hubbell
Mrs. Caliban, Rachel Ingalls
The Remains of the Day, Kazuo Ishiguro
Niels Lyhne, Jens Peter Jacobsen
Shoeless Joe, W. P. Kinsella
The Monk, Matthew Lewis
The Storyteller, Mario Vargas Llosa
Changing Places: A Tale of Two Campuses, David Lodge
The Wine of Astonishment, Rachel MacKenzie
Palace Walk, Naguib Mahfouz
The Assistant, Bernard Malamud
Love in the Time of Cholera, Gabriel García Márquez
So Long, See You Tomorrow, William Maxwell
The Rector's Daughter, F. M. Mayor
Monkeys, Susan Minot
The Enlightened Mind: An Anthology of Sacred Prose,
    Stephen Mitchell
The Enlightened Heart: An Anthology of Sacred Poetry,
    Stephen Mitchell

My Old Sweetheart, Susanna Moore
The Tree of Life, Hugh Nissenson
Under the Eye of the Clock, Christopher Nolan
The Pagan Rabbi and Other Stories, Cynthia Ozick
The Moviegoer, Walker Percy
A Glastonbury Romance, John Cowper Powys
The Tongues of Angels, Reynolds Price
Wide Sargasso Sea, Jean Rhys
Dusk and Other Stories, James Salter
Rameau's Niece, Cathleen Schine
Keep the River on Your Right, Tobias Schneebaum
The Emigrants, W. G. Sebald
The Volcano Lover, Susan Sontag
Waterland, Graham Swift
The Makioka Sisters, Junichiro Tanizaki
A Confederacy of Dunces, John Kennedy Toole
Joan of Arc in Her Own Words, Willard Trask
Frost in May, Antonia White

MARIA'S BOOKSHOP
Durango, Colorado — Founded 1984

Favorite Books of the Southwest
Angle of Repose, Wallace Stegner
Bless Me, Ultima, Rudolfo Anaya
Blue Horses Rush In, Luci Tapahonso
Cadillac Desert, Marc Reisner
Desert Solitaire, Edward Abbey
Everett Ruess: A Vagabond for Beauty, W. L. Rusho
Fire in the Sky, The Durango Herald
Hiking Trails of Southwestern Colorado, Paul Pixler
In Search of the Old Ones, David Roberts
The Lone Ranger and Tonto Fistfight in Heaven,
    Sherman Alexie
The Meadow, James Galvin
The Milagro Beanfield War, John Nichols
On the Loose, Terry and Renny Russell
One Thousand White Women, Jim Fergus
Perma Red, Debra Magpie Earling
Rain of Gold, Victor Villaseñor
Refuge: An Unnatural History of Family and Place,
    Terry Tempest Williams

Seven Arrows, Hyemeyohsts Storm
These Is My Words, Nancy E. Turner
Tomboy Bride, Harriet Fish Backus

Favorite Books for Young Readers
The Chronicles of Narnia, C.S. Lewis
Clarence Goes Out West and Meets a Purple Horse,
    Jean Ekman Adams
Click, Clack, Moo, Cows That Type, Doreen Cronin
The Girl Who Loved Wild Horses, Paul Goble
The Giver, Lois Lowry
The Giving Tree, Shel Silverstein
The Goat in the Rug, Charles L. Blood
Goodnight Moon, Margaret Wise Brown
The Harry Potter Series, J. K. Rowling
Holes, Louis Sachar
Howling Hill, Will Hobbs
I'm in Charge of Celebrations, Byrd Baylor
Is Your Mama a Llama? Deborah Guarino
The Magic Boots, Scott Emerson
Miss Rumphius, Barbara Cooney
Oh, the Places You'll Go! Dr. Seuss
The Quiltmaker's Gift, Jeff Brumbeau
The Tao of Pooh, Benjamin Hoff
Time for Bed, Mem Fox
The Velveteen Rabbit, Margery Williams

Favorite Nonfiction
Anatomy of the Spirit, Caroline Myss
The Art of Happiness, the Dalai Lama
The Artist's Way, Julia Cameron
Birthing from Within, Pam England
Breaking Clean, Judy Blunt
Endurance: Shackleton's Incredible Voyage, Alfred Lansing
Fast Food Nation, Eric Schlosser
The Four Agreements, Don Miguel Ruiz
Guns, Germs, and Steel, Jared Diamond
How to Use Yoga, Mira Mehta
I, Rigoberta Menchú, Elisabeth Burgos-Debray
The Long Walk, Slavomir Rawicz
Nickel and Dimed, Barbara Ehrenreich
The Not So Big House, Sarah Susanka
Peace Is Every Step, Thich Nhat Hanh

Touching the Void, Joe Simpson
West with the Night, Beryl Markham
When Things Fall Apart, Pema Chödrön
Where Rivers Change Direction, Mark Spragg
Wild Swans: Three Daughters of China, Jung Chang

Favorite Fiction
The Alchemist, Paulo Coelho
All the Pretty Horses, Cormac McCarthy
Chocolat, Joanne Harris
Cold Mountain, Charles Frazier
Consider This Señora, Harriet Doerr
Corelli's Mandolin, Louis De Bernières
Cowboys Are My Weakness, Pam Houston
Divine Secrets of the Ya-Ya Sisterhood, Rebecca Wells
The English Patient, Michael Ondaatje
The God of Small Things, Arundhati Roy
The House of the Spirits, Isabel Allende
I Know This Much Is True, Wally Lamb
In the Time of the Butterflies, Julia Alvarez
The Kite Runner, Khaled Hosseini
Memoirs of a Geisha, Arthur Golden
The Poisonwood Bible, Barbara Kingsolver
The Power of One, Bryce Courtenay
The Red Tent, Anita Diamant
The River Why, David James Duncan
Snow Falling on Cedars, David Guterson

Favorite Authors
Edward Abbey
Sherman Alexie
Isabel Allende
Byrd Baylor
Pema Chödrön
Noam Chomsky
Sharon Creech
David James Duncan
Louise Erdrich
Paul Goble
Kent Haruf
Will Hobbs
Pam Houston
Barbara Kingsolver

Louis L'Amour
Dalai Lama
Thich Nhat Hanh
Pablo Neruda
Mary Oliver
David Petersen
J. K. Rowling
Arundhati Roy
Shel Silverstein
Duane Smith
Mary Sojourner
Wallace Stegner
David Whyte
Ken Wilber
Terry Tempest Williams
Howard Zinn

OFF THE BEATEN PATH
Steamboat Springs, Colorado — Founded 1988

Until They Bring the Streetcars Back, Stanley Gordon West
The Truth Machine, James L. Halperin
Snow Falling on Cedars, David Guterson
A Civil Action, Jonathan Harr
Winterdance, Gary Paulsen
The Flight of the Iguana, David Quammen
Schott's Original Miscellany, Ben Schott
The Secret Knowledge of Water, Craig Childs
Buffalo for the Broken Heart, Dan O'Brien
All the Pretty Horses, Cormac McCarthy
A Great Deliverance, Elizabeth George
The Far Pavilions, M. M. Kaye
The Lymond Chronicles, Dorothy Dunnett
Train, Pete Dexter
Angle of Repose, Wallace Stegner
The Persian Pickle Club, Sandra Dallas
Continental Drift, Russell Banks
A Fine Balance, Rohinton Mistry
The Grapes of Wrath, John Steinbeck
The Joy Luck Club, Amy Tan
The Remains of the Day, Kazuo Ishiguro
Snow in August, Pete Hamill

The Bone People, Keri Hulme
The Fool's Progress, Edward Abbey
Staircase of a Thousand Steps, Masha Hamilton
A Little More About Me, Pam Houston
12 Miles to Paradise, Ted Simendinger
The Lakota Way, Joseph M. Marshall III
The Devil in the White City, Erik Larson
Rain of Gold, Victor Villaseñor

POLITICS AND PROSE BOOKSTORE
Washington D. C. — Founded 1984

Fiction: Pure Gold
Angle of Repose, Wallace Stegner
Crossing to Safety, Wallace Stegner
No Great Mischief, Alistair Macleod
A Fine Balance, Rohinton Mistry
The Known World, Edward P. Jones
White Teeth, Zadie Smith
The Corrections, Jonathan Franzen
A Dangerous Friend, Ward Just
Love in the Time of Cholera, Gabriel García Márquez
Charming Billy, Alice McDermott
The Human Stain, Philip Roth
The Hours, Michael Cunningham

Fiction: What Fun!
Enduring Love, Ian McEwan
Empire Falls, Richard Russo
The Curious Incident of the Dog in the Night-Time,
    Mark Haddon
A Landing on the Sun, Michael Frayn
The Rage of Vultures, Barry Unsworth
Morality Play, Barry Unsworth
Dinner at the Homesick Restaurant, Anne Tyler

Don't Forget the American Classics
All the King's Men, Robert Penn Warren
The Grapes of Wrath, John Steinbeck
Giants in the Earth, O. E. Rolvaag

Nonfiction Narrative
A Hope in the Unseen, Ron Suskind
The Spirit Catches You and You Fall Down,
    Anne Fadiman
Praying for Sheetrock, Melissa Fay Greene
My Own Country, Abraham Verghese
True Notebooks, Mark Salzman
Mountain Beyond Mountains, Tracy Kidder
Among Schoolchildren, Tracy Kidder

Biography/Memoir
Isaiah Berlin, Michael Ignatieff
Gellhorn: A Twentieth-Century Life, Caroline Moorehead
Bad Blood: A Memoir, Lorna Sage
Don't Let's Go to the Dogs Tonight, Alexandra Fuller
Waiting for Snow in Havana, Carlos Eire
Lost in Translation, Eva Hoffman

History
Founding Brothers, Joseph J. Ellis
The Pity of It All, Amos Elon
They Marched into Sunlight, David Maraniss

POWELL'S CITY OF BOOKS
Portland, Oregon — Founded 1971

Talking to the Sun, edited by Kenneth Koch, with art
    from Metropolitan Museum of Art
Go In and Out the Window, edited by Dan Fox
Clabbered Dirt, Sweet Grass, Gary Paulsen, illustrated
    by Ruth Wright Paulsen
Travels, Michael Crichton
Pilgrim at Tinker Creek, Annie Dillard
The Word for World Is Forest, Ursula K. Le Guin
The Earthsea Trilogy, Ursula K. Le Guin
The Handmaid's Tale, Margaret Atwood
The Heart Is a Lonely Hunter, Carson McCullers
To Kill a Mockingbird, Harper Lee
Lanark: A Life in Four Books, Alasdair Gray
Trainspotting, Irvine Welsh
The Wind-Up Bird Chronicle, Haruki Murakami

Trout Fishing in America, The Pill versus the Springhill
   Mine Disaster, and In Watermelon Sugar,
   Richard Brautigan
Ghostwritten, David Mitchell
The Magic Mountain, Thomas Mann
If on a Winter's Night a Traveler, Italo Calvino
Nymphomation, Jeff Noon

PRAIRIE LIGHTS
Iowa City, Iowa — Founded 1978

All Around Atlantis, Deborah Eisenberg
Angle of Repose, Wallace Stegner
Blood Done Sign My Name, Timothy B. Tyson
The Book of Laughter and Forgetting, Milan Kundera
The Complete Poems of Elizabeth Bishop
Crabcakes, James Alan McPherson
Daniel Martin, John Fowles
The Deptford Trilogy, Robertson Davies
Distance From Loved Ones, James Tate
Donald Justice: New and Selected Poems
The Dream of the Unified Field, Jorie Graham
Enormous Changes at the Last Minute, Grace Paley
A Good Man Is Hard to Find, Flannery O'Connor
Housekeeping, Marilynne Robinson
Jesus' Son, Denis Johnson
Lies and the Lying Liars Who Tell Them, Al Franken
The Meadow, James Galvin
Nickel and Dimed, Barbara Ehrenreich
Of Human Bondage, W. Somerset Maugham
Observatory Mansions, Edward Carey
A People's History of the United States, Howard Zinn
So Long, See You Tomorrow, William Maxwell
Stop-Time, Frank Conroy
Stuart Little, E. B. White
What We Talk about When We Talk about Love,
   Raymond Carver

RAINY DAY BOOKS, INC.
Fairway, Kansas — Founded 1975

Fiction
Jim the Boy, Tony Early
Birdsong, Sebastian Faulks
In the Time of the Butterflies, Julia Alvarez
The God of Small Things, Arundhati Roy
Tulip Fever, Deborah Moggach
Crossing to Safety, Wallace Stegner
Eden Close, Anita Shreve
Charms for the Easy Life, Kaye Gibbons
The Clearing, Tim Gautreaux
Empire Falls, Richard Russo
The Cape Ann, Faith Sullivan
Memoirs of a Geisha, Arthur Golden
Amy and Isabelle, Elizabeth Strout
I Capture the Castle, Dodie Smith
A Lesson Before Dying, Ernest J. Gaines
Roxana Slade, Reynolds Price
Peace Like a River, Leif Enger
Plainsong, Kent Haruf
The Birth of Venus, Sarah Dunant
The Secret Life of Bees, Sue Monk Kidd

Nonfiction
An Army at Dawn, Rick Atkinson
Seabiscuit: An American Legend, Laura Hillenbrand
Tuxedo Park, Jennet Conant
A Girl Named Zippy, Haven Kimmel
Life and Death in Shanghai, Nien Cheng
The Road from Coorain, Jill Ker Conway
Lost in Place, Mark Salzman
The Color of Water, James McBride
Blackbird, Jennifer Lauck
Expecting Adam, Martha Beck
Great Plains, Ian Frazier
The Alphabet Versus the Goddess, Leonard Shlain
All Over but the Shoutin', Rick Bragg
Ava's Man, Rick Bragg
The Professor and the Madman, Simon Winchester
A Walk in the Woods, Bill Bryson
Paris to the Moon, Adam Gopnik

Colors of the Mountain, Da Chen
Tender at the Bone, Ruth Reichl

Children's
Lilly's Purple Plastic Purse, Kevin Henkes
Jamberry, Bruce Degen
The Water Hole, Graeme Base
We're Going on a Bear Hunt, Michael Rosen and
   Helen Oxenbury
A Porcupine Named Fluffy, Helen Lester and
   Lynn Munsinger
Pookins Gets Her Way, Helen Lester, illustrated by
   Lynn Munsinger
Philadelphia Chickens, Sandra Boynton
Molly Moon's Incredible Book of Hypnotism, Georgia Byng
The Napping House, Audrey Wood
Orwell's Luck, Richard Jennings
A Girl of the Limberlost, Gene Stratton-Porter
Hoot, Carl Hiaasen
Dudley: The Little Terrier That Could,
   Stephen Green-Armytage
Because of Winn-Dixie, Kate DiCamillo
Time Stops for No Mouse, Michael Hoeye
The Sisterhood of the Traveling Pants, Ann Brashares
The Bear's Toothache, David McPhail
Frederick, Leo Lionni
The Kissing Hand, Audrey Penn
Old Turtle, Douglas Wood

HARRY W. SCHWARTZ BOOKSHOPS
Milwaukee, Mequon, Brookfield, and Shorewood,
Wisconsin — Founded 1927

In Alphabetical Order
Alice's Adventures in Wonderland, Lewis Carroll
American Pastoral, Philip Roth
Beloved, Toni Morrison
The Book of Ruth, Jane Hamilton
The Brothers K, David James Duncan
A Confederacy of Dunces, John Kennedy Toole
Fanny Hill or Memoirs of a Woman of Pleasure,
   John Cleland

Fifty Years in My Bookstore, Harry W. Schwartz
Girl with a Pearl Earring, Tracy Chevalier
Harry Potter and the Sorcerer's Stone, J. K. Rowling
Home Cooking, Laurie Colwin
Howard's End, E. M. Forster
Jane Eyre, Charlotte Brontë
Jude the Obscure, Thomas Hardy
The Life of Samuel Johnson, James Boswell
The Making of the English Working Class,
   E. P. Thompson
Mastering the Art of French Cooking, Julia Child
   (in two volumes)
Montana 1948, Larry Watson
Sacred Hunger, Barry Unsworth
Salmagundi, William Faulkner
A Sand County Almanac, Aldo Leopold
The Settlement Cookbook, Simon Kander
Sophie's Choice, William Styron
Talk Before Sleep, Elizabeth Berg
Then She Found Me, Elinor Lipman
Tropic of Cancer, Henry Miller
War and Peace, Leo Tolstoy
The Wind in the Willows, Kenneth Grahame,
   illustrations by Arthur Rackham

SHAKESPEARE & CO.
New York City, New York — Founded 1981

Favorite Titles
The Motorcycle Diaries, Ernesto Che Guevara
Einstein's Dreams, Alan Lightman
The Captain's Verses, Pablo Neruda
Midnight in the Garden of Good and Evil, John Berendt
A Confederacy of Dunces, John Kennedy Toole
The Name of the Rose, Umberto Eco
The New York Trilogy, Paul Auster
Low Life: Lures and Snares of Old New York, Luc Sante
Perfume, Patrick Süskind
Up in the Old Hotel, Joseph Mitchell
The Vagina Monologues, Eve Ensler
Maus: A Survivor's Tale, Art Spiegelman
A People's History of the United States, Howard Zinn

The Da Vinci Code, Dan Brown
The Satanic Verses, Salman Rushdie
Beloved, Toni Morrison
A Heartbreaking Work of Staggering Genius, Dave Eggers
The Alchemist, Paulo Coelho
Interpreter of Maladies, Jhumpa Lahiri
The Alienist, Caleb Carr
Naked, David Sedaris
Trainspotting, Irvine Welsh
The Gashlycrumb Tinies, Edward Gorey
A Brief History of Time, Stephen Hawking
The English Patient, Michael Ondaatje

SNOW GOOSE

Stanwood, Washington — Founded 1979

The World According to Garp, John Irving
Riverwalking, Kathleen Dean Moore
Inkheart, Cornelia Funke
Miss Garnet's Angel, Salley Vickers
The Accidental Tourist, Anne Tyler
The Good Rain, Timothy Egan
Stones from the River, Ursula Hegi
Birdsong, Sebastian Faulks
The Jump-Off Creek, Molly Gloss
Epitaph for a Peach, David Mas Masumoto
The Flanders Panel, Arturo Pérez-Reverte
The Voyage of the Narwhal, Andrea Barrett
Plain and Simple, Sue Bender
In Pale Battalions, Robert Goddard
The Golden Compass, Philip Pullman
The Dress Lodger, Sheri Holman
Out West, Dayton Duncan
Indian Creek Chronicles, Pete Fromm
Life Is So Good, George Dawson and Richard Glaubman
The Sparrow, Mary Doria Russell
Bachelor Brothers Bed and Breakfast, Bill Richardson
The Soul of the Night: An Astronomical Pilgrimage,
    Chet Raymo
A Lesson Before Dying, Ernest J. Gaines

SQUARE BOOKS

Oxford, Mississippi — Founded 1979

Dersu the Trapper, V. K. Arseniev
What Are People For?, Wendell Berry
Facing the Music, Larry Brown
Brother to a Dragonfly, Will D. Campbell
About Grace, Anthony Doerr
The Rock Cried Out, Ellen Douglas
Erasure, Percival Everett
A Fan's Notes, Frederick Exley
Absalom, Absalom!, William Faulkner
Gould's Book of Fish, Richard Flanagan
The Civil War: A Narrative, Volume I-III, Shelby Foote
Independence Day, Richard Ford
Cold Mountain, Charles Frazier
One Hundred Years of Solitude, Gabriel García Márquez
Ellen Foster, Kaye Gibbons
*We Wish To Inform You That Tomorrow We Will Be
    Killed With Our Families,* Philip Gourevitch
A Time to Kill, John Grisham
Trials of the Earth, Mary Hamilton
Bats Out of Hell, Barry Hannah
Legends of the Fall, Jim Harrison
Plainsong, Kent Haruf
A Very Long Engagement, Sebastien Japrisot
Life of Pi, Yann Martel
Child of God, Cormac McCarthy
*A Book of Luminous Things: An International Anthology
    of Poetry,* Czeslaw Milosz, editor
Music of the Swamp, Lewis Nordan
The Things They Carried, Tim O'Brien
The Habit of Being, Flannery O'Connor
The Patron Saint of Liars, Ann Patchett
The Moviegoer, Walker Percy
The Shipping News, E. Annie Proulx
All God's Dangers, Theodore Rosengarten
CivilWarLand in Bad Decline, George Saunders
Sophie's Choice, William Styron
A Woman of Means, Peter Taylor
The Secret History, Donna Tartt
The Third Life of Grange Copeland, Alice Walker
The Collected Stories of Eudora Welty

The Encyclopedia of Southern Culture,
  Charles Wilson & William Ferris, editors
The Duke of Deception: Memories of My Father,
  Geoffrey Wolff
This Boy's Life: A Memior, Tobias Wolff

TATTERED COVER BOOKSTORE
Denver, Colorado — Founded 1971

Nonfiction
Nine Parts of Desire: The Hidden World of Islamic Women,
  Geraldine Brooks
Traveling Mercies: Some Thoughts on Faith, Anne Lamott
The Right Stuff, Tom Wolfe
The Guns of August, Barbara W. Tuchman
Man's Search for Meaning, Viktor E. Frankl
Angela's Ashes, Frank McCourt
Mornings on Horseback, David McCullough
The Last Lion, William Manchester
Refuge: An Unnatural History of Family and Place,
  Terry Tempest Williams
Zen and the Art of Motorcycle Maintenance,
  Robert M. Pirsig
Dispatches, Michael Herr
Wild Swans: Three Daughters of China, Jung Chang
Life and Death in Shanghai, Nien Cheng
From Beirut to Jerusalem, Thomas L. Friedman
Coming into the Country, John McPhee
Surely You're Joking Mr. Feynman, Richard P. Feynman
84 Charing Cross Road, Helene Hanff
I Know Why the Caged Bird Sings, Maya Angelou
Personal History, Katharine Graham
This House of Sky, Ivan Doig

Fiction
Lonesome Dove, Larry McMurtry
Peace Like a River, Leif Enger
Cold Mountain, Charles Frazier
The House of the Spirits, Isabel Allende
Plainsong, Kent Haruf
All the Pretty Horses, Cormac McCarthy
The Prince of Tides, Pat Conroy

The Milagro Beanfield War, John Nichols
Daughter of Time, Josephine Tey
Walking Across Egypt, Clyde Edgerton
The Bean Trees, Barbara Kingsolver
A Very Long Engagement, Sébastien Japrisot
The Color Purple, Alice Walker
A Prayer for Owen Meany, John Irving
The Things They Carried, Tim O'Brien
Angle of Repose, Wallace Stegner
Sophie's Choice, William Styron
Atonement, Ian McEwan
The Joy Luck Club, Amy Tan
Even Cowgirls Get the Blues, Tom Robbins
Cowboys Are My Weakness, Pam Houston
The Remains of the Day, Kazuo Ishiguro
The Shipping News, E. Annie Proulx
The Handmaid's Tale, Margaret Atwood
The Blind Assassin, Margaret Atwood
Trinity, Leon Uris
The Caine Mutiny, Herman Wouk
The Winds of War, Herman Wouk

Childrens
Picture Books
The Snowy Day, Ezra Jack Keats
Cars and Trucks and Things That Go, Richard Scarry
The Empty Pot, Demi
Lilly's Purple Plastic Purse, Kevin Henkes
Voyage to the Bunny Planet, Rosemary Wells

Beginning Reader
Days with Frog and Toad, Arnold Lobel

Chapter Books
Babe the Gallant Pig, Dick King-Smith
Jeremy Thatcher, Dragon Hatcher, Bruce Coville
The Cricket in Times Square, George Selden
The Watsons Go to Birmingham— 1963,
  Christopher Paul Curtis
Nothing But the Truth, Avi
Esperanza Rising, Pam Munoz
Holes, Louis Sachar

VILLAGE BOOKS
Bellingham, Washington — Founded 1980

25 years of favorites (in no particular order)
Another Roadside Attraction, Tom Robbins
This House of Sky, Ivan Doig
Snow Falling on Cedars, David Guterson
Stones from the River, Ursula Hegi
The Poisonwood Bible, Barbara Kingsolver
Angle of Repose, Wallace Stegner
The Brothers K, David James Duncan
Handling Sin, Michael Malone
Lamb, Christopher Moore
Atonement, Ian McEwan
Cold Mountain, Charles Frazier
Ishmael, Daniel Quinn
The Sparrow, Mary Doria Russell
The Prince of Tides, Pat Conroy
Undaunted Courage, Stephen Ambrose
A Thousand Acres, Jane Smiley
Homestead, Rosina Lippi
The Things They Carried, Tim O'Brien
Straight Man, Richard Russo
Love Medicine, Louise Erdrich
The Killer Angels, Michael Shaara
Ship of Gold in the Deep Blue Sea, Gary Kinder
Obasan, Joy Kogawa
Staggerford, Jon Hassler
The Good Rain, Timothy Egan
Talk Before Sleep, Elizabeth Berg
A Great Deliverance, Elizabeth George (and rest of series)

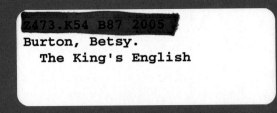